IN MEMORIAM

SO·THE·HEART·BE·RIGHT

Joanna Defrates
1945-2000

Spoiling the Egyptians

SPOILING
THE EGYPTIANS

John Marlowe

"And they spoiled the Egyptians."
Exodus, 12, 36

ANDRE DEUTSCH

First published 1974 by
André Deutsch Limited
105 Great Russell Street London wc1

Printed in Great Britain by
Tonbridge Printers Limited
Tonbridge Kent

ISBN 0 233 96601 3

Contents

List of Illustrations

Acknowledgements

Illustrations 1 and 4 are reproduced from *Egypt, Descriptive, Historical and Picturesque* by G. Ebers, (1887).

Illustrations 2 and 3 are reproduced from photographs in the possession of Radio Times Hulton Picture Library.

Illustrations 5 to 9 inclusive are reproduced from prints in the possession of R. G. Searight Esq, to whom thanks are also due for permission to reproduce the drawing by Tenniel (illustration 10) and the lithograph by Louis Haghe after David Roberts (jacket).

Introduction

THIS is the story of the technical, financial and economic colonisation of Egypt by Western Europe. The story begins with Bonaparte's invasion of Egypt in 1798 and ends with the British invasion of Egypt in 1882. At the beginning of the period Egypt was a semi-autonomous province of the Ottoman Empire in name and an almost independent oligarchy in fact. It was entirely untouched by European influence and the few Europeans who lived there were entirely at the mercy of the country's Mamluk rulers. At the end of the period Egypt was still a province of the Ottoman Empire and, formally, its ruler enjoyed at least as much autonomy as the Mamluks had done in 1798. But, in fact, the country's economy and finances were almost entirely under the control of European foreigners. It had become not a part, but a colony, of Western Europe. It was a colony in the sense that it was largely controlled by European foreigners enjoying extra-territorial immunities and privileges, and in the sense that these privileges were being used, or abused, to provide a favourable field for European investment, a protected market for European manufactures, and a cheap source of raw materials needed by European manufacturers. It was a colony in the sense that the actions of a nominally autonomous Egyptian Government were subject to usually irresistible pressures from the governments of the European Great Powers. It was a colony in the sense that its culture, its techniques, and the ambience of its ruling class had been infiltrated by, and were being permeated with, the civilisation of Western Europe. All this had come about because of the pressures which an expansionist, technically and militarily superior, industrialised Western Europe, with surplus capital to invest and surplus manufactures to sell, had been able to exert on a defenceless, easily accessible, technically backward, agriculturally rich country with a docile population despotically ruled by men who were not themselves Egyptian and who had been corrupted and seduced by the allurements of the West. It had come about because of the connection with the Ottoman Empire, itself a victim of much the same process of exploitation. It had not, to any large extent, come about because of Egypt's new-found strategic importance as a staging-post between Western Europe and the British possessions in India. The strategic interest in, and the political interference with, Egypt which led to the British military occupation in 1882 was essentially separate from, although it proceeded parallel to, and eventually coalesced with, the process of economic colonisation. The strategic interest was almost exclusively British. The economic and financial interests were international. This book is concerned with the economic and financial interests. It is a tale of bankers' parlours rather than battlefields, of pens rather than swords; not, until the end, a tale of armed invasion, but of peaceful penetration. The front of the stage is filled with diplomats and engineers, with lawyers and money-lenders and their respective victims. Until the Egyptian people started to rebel against the servitude which had been imposed on them, the warships were over the horizon and out of sight.

1

The Beginnings
of European Influence

In modern times, the intensive interest of the West in Egypt, leading, in less than a century, to the colonisation and subjugation of Egypt by the West, started with Bonaparte's invasion in 1798. For three hundred years before that, from the time of the Ottoman conquest at the beginning of the sixteenth century, Egypt had been almost entirely cut off from the West. Its rulers and its people had been unaffected by the changing culture of the West, by its scientific and technical discoveries, and by its rapidly changing social and political climate. There had been some trade with the West, and a few Western European consuls and merchants were usually resident in Egypt. Adventurous European travellers, like Pococke and Savary and Bruce, occasionally visited Egypt and published descriptions of an exotic and comparatively unknown land, rich in antiquities but presently sunk in barbarism and squalor. In Paris, and sometimes in Vienna, there had been an occasional, half-hearted interest in the possibility of occupying Egypt with a view to controlling and developing an overland route for the rich Eastern trade in competition with the long sea route round the Cape. In Paris, this interest sharpened after the Seven Years' War, which resulted in the eclipse of the French, and the establishment of the British trading empire in India. Bonaparte's invasion was a direct result of this sharpened interest.

The immediate results of this invasion were insignificant. The French occupation only lasted for three years. In another two years their British supplanters had departed. To all appearance Egypt had reverted to the *status quo ante* Bonaparte. But, in reality, Egypt's long period of isolation from the West had come to an end. Both the extent of this isolation, and its ending, are perhaps best symbolised by the introduction into Egypt, for the first time, of a printing press. 'Before the French arrived in Alexandria, not a line had ever been printed in Egypt. Bonaparte brought two printing plants with his army. One, operated by the Orientalist Marcel and a staff of thirty-one, remained at Alexandria until the end of 1798 . . . It had three sets of type – French, Arabic and Greek. On its presses all Bonaparte's proclamations were printed, as was the first book ever printed in Egypt – *Exercises in Literary Arabic* . . . In addition to Marcel's press, there was another, privately owned, which was shipped to Cairo soon after the French occupied the capital . . . [which] . . . published the more or less weekly newspaper *Le Courrier de l'Egypt* and the literary and scientific periodical *La Décade Egyptienne*, the organ of the Institute of Egypt[1].' These two journals, produced by the press which afterwards became known as *L'Imprimerie Nationale du Caire*, were 'the ancestors, the Adam and Eve, of the Egyptian Press, and of all the publications which have appeared since on the banks of the Nile, in French, in Arabic, in English and in Italian.'[2]

The introduction of the printing press was symbolic. The practical ending of Egypt's isolation from the West was brought about by two developments, one arising directly, the other indirectly, from Bonaparte's invasion.

Bonaparte's intention had been to make of Egypt a permanent French colony. To that end he had attached to his expedition a number of *savants* from almost every branch of learning, whose business it was to study and report upon every aspect of Egypt's natural and man-made resources. He needed the *savants'* researches primarily for administrative purposes and with a view to the exploitation of Egypt's economic wealth. Many of the *savants* themselves were actuated by a disinterested desire for knowledge.

Before the expedition left France these *savants* had been organised into a Commission of Sciences and Arts, consisting of 165 persons, including civil engineers, surveyors, cartographers, architects, botanists, zoologists, physicians, pharmacists, chemists and mineralogists. There were also a few artists, mathematicians, archaeologists, writers and musicians. Soon after their arrival in Egypt an inner group of the more distinguished of these *savants* formed themselves into the Institut d'Egypte, a more select and more specifically academic society than the Commission of Sciences and Arts. It had as its stated objects: 1) progress and the propagation of enlightenment in Egypt: 2) the research, study and publication of natural, industrial and historical facts about Egypt: 3) the giving of advice about various subjects on which the French administration might consult them. The Institut was divided into four sections – mathematics, physics, political economy, literature and the arts. The Institut did an immense amount of work during the years of the French occupation. It continued this work in France after the French had left Egypt and, after the war had ended, was re-established in Egypt. Its researches during the period of the occupation were given to the world in nine volumes of text and fourteen volumes of illustrations, comprising *Description de l'Egypte*, published in Paris between the years 1809 and 1828. Particularly after the end of the Napoleonic wars in 1815, these volumes had a wide circulation throughout Western Europe and contributed largely to a newly-awakened interest in Egypt being shown by educated people in nearly all Western European countries. This interest was mainly directed towards the monuments of ancient Egypt, of which the Institut had made a considerable study. The appetite for these antiquities had been whetted by the publication, in Paris in 1802, by Vivant-Denon, a member of the Institut, of *Voyages dans la Basse et Haute Egypte*. This work, consisting of two volumes of text and one of illustrations drawn by Denon himself, was an entertaining and well-illustrated account of a comprehensive inspection of Egypt's principal known antiquities. It was the first of its kind and became immensely popular. It was translated into English within a year of publication. It marked the beginning of a passionate interest in Egyptian antiquities which started to manifest itself in Western Europe as soon as the end of the Napoleonic wars made extensive travel once more practicable for Western European gentry.

This interest was shown by serious scholars, by globe-trotters, and by rich dilettantes. It led to a considerable market for Egyptian antiquities to meet the needs of museums and collectors. Many of the European residents in Egypt, including most of the consuls, both formed their own collections and catered for this market. Several European visitors, ranging from scholars to fortune-hunters, and including a number of gentlemen who joined in for the fun of it, came to Egypt to see what they could find, to take it home with them if it were sufficiently portable, or to draw or describe it if it were not. Father Geramb, a Trappist monk, is said to have remarked jestingly to the ruler of Egypt in 1833: 'Your Highness, I can see that it would be scarcely respectable, on returning from Egypt, to present oneself in Europe without a mummy in one hand and a crocodile in the other.'

The Egyptian Government regarded this process of looting tolerantly. They could see no interest or value – apart from the possible use of some of the more durable items as building material – in the carved stones, the papyrus rolls and the mummy cases on which so many of the European residents and visitors set so much store. For many years they raised no obstacles against these Europeans doing much as they liked with them, including taking them out of the country. As a result, according to Ernest Renan, writing in 1865; 'For more than half a century Egyptian antiquities have been pillaged. Purveyors to museums have gone through the country like vandals; to secure a fragment of a head, a piece of inscription, precious antiquities were reduced to fragments. Nearly always provided with a consular instrument, these avid destroyers treated Egypt as their own property.' In 1835, on the recommendation of the great French Egyptologist Champollion, Mohamed Ali, the ruler of Egypt, promulgated an ordinance forbidding the export or destruction of antiquities and providing for the creation of a Museum of Antiquities in Egypt. But nothing was done about this ordinance and it was not until 1857, under the inspiration of Mariette, another great French Egyptologist, that an Egyptian *Service des Antiquités* was formed, arrangements for the creation of a Museum of Antiquities made, and detailed regulations promulgated for the proper licensing, supervision and recording of all archaeological diggings.

Research into and evaluation of Egyptian antiquities proceeded *pari passu* with looting and collecting. The fruits of scholarship were limited until it became possible to decipher the copious hieroglyphic inscriptions on monuments and hieroglyphic writings on papyrus rolls. The possibility of decipherment was enhanced through the discovery, by Lieutenant Boussard during the period of the French occupation, in the desert sand near Rosetta, of a large basalt tablet containing three inscriptions – in Greek, demotic (later recognised as a cursive form of hieroglyphics) and hieroglyphics – of which the Greek version was a decree dating from the reign of Ptolemy V. Assuming the unknown hieroglyphic inscription to be a translation of the known Greek, the inscription was long enough to provide a basis for the study of the meaning of hieroglyphics.

The French were not allowed to keep their discovery, which was seized by the British as a spoil of war after the surrender of Alexandria in 1801. The Rosetta Stone, as it became known, was then shipped to the British Museum. Its importance was immediately recognised and it became the subject of intensive studies. The first man to make a real break-through, in 1822, was a young French archaeologist named Champollion, to whom the credit belongs for bringing the study of the ancient Egyptian language to a point at which it became possible to decipher all hieroglyphic inscriptions and writing which remained legible. This naturally gave a great fillip to Egyptological studies and marked the beginning of the long and fascinating process by which the history, the religion and the customs of ancient Egypt were gradually pieced together.

As the science of Egyptology (as it became known) advanced, the previous indiscriminate and destructive collection mania receded. Under the influence of the Egyptologists, the process of abstracting what was portable and either destroying or neglecting what was not, began to be replaced by more orderly processes designed to preserve, to record, to study and to make available both to sight-seers and scholars. It was some time before the Egyptian Government became sufficiently interested to respond by the promulgation and execution of the necessary ordinances. And, when they did, they were hampered by the international privileges and immunities which, as we shall see, were already facilitating another, and more serious, exploitation of Egypt by Western Europeans. It is ironical that the beginning of some sort of control over the indiscriminate exploitation of the relics of ancient Egypt coincided approximately with the beginning of the indiscriminate European exploitation of the resources of modern Egypt.

The archaeological invasion of Egypt was the direct result of the French invasion and the consequent interest aroused in Western Europe by the memorials of ancient Egypt publicized by the French invaders. The technical invasion, which we are about to outline, was an indirect result of the French invasion, and derived mainly from the interest in Western techniques shown by the man who, within two years of the British evacuation in 1803, established himself as sole ruler of Egypt under more or less nominal Ottoman suzerainty, and who ruled over Egypt as an enlightened, effective, but merciless despot for the next forty-four years.

Mohamed Ali was an illiterate Albanian soldier who came to Egypt with a Turkish force during the period of the British occupation. He soon rose to the command of the Albanian contingent in the Turkish army and, in the confusion which succeeded the British evacuation, managed, by an adroit process of violence and intrigue, to outmanoeuvre his various rivals. He compelled the Sublime Porte to appoint him as Pasha, or Governor, of Egypt, and to acquiesce in his virtually independent rule of a country which was, nominally, a province of the Ottoman Empire. For the next ten years, which coincided with the last ten years of the Napoleonic wars, Mohamed Ali was busy consolidating his position. He subjugated and almost exterminated the old Mamluk oligarchy which had ruled Egypt up to the time of the French invasion. He established effective and despotic direct rule over the whole of Egypt, abolishing the old system of tax-farming and feudal tenure, and reducing the marauding Beduin tribes to something like obedience to his rule. In 1807, after a British force had occupied Alexandria (still held by the Turks) in the course of a war against Turkey, he defeated it in battle and procured its evacuation, thereby adding Alexandria to his Viceroyalty and securing the tacit consent of the European Powers to the exercise of his authority over Egypt. In 1812, at the behest of his nominal Suzerain, he embarked on a successful war against the Wahhabi schismatics of Central Arabia, thereby spreading his fame throughout Islam and providing occupation for his potentially rebellious Albanian mercenaries. By the time of the battle of Waterloo his ambitions had broadened and he was thinking in terms of establishing his own dynasty in Egypt, independent of Constantinople and ruling over all the Arabic-speaking lands of the Ottoman Empire.

In order to realise these ambitions he needed an efficient army and navy and money with which to pay and equip them. To raise the money he tightened his administrative hold over Egypt by assuming control of Egypt's import and export trade and by establishing a system of monopolies. Under this system locally produced products were bought at an arbitrary price fixed by the government and sold for export at a profit by the government; imported manufactures were bought by the government and sold at a profit to the Egyptian consumer. To raise his army Mohamed Ali recruited, for the first time, Egyptian peasants from the villages and negroes from the Sudan, which he started to conquer in 1820. To train his army he engaged European officers, who were plentifully available after the end of the Napoleonic wars. He engaged Colonel Sèves, a French officer who had previously been ADC to Marshals Ney and Grouchy, to form and command an infantry training depot at Aswan. Colonel Sèves eventually became a Moslem, married a Moslem wife, reared a Moslem family, was promoted to Pasha and Major-General, became the father-in-law of a future Egyptian Prime Minister, and, as Soliman Pasha, died at a ripe old age in the 1870s. Another French officer, Colonel Varin, was made head of the Cavalry School at Giza. M. Hammont, also a Frenchman, became Veterinary Surgeon to the army. An artillery school was established at Tura under Colonel Sequera, a Spanish officer. Primarily in order to equip the army with cannon and cannon balls, an iron foundry was established at Bulaq under the direction of a British engineer, Galloway, who had several Englishmen working under him. Textile factories were set up with the original object of manufacturing uniforms for the army. M. Clot, a French physician, was engaged to set up a military hospital. Later Clot Bey, as he became, extended his activities to civilian medicine. He set up a civilian general hospital on modern lines at Qasr-al-Aini, just outside Cairo, and a civilian medical school at Abu Zaabal, north-east of Cairo. To him belongs the credit of introducing modern medical and sanitary methods into Egypt.

Mohamed Ali also attached importance to building a navy. At first he ordered all his ships from foreign dockyards. After the destruction of most of his first navy at Navarino in 1827, he engaged a French naval constructor, M. Cérisy, to build him a fully-equipped dockyard at Alexandria where he proceeded to build a second and more powerful navy. He engaged European – mostly British or French – officers to command his larger ships.

In his efforts to increase the agricultural productivity and, consequently, the taxable capacity, of Egypt, Mohamed Ali also had recourse to European experts and European techniques. In 1819 M. Jumel, a French agronomist resident in Cairo, experimented with some cotton plants growing for ornamental purposes in a Cairo garden. He produced a long-staple cotton which, it occurred to him, could be grown commercially as being particularly suitable for the new mechanical cotton looms in Western Europe. He got Mohamed Ali interested in the idea and, within a few years, cotton was being grown all over Lower Egypt as an important export crop. Under his monopoly system, the Viceroy kept the cotton export business in his own hands, buying the crop from the cultivators at low prices fixed by himself and selling it for export at a profit through European agents.

Cotton is a summer crop and requires watering during the summer season of low Nile. This necessitated an improvement in the Egyptian irrigation system and the application to it of modern European engineering techniques. To provide for this Mohamed Ali engaged the services of Alphonse Linant de Bellefonds, a French engineer from the Ponts et Chaussées who, in course of time, gathered round him a number of French assistants.

The development of cotton-growing led to the importation of mechanical pumps for irrigation purposes, to the establishment of ginning factories and spinning and weaving factories and, consequently to the setting-up of mechanical workshops for the maintenance and repair of the machinery involved. Galloway, who became Mohamed Ali's chief mechanical engineer, was responsible for the setting-up and supervision of these workshops. Most of his principal assistants were English. The industrial experiments were not altogether a success, due mainly to a failure to train sufficient Egyptian mechanics. But, in the words of one contemporary European observer (Prince Muskau), 'the cloth factories produce a coarse cloth, more durable, cheaper, and better dyed than our own.' The same observer remarked; 'One of the cotton factories formed a perfect little town within itself, with the most laudable attention to the health and comfort of the working people, to which so little regard is had in England.'

In an Egypt which he was trying to modernize, Mohamed Ali was acutely aware of the necessity of raising up a cadre of young Egyptians trained in Western methods. In 1826, under the inspiration of a Frenchman, M. Jomard, a first contingent of forty young Egyptians was sent to Paris to undergo a course of study in a school founded especially for them under the auspices of the French Government. Here they were taught French, mathematics, geography, chemistry, agronomy, physics, zoology, medicine, engineering, navigation, and civil and military administration. The instructors, and the language of instruction, were French. The first contingent was followed by others, with the result that the first cadres of European-trained technicians and administrators absorbed French methods, in the French language, from French text-books and from French instructors. Soon afterwards, a polytechnic and a medical school were set up in Egypt, also staffed mainly with French instructors.

This preponderance of French influence was largely due to Drovetti, who was French Consul-General in Egypt from 1804 to 1814 and again from 1819 to 1829. (The break was due to the Bonapartist sympathies of Drovetti, who was a Corsican.) His return to the Consulate-General in 1819 was due to the French Government's urgent desire to re-establish French influence in Egypt. Drovetti was on good terms with Mohamed Ali, probably as the result of helpful information about British dispositions which he had been able to give him at the time of the British landing at Alexandria in 1807. (He had been in Alexandria at the time and had left for Cairo immediately after the landing.) He got to know Egypt well and remained there as a private resident during the five-year break in his official career. Like Salt, his British opposite number between 1816 and 1827, he was a keen and voracious collector of Egyptian antiquities. But he served France very well as Consul-General, particularly during his second term of office. It was largely through his influence both with Mohamed Ali and with the French Government that French nationals were given preference when European nationals were engaged and that the French Government co-operated in providing educational opportunities for Egyptian students.

Neither the British Government, nor successive British Consuls-General, were much interested in the propagation of British cultural influence in Egypt. After the end of the Napoleonic wars, they were mainly interested in the development of British trade.

Immediately before Bonaparte's invasion, British trade with Egypt was virtually non-existent. The Levant Company, which had a monopoly of this trade, had ceased trading there owing to disturbed conditions, and there were hardly any British nationals resident in Egypt. Such European trade as there was, was largely in the hands of the French. During the wars, and after the battle of Abuqir, British naval supremacy put a temporary stop to French trade with Egypt. The food requirements of various British expeditionary forces in the Mediterranean area caused the British Government to appoint commercial agents in Egypt to buy wheat. This was the beginning of the long and important British trading connection with Egypt. After the end of the war several of the British purchasing agents in Egypt stayed on to trade for their own account. One of the earliest British trading firms established in Egypt after the war was Briggs & Thurburn. Samuel Briggs had been appointed British Consular Agent in Alexandria at the time of the British evacuation in 1803. He left Alexandria with Fraser's abortive expedition in 1807 and returned later for a few years in a consular capacity with the principal duty of buying wheat for the British Government. He quarrelled with them but, soon after the end of the war, he returned to Alexandria to set up business on his own account in partnership with Robert Thurburn.

Samuel Briggs played an important part in the commercial development of the long-staple Egyptian cotton bred by Jumel. He was quick to see its suitability for the Lancashire cotton mills, and the fortunes of the firm of Briggs & Thurburn were founded on the export of Egyptian cotton to England, which began in the 1820s. These exports were made through Mohamed Ali's system of monopolies. The Viceroy bought – or rather requisitioned – the crop from the cultivators and sold it at an agreed price to a select 'ring' of European merchants, who then resold it at the best price they could on European markets. It proved a very good business for those merchants within the ring, who soon found themselves banded together in a close commercial and political alliance with Mohamed Ali. The alliance was equally profitable to Mohamed Ali, who was able to use the merchants in the ring as bankers for the short-term loans which he required to finance his administrative and military expenditure. The method adopted was that the selected merchants advanced money to the government against an agreed allocation from the next cotton crop. By this means, together with high taxation and the large profit which he made out of the cultivators on his monopolies, Mohamed Ali was able to meet his large military expenditure, his payments of tribute to the Porte, and his administrative expenditure generally, without incurring any long-term debt. In this he was wiser than some of his successors.

The merchants also used some of the European currencies obtained from sales of cotton to purchase for the Viceroy's account military and naval equipment and other manufactured goods, which they sold direct to the Egyptian Government through the monopoly system. They thus had a considerable vested interest in Mohamed Ali's administration and in his system of monopolies. Most, although by no means all, of these merchants were British. By 1825 there were fifteen British merchant houses in Alexandria and some nine-elevenths of Egypt's export trade and two-thirds of its import trade was to and from Great Britain.

Samuel Briggs established himself in England in the mid-1820s, leaving the Egyptian end of the business to Robert Thurburn. He became Mohamed Ali's agent in London and, in this capacity, purchased the Egyptian Government's military and other requirements in England, transacted some political business, and acted as unofficial liaison between the Viceroy and the British Government.

European trading methods in Egypt under Mohamed Ali were quite different from those which had prevailed up to the end of the eighteenth century. Then, European merchants, organised under the auspices of their own national chartered company, had lived and worked in national communities, known in English as 'factories', under the leadership and protection of their consuls, in a particular quarter of the town more or less segregated from the native inhabitants. The British merchants were all members, and subject to the rules and discipline of the Levant Company, by whom the British Consul was appointed. The relations of these European communities with the local government and local inhabitants were, in theory, governed by the Capitulations treaties concluded between the Ottoman Government and most of the European Powers. These treaties provided that European nationals were subject to the jurisdiction of their own consuls in civil and criminal matters arising between themselves, and provided various guarantees covering freedom of religious worship, taxation, personal status, trading conditions and so on. In practice, these treaties were almost non-operative in Egypt during the second half of the eighteenth century, owing to the exiguous nature of Ottoman control, and foreign merchants usually had to rely on the length of their purses and the agility of their wits.

After Mohamed Ali's rise to power all this was changed. The new generation of European merchants traded for their own account instead of through the old chartered monopoly companies. (The English Levant Company formally ceased to exist in 1825.) They no longer acknowledged the authority, although they sometimes sought the protection, of their consuls. But, under Mohamed Ali, this protection was seldom needed. The Viceroy welcomed the European merchants, encouraged them to emerge from their ghettoes and saw that they were not molested. The merchants, although at first suspicious of the Viceroy's dominating and domineering ways, soon saw the advantages to themselves inherent in the enlarged foreign trade, in the unaccustomed law and order, and, particularly, in the system of monopolies. No longer afraid for their persons or their possessions, they began to have social and business relations with Egyptian nationals, to acquire real estate and, generally, to become acclimatised to the country. Soon, many of them were frequenting Mohamed Ali's Court and on terms of friendly intimacy with him. In many ways the Capitulations regime became modified in their favour and they enjoyed something like extra-territorial privileges. So long as they kept on the right side of the Viceroy, they were in an enviable position. But everything depended on his favour.

While Mohamed Ali was in the plenitude of his power, and before his defeat and diminution in 1840–41, European merchants, and European officials in the Viceroy's service, on the whole regarded Egypt as their adopted country and identified their interests with those of the ruler. They went to Europe comparatively seldom. They did not wish, and were indeed unable, to insulate themselves from the life of the country. There were no 'European quarters' in Cairo or Alexandria. European officials and merchants lived in Turkish-style houses, dressed in Turkish-style clothes, ate Turkish food and, in most ways, adapted themselves to the life style of their wealthier neighbours (except in respect of religious observances and the hareem). They often learnt Turkish, and sometimes Arabic, although French became more and more the language of communication between Europeans and upper-class Turks. (At this time virtually the whole of the ruling class in Cairo and Alexandria, the two main cities of Egypt, was Turkish, a term which included Circassians and Albanians. The Turks were still the master race, sharply differentiated from the subservient native Egyptians.) During the frequent visitations of plague they shut themselves in their houses like their neighbours. Owing to insanitary conditions the rate of mortality was high, particularly among women and children. The European men were accustomed to sit cross-legged on divans, smoking water-pipes and drinking coffee with local magnates. The European wives visited the womenfolk of these magnates in their hareems. The principal contacts with Europe were provided by visits received from and paid to the captains and masters of the numerous European naval and merchant ships which called at Alexandria.

Up to 1840, Mohamed Ali was a powerful prince, a rising star, whose favour had to be sought, and whose will had to be obeyed. The privileges enjoyed by European foreigners were freely bestowed, as an act of royal bounty, as a recognition of community of interest, as a return for services rendered, and not as the result of diplomatic pressures or financial necessity. The resident Europeans were few in number and were mostly educated men who did not abuse their privileges. On the whole, their services to the Viceroy were as substantial as the rewards they received from him.

After 1841, when the Viceroy was diminished, and almost deposed, as a result of forcible action by most of the European Powers acting in concert, the case was altered. In the political interest of most of the European Powers, who wished to prolong the existence of the Ottoman Empire, Mohamed Ali was shorn of much of his military and naval power, of all his territories outside Egypt, and of some of his administrative autonomy. This rendered Egypt vulnerable to those European financial and commercial interests which, with surplus money to invest and surplus goods to sell, began to look upon a rich, easily accessible, militarily defenceless, and politically powerless country as an ideal prospect for exploitation. Mohamed Ali was already an old man, and failing fast. His formidable eldest son, Ibrahim, pre-deceased him. Within ten years of the events of 1840–41, both were dead. Their successors were men of lesser calibre. Within a very few years Egypt, to all intents and purposes, became a European colony. Without a shot being fired.

Notes

1. Christopher Herold, *Bonaparte in Egypt*, pp 165–66
2. F. Charles-Roux, *Bonaparte Gouverneur d'Égypte*, p 152

2

The Overland Route
and the Suez Canal

BEFORE the Napoleonic wars, such British official interest in
Egypt as there was, was directed towards the possibility of
using the overland route through Egypt as a means of expedit-
ing despatches between England and India. This interest was
seldom more than lukewarm. But, under the stimulus of the
India Board of Control, created in 1784 as a Department of
State to supervise the management of British interests in India
by the East India Company, the British Consulate in Egypt,
abandoned in 1756, was revived in 1786 with the principal
object of arranging for the regular transit of despatches
between England and India through Egypt. A detailed scheme
was worked out by the British Post Office for establishing a
regular service. But nothing came of it, although there was an
irregular and intermittent transit of despatches by this route
both before and after the re-establishment of the British
Consulate. The more usual, although still irregular and somewhat hazardous, overland route for the speedy transit of
despatches (compared with the long-sea route round the Cape)
was between London and Constantinople by one of the regular
routes (which changed according to the exigencies of war and
diplomacy), and by Tartars (couriers) travelling, usually by
camel, between Constantinople and Basra through Ottoman
territory via Asia Minor and the Euphrates Valley. Transit by
this route was organised by the British Embassy in Constantinople, by the British Consulate at Aleppo, and by agents
of the East India Company stationed at Baghdad and Basra. It
was greatly preferred to the Egypt route by the Embassy at
Constantinople since it was not objected to by the Ottoman
authorities, who did object to the Egypt route because they
feared that it would increase the importance of their Mamluk

vassals in Egypt. The existence of this alternative route, unreliable as it was, and the Constantinople Embassy's preference for it, probably explains why the British Government and the East India Company were not more assiduous in their efforts to develop the Egypt route.

During the Napoleonic wars express despatches continued to pass intermittently between England and India both by the Egypt and by the Euphrates routes. Soon after the war the position was revolutionised by the invention and development of the steamship. Previously, it had only been possible for sailing vessels to come to Suez for about three months in the year owing to the prevalence of northerly winds in the Gulf of Suez. With the development of steam, this difficulty was removed, and the various British communities in India, for reasons both of business and convenience, became keenly interested in the possible development of a fast and regular steamship service for passengers and mail between England and India via Suez. At first, the British Government and the East India Company were not greatly interested and nearly all the initiative came from private individuals in India. In 1823 the British community in Calcutta formed a 'Steam Committee' to promote regular steamship services between England and India by whatever route was found to be fastest and most practicable. Soon afterwards, 'Steam Committees' were formed in Bombay and Madras as well. The Calcutta Committee offered a substantial money prize to any individual or company who should, before the end of 1826, succeed in establishing a regular service of steamers between England and Bengal, either by the Cape route or via Suez. As a result of this offer the steamer *Enterprise* was built and made the voyage from England to India by the Cape route. The attempt to set up a regular service was a failure, but the experiment showed that the shorter Mediterranean and Red Sea route was, at the time, a more suitable route for steamers than the ocean route via the Cape, since the Atlantic rollers made navigation difficult for paddle-steamers (the screw propeller was not in general use until about 1850).

At the beginning of 1829 the Government of Bombay sent the sailing brig *Thetis* to the Red Sea 'for the purpose of making depots of coal for steam navigation as well as for making a survey of the coasts and ports'.[1] It had been intended that

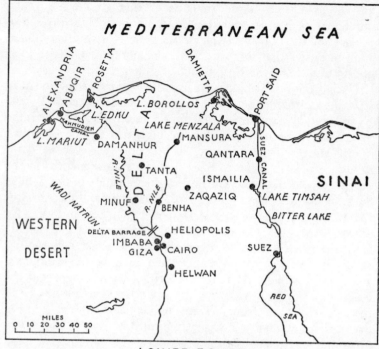

LOWER EGYPT

Enterprise, then at Bombay, should leave for Suez in November 1829 and that the East India Company should send a steamer to Alexandria to synchronise with this and pick up the mail brought by *Enterprise* from India. Transit of the mail through Egypt had already been arranged by the British Consulate.[2] But the plan fell through. *Thetis* was unable to make Suez owing to contrary winds and discharged her cargo at Qusair instead.[3] Another British sailing vessel, *Owen Glendower*, went aground in the Red Sea and eventually discharged her cargo of coal at Qusair as well.[4] The East India Company found the chartering of a steamer to go to Alexandria too expensive and the condition of *Enterprise*'s engines prevented her from leaving Bombay.[5]

At the end of 1829 Thomas Waghorn, an ex-officer of the Indian Navy who had resigned from the service to devote himself to what he always referred to as 'the steam object', arrived at Alexandria with despatches from the East India Company which he had intended to carry to India on *Enterprise*. In view of *Enterprise*'s non-arrival at Suez he returned to England. He was to come back to Egypt later.

Meanwhile, John Barker, the British Consul-General in Egypt, was being kept busy with questions about the overland route from the Foreign Office, the India Board, the British Ambassador in Constantinople, and the Governor of Bombay. In January 1829 he told Sir John Malcolm, Governor of Bombay, that 'two monsoons on the other side of the isthmus [of Suez] will always present insurmountable obstacles to rapid communication between England and India by the Suez route as long as steam navigation is not adopted'. He went on to state that mail could be passed through Egypt in three days but that, if passengers were to be carried, 'arrangements must be made for their accommodation at intermediate stations along the route'. He reported that security in Egypt was much better than along the Euphrates Valley route (Barker knew all about this as he had previously been Consul in Aleppo) and concluded that he did 'not foresee any obstacle to the regular, secure and rapid transit of packets between Alexandria and Suez under the present Government and so long as Egypt is ruled by Mohamed Ali or his son Ibrahim'. In the same despatch Barker gave details of the cost of laying down English coal at Alexandria and Suez for the bunkering of steam vessels. This worked out at £6.50 a ton at Suez and £2.50 a ton at Alexandria, based on the Suez coal being transported from Alexandria overland across Egypt.[6]

At the beginning of 1830 *Thetis*, which had been sent from Bombay with the despatches which were to have been carried by *Enterprise*, arrived at Qusair with the despatches and seven passengers.

During 1830 another marine survey of the Red Sea was carried out by HMS *Benares* of the Indian Navy, which also brought despatches to Qusair. But the most important development during the year was the first journey of a steamer between Bombay and Suez. In 1828 the Government of Bombay had started constructing at Bombay a steamer of 411 tons for the purpose of running a regular service between Bombay and Suez. This vessel was launched in October 1829 and named *Hugh Lindsay* after the Chairman of the Court of Directors of the East India Company. On 20 March 1830 *Hugh Lindsay* left

Bombay for Suez on her maiden voyage. She arrived safely at
Suez on 22 April, taking thirty-three days, of which twelve had
been spent coaling at Qusair.[7] The despatches she carried
reached England fifty-nine days after leaving Bombay.

Hugh Lindsay continued to ply regularly between Bombay
and Egypt and, on her second voyage, conveyed the retiring
Governor of Bombay from Bombay to Qusair on his way to
England, and took his successor back to Bombay. But there was
still no great enthusiasm in England for the continued development of the route. Although the Bombay Government recommended that three more steamers should be built in order to
establish a regular monthly service, no more were built for
some years, apparently on the ground of expense. Barker
recommended that the Egyptian terminal should be at Qusair
instead of Suez. A courier 'mounted on a good dromedary'
could convey mail between Qusair and Alexandria 'in seven
days in all seasons', and 'five days consumption of coal, or 50
tons, would be saved on each voyage'. Barker also, reversing
his previous opinion, told the British Government that 'the
Basra-Aleppo route is in every respect preferable to the Red
Sea route, provided that the Euphrates can be navigated in all
seasons by steamships'. He suggested a survey of the Euphrates
and made various detailed suggestions based on his previous
knowledge of the area.[8]

As a result, probably, of Barker's recommendation, the
subsequent voyages of *Hugh Lindsay* and of another steamer,
Felix, which started a regular service from Calcutta in 1834,
terminated at Qusair instead of Suez for a time. But in 1835, as
the result of a recommendation by Lieutenant-Colonel Campbell,
who had succeeded Barker as Consul-General, they returned
again to Suez.[9] Also in 1835 the British Government established
a regular steamship service between Malta and Alexandria.
Campbell was requested to secure from Mohamed Ali the
facilitation of the transit of passengers and mail overland between
Alexandria and Suez, 'as HM's Government have adopted this
arrangement with the object of keeping up a speedy and regular
communication with the British Provinces in India via the Red
Sea.'[10] A year previously, in 1834, an Austrian company had
established a regular steamer service between Trieste and
Alexandria.[11]

Mohamed Ali was enthusiastic about the development of the

overland route, since it would bring him in money and, he hoped, would improve his relations with England. He co-operated with the British Consulate in arrangements for laying down coal and for the transport of mail through Egypt. He sent a letter to the Governor of Jidda instructing him to co-operate with the Indian Navy in their survey of the Red Sea.[12] He began to ponder the possibility either of a canal or a railway between Cairo and Suez.[13] The railway had been suggested to him by Galloway Bey, an English civil engineer in his service, who spent some time surveying the route with a view to laying a double track which, he estimated, could be completed in two years.[14] The canal had been suggested to the Viceroy by Prosper Enfantin, a Saint-Simonian and a fanatical enthusiast for the idea, who visited Egypt in 1833, accompanied by several French engineers.

At the time, neither the canal nor the railway came to anything, Mohamed Ali preferring a scheme for building a barrage at the apex of the Delta in order to raise the level of summer water in the Delta for irrigating the cotton crop. Nothing immediate was done about this either, as the critical state of affairs between Mohamed Ali and his suzerain, and the consequent demands on his resources, made it impossible to pursue any major public works for the time being. Galloway went to London to try to raise money there for the construction of railways between Alexandria and Cairo and Cairo and Suez. But, at that time, the British Government were more interested in the possibility of developing the Euphrates Valley route, and Galloway received no encouragement and no money.[15]

The British Government had an almost traditional preference for the Euphrates as against the Suez route. During the 1830s this preference was reinforced by several factors. First, an increasing reluctance to enhance the importance of Mohamed Ali. Secondly, an increasing desire to instal, on some plausible pretext, a British presence along the line of the Euphrates in order to keep an eye on Russian expansion in that direction. Thirdly, the fact that the paddles which still activated steam-ships were more suitable for river than for high seas navigation. All these factors may have induced the British Government to pay more attention to Barker's recommendation in favour of the Euphrates route than they usually paid to that gentleman's views.

But Barker's views were probably less influential than those of Captain F. R. Chesney R.A. who, in 1832, produced a report on the relative advantages of the two alternative overland routes which he had just returned from surveying. Chesney had arrived in Constantinople in 1828 with the intention of assisting the Turkish army in the war which had broken out with Russia. But, when he arrived, the war was already over and he found himself at a loose end. He was therefore pleased to accept from Sir Robert Gordon, the British Ambassador, a commission to survey both the Suez and the Euphrates routes and report on their relative advantages. He proceeded first to Egypt, arriving in May 1830 at Alexandria, where Barker handed him a questionnaire which he had just received from the India Board.[16] While in Egypt Chesney investigated the possibility of transforming the overland route through Egypt into a waterway by the construction of a canal across the Suez isthmus. This was not a new idea. One of Bonaparte's instructions from the Directory when he invaded Egypt in 1798 had been to construct such a canal. In pursuance of these instructions one of his engineers, Le Père, made a survey of the route and came to the erroneous conclusion that a direct cut between the Mediterranean and the Red Sea was impracticable on account of a thirty-feet difference in level between the two seas. Chesney came to the correct conclusion that there was no appreciable difference. But he did not develop the idea of a direct cut through the isthmus as he had already become attracted to the alternative route via the Euphrates Valley. Towards the end of 1830, therefore, he asked for and obtained Gordon's permission to leave Egypt and make a survey of the Euphrates to test its navigability for steamers.

In January 1831 Chesney set out from Ana, near the Syrian border north-east of Aleppo, and down the Euphrates on an adventurous journey which brought him to Basra at the end of April. In spite of various disadvantages arising from the presence of marshes, dangerous currents and hostile Arabs, Chesney, when he returned to England at the end of 1832, reported to the British Government favourably on the Euphrates route, stating that it would be six or seven days quicker than the Egypt route, less expensive to operate (although more expensive to develop), susceptible of use all the year round, more comfortable, and possessing larger commercial possibilities.[17] Palmerston, the Foreign Secretary, was favourably impressed and a Select Committee of both Houses of Parliament was set up to consider the matter.[18]

The Committee reported in July 1834. It recommended that 'measures should immediately be taken for the regular establishment of steam communication with India by the Red Sea' which could be used for eight months of the year (paddle-steamers could not navigate the Indian Ocean during the monsoon season) and that, in order to provide a monthly service throughout the year, a steam navigation route via the Euphrates should be set up as well. It recommended that Parliament should vote £20,000 for making a trial with steamers on the Euphrates. The House of Commons, on the motion of the President of the India Board, duly voted this sum.

The India Board, which had the responsibility for directing the project, selected Chesney, who was promoted to Lieutenant-Colonel, to lead the expedition. The components of two river steamers were to be constructed in England, shipped out to Selucia at the mouth of the Orontes in northern Syria, transported by land from there to the highest navigable point on the Euphrates, and there assembled for the voyage to Basra. The British Ambassador in Constantinople obtained a Firman from the Sultan to 'permit two steam vessels to navigate the Euphrates alternately and this navigation may continue as long as it results in no inconvenience'. The British Consul-General in Egypt was instructed to obtain the co-operation of Mohamed Ali, who at that time occupied Syria and through whose dominions the expedition would have to pass in order to reach the Euphrates.

The expedition was a failure. After overcoming the physical and other difficulties of transporting the components overland from Seleucia to Bir, on the Euphrates, the two ships, *Tigris* and *Euphrates*, were assembled and launched in March 1836. They proceeded as far as Deir-ez-Zor but, just downstream of Deir, on 21 May, *Tigris* capsized and sank in a sandstorm. Several members of the expedition were drowned. *Euphrates*, on 19 June, reached Basra, where it met *Hugh Lindsay* which had come from Bombay and which had been waiting for some weeks with despatches for the expedition to take on its return journey. But *Euphrates* was unable to return immediately as its engines needed overhauling, and *Hugh Lindsay* left with the despatches for Suez, by which route they eventually arrived in England. *Euphrates*, after its overhaul, steamed up the Tigris to Baghdad with some newly-arrived Indian mail, which was despatched from Baghdad to Beirut via Palmyra and Damascus, thus opening a third alternative route, which continued to be used fairly regularly for some years. The opening of this new route was the sole useful result of the expedition. *Euphrates* returned in October to Basra, where *Hugh Lindsay* was again awaiting it with mail from India. On its return journey up the Euphrates the steamer's engines broke down. One of the party volunteered to carry the mail overland to the Mediterranean. After being attacked and robbed on the way, he reached the Syrian coast and forwarded the mail to England. *Euphrates* returned to Basra and the expedition was finally abandoned on 19 January 1837. It had cost £43,000, more than twice the sum originally voted by Parliament. From then onwards the British Government and the East India Company began to take the Egypt route seriously.

By the end of 1837 there were three steamers – *Hugh Lindsay*, *Atalanta* and *Berenice* – all belonging to the East India Company, in regular service between Bombay and Suez, taking about twenty days on the voyage each way. There was also a regular monthly service of steamers between England and Alexandria, although it had not yet been found possible to synchronise the two services.[19] Waghorn returned to Egypt in 1837 as Deputy Agent for the East India Company (Campbell, as Consul-General, was *ex officio* Chief Agent) to organise the transit of passengers and mail, to arrange for the laying down of coal, and to supervise the local agents of the Company at Cairo, Suez, Qusair and Jidda.

The laying down of coal was a prime necessity in the organisation and administration of the steam route. At first, this was done by the Indian Navy with coal brought from England by the Cape route. *Hugh Lindsay* had only small coal bunkers and could only steam short distances without refuelling. Coal depots were consequently established by the Indian Navy at Socotra, Aden, Kameran, Mocha and Qusair. Subsequent additions to the fleet had larger bunkers and only one coaling stop became necessary between Bombay and Suez. It was largely in order to establish this one coaling stop on a secure basis that Aden was occupied by the Government of Bombay in 1838. It was found cheaper to lay down coal at Suez with supplies brought to Alexandria from England and transported overland than to lay down stocks at Qusair brought from England by sea via the Cape. One of Waghorn's principal duties was to arrange this, which he did by organising the transport from Alexandria to Cairo by Nile and from Cairo to Suez by camel In doing this he fell foul of Campbell, who objected to his making arrangements direct with Mohamed Ali, and to his rather autocratic behaviour generally. After several months of bickering Waghorn resigned. Henceforward he worked for his own account, organising facilities for the transit of the ever-increasing number of passengers passing through Egypt on their way to and from India.[20]

In spite of the worsening relations between the British Government and Mohamed Ali over the latter's quarrel with his suzerain, the Viceroy continued to be extremely co-operative over the development of the steam route. He provided coal storage facilities at Cairo, Suez, Qusair and Kameran. He requisitioned camels for the Company to transport coal from Cairo to Suez, thus reducing the cost from 10s to 5s per camel per trip. He offered to lend coal to the Company from the Egyptian Government stores at Bulaq when supplies at Suez ran short (this sometimes happened as coal could only be transported by river from Alexandria during the season of high Nile). He put the resources of the Egyptian Government's workshops at the Company's disposal when one of *Berenice*'s engines needed repair.

The increasing use being made of the overland route naturally revived interest in the possibility of a railway, which had been pressed on the Viceroy for some years by Galloway Bey. In 1838 Campbell disapproved of the idea as 'needless and super-fluous' on the ground that 'it is not probable that Egypt will ever be the channel of heavy traffic between Europe and India, and light goods can always be transported between Suez and Cairo in 2 to $2\frac{1}{2}$ days'.[21] He attributed Galloway's enthusiasm to the fact of his father being an iron-founder and destined to supply the rails, and regarded the whole scheme as one of those 'chimerical projects' in which 'interested people deceive the Pasha and lead him into heavy expense for their own private ends, such being the object of nearly all Europeans here'. Like many such schemes, the railway came to nothing, although 'a

B

great part of the iron necessary for the work has been sent out and now lies useless'.

The idea of a canal was still in the air. Enfantin had left Egypt in 1836 but, towards the end of 1838, Campbell reported that Mougel, a French engineer from the Ponts et Chausseés who had just entered the Pasha's service, was 'a great advocate for a fresh water canal to connect the Red Sea with the Mediterranean'.[22] Linant de Bellefonds, another French engineer who had been in the Viceroy's service for some twenty years, was also an enthusiastic advocate, and had made a survey of the possibility of such a canal which he published, at Mohamed Ali's request, in 1840.

Meanwhile, the overland route continued to develop by a mixture of private enterprise and official action. At the western end, between 1837 and 1840, mail and passengers were transported between Falmouth and Gibraltar by monthly sailings of steamers of the Peninsula Steamship Company, and between Gibraltar and Alexandria via Malta by Admiralty packets. At the eastern end the steamship service was run by the East India Company. The overland transit of mail through Egypt was managed by the East India Company, which also laid down coal at Suez and Qusair. Passengers and goods were transported across Egypt by private contractors. A private company ran a service of horse-drawn barges along the Mahmudieh Canal between Alexandria and Atf, on the Rosetta branch of the Nile. Waghorn had a service of sailing boats on the Nile between Atf and Cairo. Two Englishmen, Richard Hill and Henry Raven, had a hotel in Cairo and, in 1838, contracted with the Bombay Steam Committee to run a regular service of passengers by mule-drawn vans between Cairo and Suez and to manage a series of rest-houses and staging-posts built along the Cairo–Suez road by the Bombay Steam Committee,[23] Waghorn competed with Hill and Raven on the Cairo-Suez road and both competitors built hotels at Suez. But Waghorn was not allowed to use the rest-houses and sometimes, in revenge, succeeded in commandeering all the available mules.

In 1839 a Postal Convention was signed between the British and French Governments providing for the passage of mails across France to and from India. In 1840 the Peninsula Steamship Company received a Royal Charter, constituting it as the Peninsula & Oriental Steam Navigation Company, with the object of organising a unified, fast and regular steam service between England and India, operating on both sides of the Suez Isthmus. It was also given a five-year contract for the carriage of mails between Marseilles and India. A year later it absorbed the East India Steam Navigation Company, which had been formed in Calcutta to supplement the not very satisfactory service run between Bombay and Suez by the East India Company.

At the end of 1840 Arthur Anderson, Managing Director of the new company (which became known as the P. and O.), went to Egypt with the object of improving the overland service (which had not been at all affected by current political events). As a result of his negotiations with the Egyptian Government he arranged that goods in transit between England and India should only pay ½ per cent customs duty instead of the 3 per cent laid down in the Capitulations (which made no distinction between imported goods and goods in transit). He started a service of barges drawn by steam tugs along the Mahmudieh Canal, which was an improvement on the horse-drawn barges, and put two river steamers – *Lotus* and *Cairo* – into service between Atf and Cairo. He arranged for the repair of the road between Cairo and Suez and for the installation of a semaphore telegraph system between the two places.[24] He also became interested in the possibility of piercing the Suez Isthmus by a ship canal.

Just after Anderson's visit, Waghorn on the one side and Hill and Raven on the other, no doubt foreseeing the prospect of severe competition from P. and O., amalgamated their services under the style of Hill & Co. and, in 1841, had a steamer – *Jack O'Lantern* – built for the Cairo–Atf service. They also took over the horse-barge company on the Mahmudieh Canal and started a steam tug service in competition with P. and O.

By this time the number of passengers transiting Egypt between England and India was nearly 1,000 a year. In 1843, as a first step towards getting the transit business into his own hands, Mohamed Ali advanced a sum of £20,000 to an English merchant, Robert Thurburn, to enable him to set up a Transit Company. Hill & Co., 'being called upon either to sell or run the risk of being overpowered by a Company established under the protection of Government'[25] sold out to Thurburn, who also

took over the lease of the Cairo–Suez rest-houses from the
Bombay Steam Committee. 'In most respects the service was
better conducted by the Transit Co., but the fares went up
from £12 to £15 and, from the first, there was a disposition
to monopolise every means of transit'.[26]

In December 1844 a Postal Convention was negotiated
between the British Post Office and the Egyptian Government
for regulating the conditions of transit of British–Indian mail
through Egypt. The British Government, as a condition of
ratifying this Convention, stipulated that British companies and
individuals should be allowed a free choice in arranging for the
transit of passengers and goods through Egypt, subject to
reasonable arrangements to guard against evasion of customs
duties. But the Egyptian Government insisted that all passengers, goods and mail should be transported by Thurburn's
Transit Company, which they had themselves set up. As a
result the British Government refused to ratify the Convention.
In spite of further negotiations, neither side gave way and
mail continued to be carried as before under East India Company
arrangements until 1848, when an agreement was arrived at by
which the Egyptian Government became responsible for the
transit of mail through Egypt against an annual lump sum
payment by the British Post Office.[27]

After the Postal Convention negotiations had broken down,
Mohamed Ali, who once admitted to the British Consul-
General that, in advancing Thurburn the money to buy out
Hill & Co., he had the eventual intention of taking the transit
business into his own hands,[28] first refused to allow P. and O.
to put a third steamer into service on the Nile and, a few weeks
afterwards, 'forcibly dispossessed Mr Thurburn of all control,
made a compulsory purchase of all his stock, and took possession
of the station-houses on the Suez road'.[29]

P. and O., having tried without success to get some support
from the British Government, abandoned the fight and sold
their river steamers and the Mahmudieh Canal barges to the
Egyptian Government, which thus acquired a virtual monopoly
of the overland transit, by this time handling some 2,300
passengers and 2,500 camel-loads of goods a year, apart from
mail.

In England, in the summer of 1846, the Conservative
Government headed by Sir Robert Peel, with Lord Aberdeen as

Foreign Secretary, which had been in office since 1841, fell. Palmerston came back to the Foreign Office and with him all the old suspicions of French designs in Egypt, which were revived in his mind both by the interest of various French nationals in a ship canal and by the influence believed to have been exerted by French officials in the Egyptian service in inducing Mohamed Ali to take over the transit business as a means of getting it out of British hands.

In Egypt, a new Consul-General, Charles Murray, who succeeded Colonel Barnett in 1846, shared Palmerston's views. Towards the end of 1846 he sent Palmerston a despatch giving his version of how things were going on.[30] 'The Pasha, guided partly by his own shrewdness and still more by the counsels of his French advisers, has steadily adhered to one line of policy, the object of which is to keep the overland communication entirely under his own control and to prevent England from obtaining any solid or permanent footing within his dominions . . . It was with this view that he has bought out the Transit Co., and it was with the same view that he forbade the P. and O. to add a third steamer to the two they have on the Nile.'

Murray went on to deal with the question of the railway. Three years before, in 1843, the idea of a railway between Cairo and Suez had again been raised by J. A. Galloway, a brother of Galloway Bey, who had died in 1838. J. A. Galloway, who was a partner in a British merchant house in Alexandria, continued his brother's canvassing for the railway, both in England and in Egypt, arguing that it was a cheaper and generally preferable alternative to a ship canal as a means of speeding up the India route.[31] Towards the end of 1843 Lord Aberdeen, in response apparently to an application by the Galloway family in London, instructed Colonel Barnett, the Consul-General, to 'give every proper countenance to so useful an enterprise' and added that 'should opposition, either overt or secret, be made to it, or arguments urged against it on the part of any foreign agent', he should 'encourage the Pasha to complete an undertaking which promises to confer great advantages on Egypt and be eminently useful to the whole Western world'.[32]

In Egypt there was little enthusiasm. Artin Bey, one of the Pasha's Armenian *hommes de confiance*, told Barnett that the Pasha had already given an order to Galloway for the rails but that he (Artin) had advised him to cancel it. He went on to say that Mohamed Ali was too ready to adopt hastily any wild-cat scheme that was suggested to him and that no proper cost calculations had been made. He added that, if the British Government wanted the railway, they might be prepared to guarantee a certain annual sum towards its upkeep. Barnett, reporting this conversation to Aberdeen, expressed the view that Artin's advice to the Pasha had been judicious and suggested that a canal might be a preferable alternative.[33]

During the course of the Postal Convention negotiations Mohamed Ali showed some interest in the idea of a railway and allowed Galloway to make a survey.[34] Aberdeen, no doubt pressed by the Galloways, and ignoring Barnett's lack of enthusiasm, continued to support the idea. He told Barnett that 'although HM's Government do not propose to interfere directly in the matter . . . they take the deepest interest in accelerating the transit of mail and passengers across Egypt . . . leaving it to the Pasha to judge whether and how such a measure may be rendered practicable and advantageous.'[35]

After the British refusal to ratify the Postal Convention Mohamed Ali lost interest in the railway. Artin told Barnett that Galloway had been informed that 'HH declined for the present commencing work on the railroad, alleging as a reason the high price of iron in England.' When Galloway proposed that he should build the railway at his own expense 'upon certain conditions', the Pasha refused to consider any such arrangement.[36] Barnett added that Galloway had blamed him for not giving him enough support.

What had happened was that Mohamed Ali had decided to go ahead with the Delta barrage instead of either a canal or a railway. In April 1845 he sent Mougel, a French engineer in his service, to Paris 'for the purpose of submitting to the Council of Civil Engineers in that city a new plan for the construction of the barrage'.[37] This was a repetition of a similar decision made ten years previously, when the Viceroy was being pressed by Galloway Bey to build a railway and by Enfantin to build a canal. At that time, trouble with the Porte over Syria had intervened to prevent a start being made on the barrage.

Murray thought it improbable that the railway could be urged with reasonable prospects of success. He told Palmerston that 'France has pronounced herself determinedly opposed to it, and in this opposition she has been supported by the agents of the other great Continental Powers who are rather concerned in the plan for a ship canal between the Levant and the Red Sea.'[38] This was a reference to the formation, in Paris in November 1846, under the influence of Prosper Enfantin, of a Societé d'Etudes for working out a plan for a ship canal. The Societé consisted of five Frenchmen, ten Germans and two Englishmen. They were in correspondence with Linant de Bellefonds, and with Laurin, the Austrian Consul-General in Egypt, who was keenly interested in the canal and writing to Metternich about it. Murray concluded 'from the opinions of the best-informed professional men to whom I have spoken', that such a canal would be more expensive than a railway. He asked for instructions; whether HMG wanted to maintain the employment of British capital and British agency in the transit business or whether they were content to see it pass entirely into the Viceroy's hands; whether HMG agreed that P. and O. should sell their ships to the Egyptian Government (he reported later that the sale had gone through); and whether the building of a railroad between Cairo and Suez 'is held to be highly desirable to British interests and to be pressed on Mohamed Ali as a matter in which HMG are interested, or whether I am to consider it as an affair between Mr Galloway and the Pasha and therefore not calling for interference on my part.'

In reply, Palmerston told Murray; that it was certainly HMG's wish to maintain as far as possible British capital and British agency in the transit business, 'but, as a contrary policy seems to have been acted on in late years, you must act with discretion and prudence in endeavouring to get back what has been given up and you must wait for and watch for opportunities'; 'that the P. and O. Company had already sold the steamers before I could advise them not to do so'; that, with regard to the railroad, 'HMG would be glad to see the undertaking commenced but, as the work would be done at the expense of the Pasha, and as he is at present engaged in an expensive operation for damming the Nile, it is not likely that he will just now be induced to enter upon the construction of a railway'; and that, with regard to the ship canal, 'you should lose no opportunity of enforcing on the Pasha and his Ministers the costliness, if not the impracticability, of such a project . . . The persons who press upon the Pasha such a chimerical scheme do so evidently for the purpose of diverting him from the railroad, which would be perfectly practicable and comparatively cheap.'[39]

In the event, nothing effective was done, either by HMG or by anybody else, about limiting the extent of the Egyptian Government monopoly of the means of transit on the overland route, which was enforced by withholding the $\frac{1}{2}$ per cent transit dues concession obtained by Anderson and insisting on the full 3 per cent on all goods transported otherwise than by the government Transit Administration. There were at first a good many grumbles from the British Post Office representative at Alexandria and from others about inefficiency and delay but, generally, the service seems to have been an improvement on the past.[40] Instead, British interest in the overland route gradually became concentrated on advocacy of a railway and opposition to a ship canal. This had little or nothing to do with the technical or commercial merits of the two alternatives. The railway was advocated because it was put forward by, and for the benefit of, British capitalists; the canal was opposed because it was believed to be supported by the French Government with a view to the consolidation of French influence in Egypt.

The possibility of a canal first came officially to HMG's notice in 1833 when Campbell advised them that Mohamed Ali was contemplating it. On that occasion the India Board, while suggesting that the prospect was only a distant one, minuted to the Foreign Office that it 'anticipated none but desirable consequences from the accomplishment of such a work'.[41] Mohamed Ali was therefore told that HMG had no objection to his plan, of which no more was heard for the time being. In 1841, after Enfantin and his entourage had left Egypt, and after Linant had published his canal studies, Arthur Anderson, on his return from a visit to Egypt on P. and O. business (see p.35), wrote two letters to Palmerston dated 25 March 1841 and 23 April 1841 respectively, putting forward in some detail a proposal for a ship canal to be built by British capital in the name of the Sultan, with the profits divided fifty/fifty between the Sultan and the concessionary company.[42] This proposal only received a formal acknowledgement from Palmerston and the project seems to have been dropped. In 1843 a similar project was taken up with Mohamed Ali by the Austrian Consul-General on Metternich's instructions. But this too came to nothing. In 1845 a canal project was again put forward to the Viceroy by a group of Leipzig business men, who met with no encouragement from the Viceroy. Then, in 1846, came the formation of the Societé d'Etudes. This was followed in 1847 by the arrival in Egypt of three Societé d'Etudes groups – one under an Englishman, Robert Stephenson, one under a Frenchman, Paulin Talabot, and one under an Austrian, Negrelli – each charged with making a detailed survey of some particular aspect of the subject. While they were at work, Murray reported to Palmerston that the Egyptian Government 'have a plan for a canal under consideration prepared by M. Linant, a French official who has superintended the construction of all the bridges, canals and aqueducts which the Pasha has made in Egypt. M. Linant's plan has been submitted to three eminent engineers – one French, one Austrian and one British . . . I have not heard that the French and Austrian Governments have interfered directly, but there is no doubt that it is countenanced by both, especially the latter, and Negrelli has been favoured with letters of introduction from Vienna . . . In the present advanced state of science I dare not take it upon myself to assure Your Lordship that the undertaking is as impracticable as it would have been some years ago.' Commenting that such an undertaking would 'if successful exercise a vast influence over our Indian interests', Murray asked for instructions about the attitude he should adopt.[43]

Palmerston, in a detailed reply, told Murray that it was difficult for HMG 'to form an accurate judgement as to the practicability of making the canal or to foresee with certainty the effect which [it] would produce on British commercial and political interests' and recommended that 'the most prudent course for you to pursue is to remain entirely passive on the subject and to say that you have no instructions from your Government either to support or oppose it, but that in HMG's opinion the commercial advantages to be derived from it would be attained nearly as well and at much less cost of time and money by a railway across the desert from the Nile to the Red Sea'. After describing the technical difficulties of a canal, Palmerston went on; 'But it would be a bold thing to affirm that all these difficulties would not be overcome if sufficient funds are applied for the purpose . . . The Austrian Government is favourable . . . because they think that the commerce of India and China could be brought by the Red Sea to the Mediterranean instead of going round the Cape, and Trieste would become a great emporium for commerce between Asia and Europe. But any new arrangement which would facilitate commerce in general and shorten communications and cheapen transport would necessarily be advantageous to England, the greatest commercial country in the world. The French Government is anxious for the execution of the scheme because they see in its completion a great many naval and military advantages, inasmuch as it would place them, as a military and naval Power in the Mediterranean, much nearer to India than England would be. The French may however overrate the political advantages they would thereby gain and, if England were superior at sea, she might possibly profit by the canal to a greater degree than France.' Palmerston concluded that 'on the whole, HMG do not wish to oppose the canal absolutely, but would greatly prefer the railway'.[44]

Palmerston made enquiries in Constantinople through Lord Cowley, the British Ambassador, who reported that Rashid Pasha, the Grand Vizier, had been told by Mohamed Ali that 'he had been urged by foreign Powers to construct the canal and had turned a deaf ear, but thought of undertaking the work himself whenever the work he had on hand [the Delta barrage] was completed'. The Viceroy had also asked Rashid to discourage the idea if it were put up to the Porte by any foreign Power. Rashid assured Cowley that the canal was unlikely to be built for years and promised that he would put a word in with Mohamed Ali in favour of the railway.[45] Later, Rashid told Cowley that Mohamed Ali was equally opposed to a canal and to a railway.[46]

There was no further development in either project until after Mohamed Ali's death in 1849. The Societé d'Etudes reports were duly published, recommending a canal from the Nile to the Red Sea instead of a direct cut across the isthmus. By that time Talabot had quarrelled with Linant and Stephenson had quarrelled with the Societé, having become interested in a railway between Alexandria and Cairo, as being a better economic proposition than a Cairo–Suez railway, which had no economic justification apart from the transit trade.[47] Enfantin hawked the idea of a canal round Europe without success. But he did secure the interest of a retired French diplomat, without money or political influence, who had served in Egypt about fifteen years previously, during the time of Enfantin's mission there. His name was Ferdinand de Lesseps.

During the last eight years of his life, from 1841 to 1849, Mohamed Ali's physical and mental powers steadily deteriorated. His temper became more and more uncertain and he became estranged from his eldest son Ibrahim. Because of this, he did not permit Ibrahim to play that part in the running of the State for which he was eminently fitted. Until 1844, when he had a severe brainstorm, the Viceroy kept the management of affairs very much in his own hands, to their great detriment. Thereafter, the Egyptian Government's relations with foreign Powers and the foreign communities were mainly dealt with by Artin Bey, who succeeded Boghos Yusef as Foreign Minister and Minister of Commerce after Boghos' death in January 1844. Artin was the second of a series of Armenian *hommes de confiance* – Boghos being the first – who formed the principal link between the Viceroy and the European consuls. Whereas Boghos' background had been British, Artin's was French. During the period of his predominance, which lasted from the beginning of 1844 to the end of 1848, the French officials in the Egyptian service had things very much their own way and the British Consul-General had a correspondingly difficult time over the negotiation of various outstanding matters. During these years, increasing French influence was, in the eyes of the British Consul-General, demonstrated in the favouritism shown to French contractors in the award of government tenders,[48] in the commencement of work on the Delta barrage in April 1847 according to French plans and under the supervision of a French engineer,[49] and in the strengthening of the fortifications of Alexandria by Gallice Bey, a French engineer in the Egyptian service, according to plans drawn up in Paris.[50] Murray complained that 'every department of the public service is more or less in the hands of the French; the younger members of the reigning family were all educated either in Paris or under French instructors; the medical, education and engineering branches are all entirely French; Alexandria has been fortified by a Frenchman; the effective C-in-C of the army (Soliman Pasha) is a Frenchman by birth and the Foreign Minister

(Artin) is a Frenchman by adoption; it only remains to officer the troops with Frenchmen to make Egypt another Tunisia as a preliminary to its becoming another Algeria'. (Algeria was a French possession and Tunisia a French protectorate.)

In May 1848, as a result of the state of Mohamed Ali's health, a special meeting of the Divan (Viceroy's Council) decided that Ibrahim should administer Egypt in his father's name.[51] This decision was later ratified by the Sultan who issued a Hatti Sherif nominating Ibrahim as Viceroy.[52] But Ibrahim also was a dying man and the question of the succession was causing much uneasiness. Murray reported: 'I am convinced that the hereditary succession in the present family beyond the life of Ibrahim Pasha is a delusion. His brothers, sons and nephews are all equally odious and incapable, they are all at variance with each other, and at his death anarchy and civil war can only be averted by armed intervention from without.' He went on to suggest that there were three possible forms of intervention: the reversion of Egypt to the direct rule of the Porte; occupation by a French force, 'taking possession of the fortifications of Alexandria which they have long since planned and constructed with this object'; or a British occupation to maintain the security of Anglo-Indian communications.[53]

According to the terms of the 1841 settlement the succession went to the eldest surviving male in the direct line of descent. In the event of Ibrahim's death this would be Abbas, son of Tusun, Mohamed Ali's second son. The two males in direct line nearest him were Said, a son of Mohamed Ali, then about twenty-five years old, and Ahmed, Ibrahim's eldest son, who was about a year younger. There were also Ismail and Mustafa Fazil, Ibrahim's younger sons, who were in their late teens. Abbas, besides being the eldest, was also the most experienced, having been Governor of Cairo for some years. According to Murray, he was 'selfish and tyrannical, and notoriously addicted to the filthy sensualities which degrade so many of his caste', but 'a man of considerable shrewdness and energy who might be able to control the elements of discord', since 'the fact that he is so hated is a proof that he is somewhat feared, whereas the other two would depend altogether for success on the support which they might eventually receive either from the Porte or from the Powers'.[54]

From Murray's point of view, Abbas was also preferable

for personal reasons. Murray, unlike any of his fellow-consuls, spoke Turkish fluently. Abbas spoke no European language, whereas Ahmed had been educated in France and Said had had a French tutor.

When Ibrahim died in November 1848 the ambassadors in Constantinople, on the recommendation of the consuls-general, agreed with the Porte that Abbas should have the succession; and a Hatti Sherif to that effect, which also appointed Abbas as Regent for his grandfather, was immediately sent to Egypt.

The regency of Abbas seemed to HMG to be a suitable occasion to raise the question of a railway. The Galloway family had now departed from the scene and the old idea of a railway between Cairo and Suez had been replaced by the idea of one between Cairo and Alexandria. The man behind it was Robert Stephenson, a Member of Parliament and son of the great steam locomotive pioneer. He had broken with the Societé d'Etudes and was putting the weight of his influence behind the railway. Immediately on Abbas assuming the regency Palmerston wrote to Murray suggesting that he take a suitable opportunity of pointing out to Abbas how 'improved means of communication have everywhere created proportionate increases in traffic' and warning him that 'it is not impossible that, if the railway from Alexandria to Suez is not made, some other line of railway communication may be thought of which, by giving a line of passage from England to India shorter in point of time, might entirely divert the stream of passengers and merchandise from Egypt'.[53] It was already in Stephenson's mind that, once the Cairo–Alexandria line had been completed, it should be followed by the construction of a Cairo–Suez line.

At first, this suggestion bore little fruit. In April 1849, when Sir John Pirie, a director of P. and O., visited Egypt, Murray felt obliged to warn Palmerston lest Pirie had been led by some conventionally polite remarks made to him by Abbas during an audience to take a too optimistic view about the prospects for a railway. 'It was quite evident to me, who understood HH's language, that the idea of a railway was distasteful to him.' He added that 'the suggestion of a railway by means of finance raised in England would not be listened to by him for a moment . . . HH is of the opinion that a railroad would immensely increase the influence exercised by England over Egypt, and this impression would be materially strengthened if English capital were offered for its construction.'[56] Stephenson took the point and, thereafter, planned in terms of a railway constructed, owned and operated by the Egyptian Government, with British interests acting as contractors and suppliers of material.

But it did not appear that Abbas would agree to a railway on any terms. He had none of his grandfather's enthusiasm for modernisation. During the first few months of his regency he 'abandoned almost all the works commenced by the old Pasha; schools are abolished, factories done away with, and I expect shortly to hear that the famous barrage will be abandoned'. He also started reducing the size of the army from the 80,000 at which it had stood during Ibrahim's short regency to 27,000, and cancelled the new conscription which Ibrahim had ordered.[57] As a set-off against these economies, Abbas spent a good deal of money on personal extravagances but, on the whole, the reduced expenditure on the army and navy (he laid up, or got rid of, most of the line-of-battle ships Mohamed Ali had loved) and on public works, benefited the country in that it led to a reduction of taxation and in the number of hands taken away from agriculture. The turning away from modernisation also led to the dismissal of many of the French experts in government service and to a consequent diminution in French influence.

On 2 August 1849 the old Pasha died at the age of eighty and Abbas formally assumed the Viceroyalty. As was normal in a new reign, the new ruler turned against his predecessor's most trusted servants. Sami Bey, who for years had been Mohamed Ali's secretary and right-hand-man, fell out of favour and managed to obtain from Constantinople a Balkan pashalik for himself. The head of the Transit Administration was dismissed. Artin fell into disgrace and, in August 1950, fled the country. (After his departure, the Ministries of Foreign Affairs and Commerce, which had been combined under Boghos and Artin, were divided. Stephan Bey, another Armenian, became Foreign Minister, and Edhem Bey, a Moslem Turk, Minister of Commerce.)

Although there had been little or no overt opposition to Abbas' succession, it was not long before intrigues were set on foot against him. His relatives were jealous of him. The most formidable of them, Nazli Khanum, Mohamed Ali's favourite and widowed daughter who, in her father's lifetime, had been regarded as the first lady in Egypt, was outraged at the public honours which Abbas heaped on his mother, Tusun's widow. In Constantinople, Sami and Artin moved the Grand Vizier, Rashid, who was supposed to be a creature of Stratford Canning, against Abbas.[58] Rashid was anxious to use the opposition to Abbas as a means of restoring effective Ottoman authority in Egypt under cover of the 1841 settlement, which had never been fully carried into effect during the lifetimes of Mohamed Ali and Ibrahim. He therefore started harassing Abbas in a number of vexatious ways. He adopted what afterwards became an Ottoman habit of inviting various members of the Viceroy's family to live in Constantinople and form the nucleus of a permanent opposition to and centre of intrigue against the reigning Viceroy. He complained about the size of the Egyptian army which, although cut down by Abbas, was still in excess of the 18,000 laid down in the 1841 settlement. He attempted to insist that the Tanzimat – an Ottoman legal code which, as a result of the representations of the European Powers, had been theoretically imposed on all the Ottoman provinces – should be applied in its entirety to Egypt.

Murray saw the disgrace of Artin Bey, and the opposition to Abbas developing at Constantinople, as an opportunity to enhance British influence in Egypt by taking Abbas' side in Constantinople. In particular, he saw it as an opportunity to get Abbas to build the Cairo–Alexandria railway as a *quid pro quo* for British support in Constantinople. Profiting by his knowledge of Turkish, he was soon in confidential relations with Abbas, with whom he habitually conversed without any other person being present. In February 1851 Abbas sent for Murray and asked for HMG's assistance in combating the intrigues with which he was surrounded. Murray recommended to Palmerston that this assistance be given. Although Abbas was 'far from being a virtuous Ruler', he was not as bad as he was being painted and should be supported, both for the sake of British interests in Egypt and in the light of his treaty rights as laid down in the 1841 settlement to which HMG had been a party.[59] Palmerston assured Murray that Stratford Canning (whom Abbas had accused of favouring his enemies in Constantinople) had been instructed to support Abbas against any intrigues in Constantinople, but that 'he would not support Abbas in resisting the application of the Tanzimat to Egypt'.[60]

This was not surprising, since Stratford Canning had been instrumental in imposing the Tanzimat on the Porte. In the meantime, Murray had told Stratford Canning that Abbas' support of British interests in Egypt was conditional on British support for Abbas' interests in Constantinople.[61] 'The Viceroy solicits Your Excellency's friendly aid in relieving him from two immediate humiliations with which he is threatened.' These were the application of the Tanzimat to Egypt, and the summoning of junior members of his family to Constantinople without his consent. In an immediately following private letter to the Ambassador, Murray put the position frankly; 'If Your Excellency is disposed to give the Viceroy the support of your influence we shall get the whole credit and secure a footing of advantage here that will not easily be shaken; if we delay the opportunity will be lost, and even if the objective desired by Abbas is ultimately attained, he will not be indebted primarily to England for this.'[62]

What Murray was really after was the railway. He seems to have persuaded Abbas to sign contracts with British firms for it on condition of British support in Constantinople. Nubar Bey, a rising official in the Egyptian service who had previously been one of Mohamed Ali's interpreters, and who was a nephew of Boghos Yusef, was about to go to London with authority to sign contracts for the supply of material. Stephenson was negotiating a contract with the Egyptian Government for supervising the work of construction.

Stratford Canning was not entirely convinced by Murray's arguments. He had a proprietorial feeling about the Tanzimat, and he had become identified, during his years as Ambassador at Constantinople (he had been there, with one short interval, since 1841 and had had two previous spells there), with the traditional British policy of supporting the Sultan against his Egyptian vassal. On the basis of this policy he had achieved a firm alliance with the Grand Vizier, Rashid Pasha, which seemed to assure, for the time being, the predominance of British influence at Constantinople. He was not prepared summarily to reverse this policy, and to jeopardise the advantages accruing from it, for the sake of British investment in an Egyptian railway. Nor was he prepared to associate himself, with Murray, in a free-for-all competition with France when he needed the assistance of French influence at Constantinople to counterbalance the ever-present threat of Russian power to the north. So the support which he gave to Abbas was by no means as whole-hearted as Murray desired. Apart from the Tanzimat dispute (which resolved itself into a long argument as to whether or not Abbas should have the power of executing the death-penalty in Egypt without the Sultan's confirmation), the size of the army and the control of the junior relatives, the Porte demanded of Abbas that the railway should not be built without a Firman from the Sultan. They sent an emissary, Mukhtar Bey, to Egypt to tell him so. Murray protested bitterly to Palmerston: 'In fighting this battle I find myself absolutely alone, for I learn that the Representatives of all the other Powers have instructions, either secret or open, to oppose it [the railway], and it is not to be wondered at that Abbas should feel some hesitation in commending an undertaking which is distasteful to all the Continental Powers and also to the Sublime Porte. But, as I have received instructions more than once from Your Lordship to press this undertaking on HH, and as I feel a conviction that it will be a great advantage to the internal trade of Egypt as it will be to our Anglo-Indian intercourse, I have not hesitated to insist firmly on his keeping the promise that he has given and to give him the assurance that HMG would afford him their assistance and support in carrying out a great internal improvement which can give no legitimate cause of offence either to the Sublime Porte or to other European Powers. Mukhtar Bey said that the Viceroy could not commence such a work without obtaining the sanction of the Porte. Abbas objected that Mohamed Ali had carried out all sorts of improvements in Egypt without the Porte's sanction. He is determined to proceed and is sending Nubar to England armed with full powers to make the necessary contracts for rails, carriages &c. under the advice of Mr Stephenson, whom Abbas has requested to accept the charge of Chief Engineer. In encouraging HH to take this step I hope I have not exceeded the spirit of Your Lordship's instructions, and if, in taking it, HH shall find himself exposed to vexation from other quarters, I trust he will meet with that firm support from HMG which he deserves for undertaking, in spite of so much opposition, a work which is of the highest importance to British interests.'[63]

Stratford Canning, who clearly thought that British interests in Egypt, as well as in the rest of the Ottoman Empire, were better safeguarded by being directed from Constantinople, warned Murray that he had given the Grand Vizier an undertaking that work on the railway would not be started without the Sultan's authorisation, but indicated that he would probably be able to obtain it if HMG approved of the project.[64]

This was not what Abbas wanted, for he saw that this insistence on the Sultan's authority was part of the Ottoman plan to bring Egypt into a state of complete subjection to the Porte, over and above what had been laid down in 1841, and far more than had been the practice during his grandfather's reign. It was not what Murray wanted either, for he had in effect committed himself both to Abbas and to Stephenson. On receipt of the Ambassador's letter he protested to Palmerston that 'the Viceroy's agent has been for some time in England treating with our most eminent engineers with the cognizance of HMG for the necessary men and materials', that in all Mohamed Ali's public works, including the barrage, the Sublime Porte 'had never even ventured to offer a remonstrance', that 'in the construction of the fortifications of Alexandria and Rosetta by French advisers and French engineers at a cost scarcely less than that of the barrage, neither the Sublime Porte nor HMG ever interfered or protested' and that 'now, when the Viceroy, with an income considerably exceeding expenses, and with the agriculture and commerce of the Province in a most flourishing condition, proposes an undertaking for the benefit of both . . . the Sublime Porte, moved by the jealousies and intrigues of France, step in and forbid the undertaking unless with the prior sanction of the Sultan.'[65]

Palmerston supported Murray. He told Stratford Canning that Musurus Bey, the Ottoman Ambassador in London, had been informed that HMG's view was that the necessity for the Sultan's authorisation 'could only be considered applicable to matters which . . . would have an important political bearing on the condition of Egypt as part of the Ottoman Empire, and can scarcely be construed as applying to so simple a domestic improvement as the construction of a railway. A ship canal from the Mediterranean to the Red Sea . . . would be a different thing, as such a work, changing as it would the relative position of some of the maritime Powers of Europe towards each other, would involve the possibility of political consequences of great importance and might seriously affect the foreign relations of the Ottoman Empire.'[66]

Eventually, after an inconclusive wrangle as to whether Mohamed Ali had or had not asked the Sultan's permission to build the barrage, Abbas, on the British Government's advice, wrote 'a most respectful and deferential letter' to the Sultan asking for permission to build the railway. The result, as Murray and Abbas had feared, was a long questionnaire asking for detailed information about Egypt's finances. After an agitated correspondence between Stratford Canning and Murray, and after Murray had told Palmerston that 'the honour of England is to a certain extent implicated in the carrying out of this undertaking', the Firman was obtained, as a result of Stratford Canning's representations, in November 1851.[67] Abbas was delighted and told Murray of having received reports from Constantinople that the British Ambassador 'had taken up the cudgels in his favour in right good earnest, and had not only reprobated in the strongest terms the insolent behaviour of some of the junior members of the family towards Abbas, but had also promised to procure a favourable consideration for all Abbas' demands over the Tanzimat'.[68]

It was well for Abbas and for Murray that the Firman had been obtained so quickly for, in the previous July, the contract for the construction of the railway had been signed between Stephan Bey and Stephenson's representative, providing for completion within three years. The Egyptian Government had stipulated that the railway, when completed, should be owned and operated by them.[69]

Up to a point, Murray, swimming against the strong tide of traditional British policy in Constantinople and in Egypt, had got his way. But Palmerston made it clear that this policy, while it might occasionally be twisted to suit the needs of a short-term situation, still held the field. In advising Abbas to apply to the Sultan for a Firman, he had reminded Murray that 'the interference of a foreign Government between a Sovereign and his subject cannot go beyond certain limits . . . HMG could not hold out to the Pasha any expectation of physical aid if he were involved in a rupture with the Sultan in such a question and can only recommend him to comply with the request of the Sultan.'[70] Stratford Canning saved the situation by successfully insisting on the immediate grant of the Firman. Without that insistence, the Porte would have procrastinated interminably, as they did later over the canal, and Abbas' cause would have been lost. For the railroad had become a test, not only of British influence in Egypt, but of Abbas' ability to retain his throne.

In foreign circles in Egypt the grant of the Firman was seen as a victory for British as against French influence and helped to perpetuate that tradition of Anglo-French rivalry, the observance of which had already become, and was for long to remain, an obligation almost of honour for successive British and French consuls-general. Stratford Canning was remarkably free from the francophobia which afflicted so many British officials in the Levant. After the grant of the railway Firman he wrote a private letter to Murray advising him to try to get on better with Le Moyne, his French colleague. Murray replied unrepentantly in what had become the traditional accents of British officialdom in the Levant. He stressed his good personal relations with Le Moyne, expressed admiration for 'his charming wife', and complained that the French could 'not reconcile themselves to having lost that influence which they previously possessed in Egypt'. Le Moyne, for his part, took the view that Murray had taken an unfair advantage of his knowledge of Turkish to steal a march on his colleagues in his relations with Abbas.[71] A diplomatic observer of the scene noted that 'one had the curious spectacle of the British Government, which had taken the lead in imposing the 1841 Hatti Sherif on Mohamed Ali, encouraging Abbas to assert his independence of the Porte, while France, who would have gone to war with all and sundry for the interest of Mohamed Ali, intrigues to tighten the bonds of vassalage'.[72] What had really happened was that private financial and commercial interests in England and France were beginning to exert more influence on policy than supposed strategic advantages.

During the next two years various events combined to reduce political tensions between Egypt and Constantinople. Mainly as the result of Stratford de Redcliffe's efforts (Stratford Canning was elevated to the peerage as Lord Stratford de Redcliffe in 1853), a compromise was arrived at between the Sultan and Abbas over the Tanzimat and over the financial position of Abbas' family (Abbas was given the right of confirming death sentences in Egypt for a period of five years,

and allowances amounting to a total of about £700,000 a year
were fixed for members of the family). England and France
became allied with each other, and with Turkey, in the Crimean
War against Russia. Abbas loyally supported his Suzerain
during the war and sent him a naval squadron consisting of one
battleship, four frigates and two corvettes from the run-down
and debilitated Egyptian fleet, together with 10,000 troops.[73]
He later sent military reinforcements, and a total of some
30,000 Egyptian troops went to the war.[74] Murray left Egypt
in March 1853 and was succeeded as British Agent and Consul-
General by the Hon F. W. A. Bruce in December of that year.

Lord Clarendon, Foreign Secretary in a coalition government
under Lord Aberdeen which took office in the spring of 1853,
instructing Bruce about British policy in Egypt, told him:
'HMG do not desire political influence and seek no exclusive
advantage in Egypt; and still less do they wish to disturb those
good relations that now so happily subsist between the Sultan
and the Pasha. But HMG have a right to expect and are
resolved to secure a fulfilment of treaties and a perfect justice to
British subjects . . . England has no other desire than to see
Egypt prosperous and progressive and that it should continue
to be the high road to India.'[75]

Bruce was at pains to improve Anglo-French relations. He
noted that the persistence of Anglo-French rivalry had 'led to
the formation of two parties, one consisting of French employees
of the Egyptian Government who make it their business to
suggest to the Viceroy that every improvement prompted by
England is destined to forward secret views of acquisition of
the country which they impute to England; while those who
profess to be friendly to English influence lose no opportunity
of misrepresenting every step taken by the French Agent in
defence of the rights and interests of French subjects. In this
way the Pasha is led to look with jealousy and suspicion at the
improvements in the internal administration which are suggested to him, to exaggerate the importance attached to general
expressions of friendship and goodwill, and to flatter himself
that, by taking advantage of the reluctance to endanger the
influence which may be acquired by being on good terms with
him, he will be able to persevere in refusing satisfaction for
repeated acts of injustice to individuals in his endeavours to
restore the monopoly of trade.' (At this time one of HMG's

principal interests in Egypt was to prevent any revival of Mohamed Ali's monopolies, particularly on cotton.) He went on to express the view that a good understanding with Sabatier (who had replaced Le Moyne as French Agent and Consul-General) would put a stop to this tactic of taking advantage of Anglo-French rivalry. He expressed approval of Sabatier's attitude, which showed that he was 'determined at all costs to insist on respect for treaties', and which had the effect of making him most unpopular with Abbas, who dismissed a great many French officials and officers from his service. He added that Sabatier had no objection to the Cairo–Alexandria railway, and would have no objection to the extension of this railway from Cairo to Suez, provided that the privileges granted to P. and O. were extended to the French Messageries and that the ½ per cent transit dues privilege were extended to all goods in transit through Egypt.[76]

Bruce was anxious to see the Cairo–Alexandria railway completed and to get the Viceroy's approval for its extension between Cairo and Suez. But he resisted Stephenson's attempts to employ European engineers in the construction of the railway since 'any such arrangement would be made use of by opponents of the railway to dissuade the Pasha from carrying on with it on the grounds that he will thereby establish a foreign interest in the country'. Bruce recognised that the construction of the railway was proving a considerable drain on the country's man-power and anticipated some difficulty in persuading Abbas to carry the line on to Suez. Unlike Murray, he attached great importance to the Cairo–Suez line, considering that it was 'absolutely necessary to the improvement of communications with India' and that 'little will have been gained from that point of view by the line between Cairo and Alexandria'.[77] In the event he and Stephenson persuaded Abbas to build a line between Cairo and Suez, although this had not been started, and the Cairo-Alexandria line had not been completed, when Abbas died in 1854. But his successor, Said, honoured Abbas' commitments. The Cairo–Alexandria line, including a bridge across the Damietta branch of the Nile at Benha, was completed in 1855. The crossing of the Rosetta branch at Kafr-ez-Zayat was at first accomplished by steam-ferry, but a bridge was built later and completed in 1859. The Cairo–Suez line was started in 1856 and completed in 1858. The necessary funds were found principally out of the profits of the Transit Administration.[78]

During Abbas' reign the Transit Administration was run by Abdulla Bey, an English renegade. Together with most of Abbas' senior officials, he was dismissed by Said and replaced by Mr Lee Green, a brother of the British Consul in Alexandria. By this time the traffic passing over the overland route had very greatly increased. Not only mail and passengers but also a large quantity of merchandise was being handled. Gold from the new Australian fields came to England by this route, as well as silk from China. It was the regular route for passengers between Europe and most destinations east of Suez. In 1855 two regiments of cavalry were transported by it on their way from India to the Crimea. Two years later several regiments of infantry were transported from England to India to reinforce the British garrisons there during the Mutiny. The French had a line of steamships, the Messageries Imperiales, operating both east and west of Suez and they, as well as the P. and O. and the Royal Mail Co., used the route for mail, passengers and goods.

There were some complaints against the Transit Administration on grounds of delay, theft and general incompetence. Some of these came from Turks and Egyptians who resented the employment of a European manager and many European senior staff; some came from European speculators who wanted to see the Administration de-nationalised and turned into a private company; some, embarrassingly for Bruce who was afraid that complaints might cause Said to change his mind about the Cairo–Suez line, came from the British Post Office and the East India Company. The British complainants were, at Bruce's request, suitably 'spoken to' by the British Government and told to keep quiet.

Towards the end of 1857 Mr Lee Green retired as head of the Transit Administration on grounds of ill-health[79] and was replaced by Nubar Bey, one of the Viceroy's principal *hommes de confiance*. By the time Nubar took over, the goods-carrying side of the business was more lucrative to the Egyptian Government, and almost as important to the British Government, as the mails. Most of the goods were being handled by the P. and O. and there was continual friction between P. and O.

and the British Post Office since each thought that the interests
of the one were being sacrified to the other. The Post Office
representative was particularly clamorous. Bruce, who was
intent on keeping the Egyptian Government sweet in order to
get the Cairo–Suez railway completed, had very little patience
with either.

In 1858 the ten-year Postal Convention signed in 1848 for
the carriage of mails through Egypt was renewed, the Egyptian
Government receiving a lump sum of £12,000 a year for the
service. By this time HMG had reconciled themselves to
Egyptian Government ownership and management of the
Transit Administration, partly because they were gratified at
the Egyptian Government's co-operative attitude over the
passing of British troops and military equipment through Egypt
at the time of the Indian Mutiny. After the Mutiny troops and
equipment continued to be passed both ways from time to time
by the overland route and HMG attached great importance to
this occasional, but valuable, means of rapid communication.

Within a few months, Nubar was dismissed from the Transit
Administration on the complaint of a foreigner, and was
thereafter employed by Said as his secretary, frequently going
to Europe on his behalf and becoming well acquanted with
European bankers and statesmen as a result. He was replaced
as head of the Transit Adminstration by a Turk who knew no
foreign languages, but most of the work was done by Betts
Bey, an Englishman, who was his deputy.

From time to time offers were made to Said by foreign
individuals and syndicates who wanted to be given a concession
for the operation of the railway, sometimes in return for a loan.
But Said, usually with the support of the British Consul-
General, turned them all down, partly because he regarded the
railway as something of a plaything, partly because he had been
forbidden by the terms of the Firman authorising its construction
to relinquish control of it, and partly because Bruce warned him
that such a concession would probably be followed by a demand
for an indemnity on some pretext that the concession was
proving less profitable than expected.

In 1861, Said's ill-considered economies began to cause
railway operation and maintenance to be neglected. This, and
the existence of the French Suez Canal Company, caused HMG
to look with more favour on the possibility of a concession for

the operation and, possibly, for the ownership of the railways being granted to an English company. There were several more proposals to this end, but again none of them came to anything. By that time, the railway revenue was estimated by the British Consul-General at £190,000 a year, 'in spite of the Egyptian Government's mismanagement'.[80] During the first few years of the reign of Said's successor, Ismail, the railway was extended into Upper Egypt as far as Qena and branch lines were constructed in the Delta. In 1866 the railway revenues were pledged as security for one of Ismail's numerous loans.

Soon after Said's accession, a new aspect of the overland route came into prominence with the invention of the electric telegraph. In 1855 the Egyptian Government contracted with an English company to lay land lines between Cairo and Alexandria and Cairo and Suez.[81] In 1856 England and Europe were linked to Egypt by a submarine cable to Alexandria laid by the Eastern Telegraph Company, which also had plans for laying a submarine cable between Suez and Bombay. In anticipation of this, Mr Gisborne, a representative of the Eastern Telegraph Company, negotiated with the Egyptian Government for a fifty-year concession for the operation of land lines across Egypt linking the Alexandria and Suez cables. But he got no support from HMG and had to be content with facilities for operating special lines for through traffic in the Egyptian Government system. In this, and in other cases, HMG were generally consistent in refusing to support any proposal for the grant of monopolistic public utility concessions, even when the firms or individuals concerned were British.

During the Indian Mutiny, when rapid communication of information between England and India was of vital importance, Indian news arriving at Suez by sea was telegraphed to Alexandria by the British Consul at Suez and thence cabled to London by the British Consul at Alexandria. A submarine line under the Red Sea from Suez, via Qusair, Suakin and Massawa to Aden was laid in 1859–60, but gave a lot of trouble through breakages. For this reason, although Aden and Bombay were linked by cable in 1862, telegraphic communication between England and India was first achieved by the Indo-European land line through Mesopotamia, Persia and the Persian Gulf.

During the whole of Abbas' reign the question of a ship canal had been in abeyance. The Societé d'Etudes, after the detailed studies and plans made in 1846, made no further progress. Stephenson deserted the Societé and became absorbed in the railway. Enfantin continued to pursue a quest which looked more and more hopeless. Then Ferdinand de Lesseps came on the scene. After his retirement from the French foreign service he devoted himself to the study of the ship canal. He read everything on the subject. He got in touch with Enfantin and with various members of the Societé d'Etudes. He also, through intermediaries, approached the Ottoman Government in Constantinople and Abbas in Cairo. But he got no encouragement in either quarter. His opportunity came with the accession of Said in 1854. He had got to know Said well during his time as Consul in Egypt twenty years before and had kept up a correspondence with him since. Almost immediately on Said's accession he solicited and obtained an invitation to come to Egypt and visit him. A very few weeks after his arrival, in November 1854, Lesseps obtained from Said a concession conferring on him 'the exclusive right to form and direct a *compagnie universelle* for the construction and operation of a canal through the isthmus of Suez'. This concession, which was for ninety-nine years, provided that the company would finance, construct and operate the canal, that the Egyptian Government would provide such lands as might be required, and would receive in return 15 per cent of the net profits. It was also provided that the concession would have to be ratified by the Sultan, and Lesseps was informed that work must not be started until the authority of the Sublime Porte had been obtained.

In January 1856, after an 'international scientific commission' appointed by Lesseps had made a study of the technical problems involved, a second concession was awarded to Lesseps by Said in amplification of the original one. This provided, *inter alia*, that the canal should be a direct cut between the Mediterranean and the Red Sea, that a fresh-water canal should be dug from the Nile to the Suez isthmus and there run parallel to the ship canal, that four-fifths of the workers employed should be Egyptian, that the canal dues should be fixed by the concessionary company up to a maximum of 10 francs per ton, and that the canal should be open to merchant ships of all nationalities without discrimination. The Statutes of the Company, published at the same time, fixed the capital at 200 million francs, being the cost of construction as estimated by the 'international scientific commission', divided into 400,000 shares of 500 francs each, and provided that the company's legal domicile should be in France. Seven months later, in July 1856, a secret agreement was arrived at between Said and Lesseps and published in a Viceregal degree, providing that the Egyptian Government would, after taking into account the seasonal requirements of Egyptian agriculture, supply all the labour required by the company, subject to the provision of accommodation and the payment of fixed wages by the company. This labour could only be supplied by means of *corvées* – levies of forced labour – as had been done for the railways, for the barrage and, indeed, for all major public works undertaken by the Egyptian Government. The important difference was that, this time, the *corvée* would be for work done, not by the Egyptian Government but by a foreign concessionary company operating for its own account.

The official British attitude was, at first, one of cautious disapproval. Lord Cowley, British Ambassador in Paris in reply to a complaint from Drouyn de Lhuys, the French Foreign Minister that Bruce, the British Consul-General, had been openly opposing the canal, acknowledged that HMG disapproved but said that British opposition would not be pushed 'beyond the bounds of courtesy'.[82] In Constantinople, Stratford de Redcliffe was told that 'in the opinion of HMG it would not be expedient to make any official protest against the scheme'.[83] The French Government's attitude was one of almost equally cautious approval, and the instructions given to the French representatives in Constantinople and Cairo provided that, while the project was to receive such official backing as might properly be given to any respectable scheme put forward by a private French citizen, the French government were not to be identified with it, and no pressure was to be employed or intimidation attempted in order to advance it. Stratford de Redcliffe reported that 'the language of the French Embassy tends to promote its success while disclaiming all interest or official participation in the scheme'.[84]

This official moderation was imposed by the necessities of the Anglo-French alliance in the Crimean war. Privately, Palmerston, who became Prime Minister at the beginning of

1855 after the fall of the Aberdeen Government (Clarendon remained as Foreign Secretary under Palmerston), expressed two specific objections: in the event of a quarrel between France and England, France, being so much nearer the canal, 'would have much the start of us in sending ships and troops to the Indian seas'; [85] and 'It is quite clear that the scheme is founded on intentions hostile to British views and interests, and the secret intention no doubt is to lay a foundation for the future severance of Egypt from Turkey and for placing it under French protection . . . A deep and wide canal interposed between Egypt and Syria studded with fortifications would be a military defensive line which, with the desert in front of it, would render the task of a Turkish army very difficult . . . If land is to be conceded to the French company, a French colony on French territory would be interposed between Turkey and Egypt and any attempt by Turkish troops to cross that line would be held to be an invasion of France. From the moment the enterprise was completed Egypt would be completely cut off from Turkey and would be placed under the protection of France.' [86]

For the next ten years, until his death in 1865, during most of which time he was Prime Minister, Palmerston persistently opposed the construction of the canal on the ground that it was a French plot designed to separate Egypt from the Ottoman Empire, to impose a French protectorate over Egypt, and, in the event of a war with England, to enable the French effectively to attack British interests east of Suez. He defended his view by referring to the strengthening of the fortifications of Alexandria a few years earlier by Gallice Bey, a French engineer in the Egyptian service, according to plans drawn up in Paris, and to the building of the Delta barrage by a French engineer and by French advice. He formed the fantastic idea that the barrage was designed by the French, not as an irrigation work but as a military one which would enable the Delta to be flooded in the event of a Turkish or a British invasion.

Lesseps, after interviews with Stratford de Redcliffe in Constantinople, with Clarendon in Paris, and with Palmerston in London, at which he tried and failed to mitigate British opposition, and after various lobbyings in Paris at which he tried and failed to secure French diplomatic support, proceeded to go ahead and create his *fait accompli*. In August 1858 he arrived in Paris, put out his Prospectus and opened his sub-scription list. Because of British opposition, because the Sultan's Firman had not been obtained, and because the international banking world had little confidence in Lesseps, the subscription was a failure. Of the 220,000 shares allotted to French nationals, only 207,111 were taken up. Said, on behalf of the Egyptian Government, agreed to take, and was allotted, 64,000 shares. Of the balance of some 116,000 shares, which were to have been taken up through various banking houses in other European countries and the United States, only 15,247 were subscribed. No shares were taken up in Great Britain, Austria, Russia or the United States and, apart from the Viceroy's 64,000 shares, none in the Ottoman Empire. There were therefore 113,642 unsubscribed shares left on Lesseps' hands. Relying on a verbal promise of Said's to take up any unsubscribed shares, Lesseps applied to the French Ministry of Commerce for the registration of the company, which involved making a declaration that its authorised capital had been fully subscribed. He then went to Egypt and, in April 1859, started preliminary construction work on the canal. He soon found himself in difficulties. HMG, on hearing that the work had started, instructed Sir Henry Bulwer, who had replaced Stratford de Redcliffe as Ambassador at Constantinople in July 1858, to press the Porte to 'give positive orders to stop a work which is a political and private piece of swindling'.[87] As a result the Grand Vizier wrote to Said pointing out that 'enterprises of this importance must not be proceeded with before the Sultan's Firman has been obtained' and urging him not to do anything to 'increase those political complications everyone is trying to straighten out'.[88] Said, alarmed by this communication, and annoyed by a tactless and threatening letter from Lesseps, caused a letter to be written to the canal company, with copies to all members of the Consular Corps, ordering all work to cease on the canal. The company asked Walewski, the French Foreign Minister, that 'the Emperor, by the exercise of his powerful authority, should uphold the rights of the company' and warned him that a public set-back for the canal would be regarded by the world as a set-back for France.[89] Walewski told the company that 'it would be difficult for the Government of the Emperor to make a request to the Egyptian Viceroy which is incompatible with his obligations to the Porte'.[90]

For the next few weeks the future of the canal hung in the balance. Lesseps went to Paris to mobilise all the support he could get (including that of the Empress Eugénie, a distant relative of his), for a final appeal to the Emperor. If that were unsuccessful, the company would have to be wound up. Mukhtar Bey, an emissary from Constantinople, arrived in Egypt in October with a most peremptory letter to Said from the Grand Vizier demanding the immediate cessation of all work on the canal (which had been going on all through the summer) and calling on the Consular Corps to co-operate by the removal from the isthmus of all foreign nations working for the canal company. 'To this demand Sabatier, the French Agent, declared that he at once acceded.'[91]

By this time the French Government, realising that Lesseps would have to be rescued from the predicament in which he had (deliberately) placed himself, were moving to his support. Walewski intimated to HMG that 'it would be quite impossible for the French Government to abandon the interests of the company which had claimed their protection' and added that Sabatier had received positive instructions to insist that the company's workshops and so on should not be removed.[92] On 23 October, just after news of Mukhtar Bey's mission had been received in France, Lesseps and some members of the company's Conseil d'Administration had an audience with Napoleon III in which the Emperor assured them of his support and protection. Fortified with this, and with the dismissal of Sabatier, which he had successfully urged on the Emperor, Lesseps went to Constantinople where Thouvenel, the French Ambassador, had received instructions to support Lesseps more decisively than before. Bulwer reported that 'it will be difficult to get the Porte to resist the French Government in any decided and positive manner unless we give them a clear and positive assurance that we will stand by them whatever the consequences may be'.[93] But HMG were already beginning to retreat, and Bulwer was told that 'Great Britain cannot undertake to make on behalf of her secondary interest a resistance to a scheme which Turkey, on behalf of her primary interest, should decline to make.'[94] Early in the New Year the Porte told Musurus Bey, the Turkish Ambassador in London, that the Sultan would not issue his Firman until agreement had been reached between the British and French Governments.

Meanwhile, in Egypt, the immediate crisis had passed and work on the canal went steadily, if slowly, forward. But all was not plain sailing. Said proved obstinate about taking up the additional shares which Lesseps was trying to unload onto him. In 1861, when *corvées* had to be raised in accordance with Lesseps' labour agreement with Said, HMG objected and the Porte, moved by the British Ambassador, began to ask awkward questions. By this time HMG, in their campaign against the canal, were concentrating on what Bulwer described as 'its features of colonisation and forced labour'.[95] By 'colonisation' he meant the grants of land by the Egyptian Government to the company which HMG professed to believe were intended to be developed by French, or by French-protected, cultivators.

In January 1863 Said died and was succeeded as Viceroy by his nephew Ismail, the eldest surviving son of Ibrahim.[96] The new reign inaugurated a new phase in the history of the canal and of Egypt generally.

Notes

1. Moresby-Barker, 1.5.29, FO 78/184
2. Barker-Governor of Bombay, 22.5.29, *ibid*
3. Barker-Gordon, 3.6.29, *ibid*
4. *ibid*
5. Hoskins, *British Routes to India*, p 197
6. Barker-Malcolm, 23.1.29, FO 78/184
7. Hoskins, *op cit*, p 109
8. Barker-Aberdeen, 2.5.30, FO 78/192
9. Campbell-Palmerston, 18.12.34, FO 78/245, and Campbell-Wellington 14.2.35, FO 78/257
10. FO-Campbell, 1.11.34, FO 78/244
11. Campbell-Palmerston, 3.11.34, *ibid*
12. Barker-Captain of *HMS Benares*, 3.2.30, FO 78/192
13. Barker-Palmerston, 27.10.33 and 17.11.33, FO 78/213
14. Campbell-Palmerston, 1.11.34, FO 78/244
15. *ibid*, 22.5.35, FO 78/257
16. India Board-Barker, 16.12.29, FO 78/184
17. Hoskins, *op cit*, p 155
18. For a report of the evidence see Parliamentary Papers 1834 No 478
19 A regular French steam service between Marseille and Alexandria was also set up in 1837
20. Waghorn indulged in a certain amount of political intrigue, encouraging Mohamed Ali in his ideas of independence and exaggerating his own influence with HMG. Campbell complained to HMG about this and was authorised to warn Mohamed Ali that he 'would not act wisely if he were to place reliance on Mr Waghorn's assertions of influence either in England or India'. Palmerston-Campbell, 12.5.38, FO 78/342
21. Campbell-Bowring, 18.1.38, FO 78/342. Dr (afterwards Sir John) Bowring had been sent by HMG on an official mission to report on economic and administrative matters in Mohamed Ali's dominions
22. Campbell-Palmerston, 26.12.38, FO 78/343
23. Hill and Raven budgeted for carrying 16 passengers a month from Suez to Cairo and 5 passengers a month from Cairo to Suez, plus children and servants. They allowed passengers 2 cwt of baggage each, provided breakfast, dinner, and tea or supper on the 90-mile journey, which took about 22 hours, and charged £6 per head inclusive, with children and servants half-price and alcoholic drinks extra. They estimated that they would make a gross profit of £35 a month, from which an initial capital expenditure of £1,000 for the purchase of four passenger vans, two luggage vans, and forty mules and harness, would have to be amortised
24. Barnett-Aberdeen, 5.12.42, FO 78/502. The system consisted of seventeen towers each with two semaphore arms. A semaphore telegraph between Cairo and Alexandria had already been in existence for some years
25. See report on Overland Transit by Mr Walne, East India Company Agent and British Consul in Cairo, enclosed with Murray-Palmerston, 6.6.47, FO 97/408

26. *ibid*
27. For correspondence re this Convention see FO 78/582 and 623
28. Barnett-Aberdeen, 6.6.45, FO 78/623
29. See Walne's report (note 25 above). Thurburn protested to HMG about his expropriation, but Palmerston, taking the view that he had been an instrument of Mohamed Ali's monopolistic policy, gave him a very cold reply, telling him that 'if British subjects involve themselves in complicated pecuniary transactions with foreign governments, or with subordinate officials of foreign governments, they must abide by the consequences of their own imprudent speculations'. FO 97/408
30. Murray-Palmerston, 4.11.46, FO 97/408
31. See, *inter alia*, a pamphlet published in London in 1844 'Observations on the Proposed Improvements in the Overland Route via Egypt with Reference to the Ship Canal, the Boulac Canal & the Railroad', by J. A. Galloway, FO 97/411. The interest of the Galloway family in the railway derived from the fact that they were iron-founders
32. Aberdeen-Barnett, 31.10.43, FO 78/541. The FO had clearly been oversold on the railway by the Galloway family who had convinced them that opposition to it was due to foreign, and particularly French and Austrian, preference for a ship canal
33. Barnett-Aberdeen, 1.12.43, *ibid*
34. *ibid*, 17.1.45 and 18.3.45, FO 78/623
35. Aberdeen-Barnett, 16.8.44, FO 78/582
36. Barnett-Aberdeen, 7.4.45, FO 78/623. There was obviously the prospect of a big profit in it for Galloway. Thurburn, whose Transit Company had been expropriated, and who had a finger in a number of Egyptian pies, was also interested. See Barnett-Aberdeen 17.1.45, *ibid*
37. Barnett-Aberdeen, 12.4.45, FO 78/623
38. See the French CG's views as reported in Barnett-Aberdeen, 19.3.44, FO 78/582
39. Palmerston-Murray, 8.2.47, FO 97/408
40. See Walne's a/q report (note 25 above)
41. India Board-FO, 18.8.33, FO 97/411
42. See these letters and a memo accompanying the second letter in FO 97/411
43. Murray-Palmerston, 3.5.47, FO 97/411
44. Palmerston-Murray, 27.5.47, FO 97/411
45. Cowley-Palmerston, 3.7.47, *ibid*
46. *ibid*, 17.10.47, *ibid*
47. There is a letter in FO 97/411 dated 13.3.47 from Waghorn to Stephenson expressing indignation at Stephenson's connection with the canal project, and pressing on him the idea of a railway as an alternative. Waghorn's language was habitually intemperate and in this letter he attributed both the canal and the barrage to sinister French machinations. Waghorn's views, which were publicised in England, may have had some influence on Palmerston. Waghorn died in 1850, a disappointed and financially ruined man.
48. Murray-Palmerston, 25.3.47, FO 78/706
49. *ibid*, 3.5.47, FO 78/707
50. Murray-S. Canning, 7.12.48, FO 78/757
51. Murray-Palmerston, 9.4.48, *ibid*

52. *ibid*, 4.10.48, *ibid*
53. *ibid*, 6.7.48, *ibid*
54. *ibid*, 4.10.48, *ibid*
55. Palmerston-Murray, 21.12.48, FO 78/756
56. Murray-Palmerston, 19.4.49, FO 78/804
57. *ibid*, 19.4.49, *ibid*
58. Stratford Canning had returned to Constantinople for his fourth and last term as British Ambassador
59. Murray-Palmerston, 6.2.51, FO 78/875
60. Palmerston-Murray, 20.2.51, *ibid*
61. Murray-S. Canning, 14.2.51, *ibid*
62. *ibid*, 15.2.51, *ibid*
63. Murray-Palmerston, 17.4.51, FO 78/840
64. S. Canning-Murray, 4.6.51, *ibid*
65. Murray-Palmerston, 15.6.51, *ibid*
66. Palmerston-S. Canning, 24.7.51, FO 97/411
67. Murray-Palmerston, 7.11.51, FO 78/876
68. *ibid*
69. *ibid*, 16.7.51, FO 78/840
70. Palmerston-Murray, 29.9.51, FO 78/876
71. Le Moyne-Drouyn de Lhuys, 30.11.50, Egypte Corres. Politique 22
72. Austrian Ambassador in London quoted by Hallberg, *The Suez Canal*, pp 111–112
73. Green-Clarendon, 20.7.53, FO 78/965
74. Green-de Redcliffe, 7.11.53, *ibid*
75. Clarendon-Bruce, 31.3.54, FO 78/1034
76. Bruce-Clarendon, 16.3.54, FO 78/1035. In fact, P. and O. got transit dues reduced from $\frac{1}{2}$ per cent to $\frac{1}{4}$ per cent but it is not clear whether this applied to all goods or only to British goods. See Bruce-Clarendon, 2.5.54, *ibid*
77. *ibid*, 16.2.54, *ibid*
78. After Stephenson was awarded the contract for the Cairo-Suez railway, the Galloway family, represented by J. A. Galloway, lodged a claim for an indemnity on the ground that in 1835 the Galloway firm had been given a contract for the construction of this line by Mohamed Ali. As a result of Bruce's intervention the Galloways received compensation of £110,000. See Bruce-Clarendon, 28.5.56, FO 78/1222. In addition the Galloways received a £100,000 order for materials for the line. Bruce-Clarendon, 2.2.58, FO 78/1313
79. He received a parting present of £10,000 from the Viceroy.
80. Colquhoun-Russell, 29.7.61, FO 78/1590
81. Green-Clarendon, 10.10.55, FO 78/1123
82. Cowley-Clarendon, 19.1.55, FO 78/1156
83. Clarendon-de Redcliffe, 9.3.55, *ibid*
84. de Redcliffe-Clarendon, 12.2.55, *ibid*
85. Minute by Palmerston on de Redcliffe-Clarendon, 22.2.55, *ibid*
86. Minute by Palmerston on de Redcliffe-Clarendon, 26.5.55, *ibid*
87. Malmesbury-Bulwer, 17.5.59, FO 78/1489. The Palmerston Government had been replaced in February 1858 by a Conservative Government headed by Lord Derby in which Lord Malmesbury was Foreign Secretary
88. Lesseps, *Journal*, Vol III, p 156

89. Albufera-Walewski, 18.7.59, *Memoires et Documents Egypte,* Vol XIII
90. Walewski-Albufera, 28.7.59, *ibid*
91. Colquhoun-Bulwer, 6.10.59, FO 78/1489. This attitude of Sabatier's was in accordance with the instructions given him by Walewski who had warned him against any political interference on behalf of the canal company
92. Cowley-Russell, 20.10.59, *ibid.* The Derby Government had fallen in June 1859 and Palmerston was back as PM with Lord John Russell as Foreign Secretary
93. Bulwer-Russell, 22.11.59, *ibid*
94. Russell-Bulwer, 21.12.59, *ibid*
95. Russell-Bulwer, 28.12.59, FO 78/1489
96. Ismail's elder brother, Ahmed, had been killed in an accident on the Cairo–Alexandria railway in 1859. Several members of the royal family were returning by special train from Alexandria to Cairo after an entertainment given by Said, the Viceroy. One of the train coaches overturned into the Nile from a ferry conveying the train across the Rosetta branch of the Nile at Kafr-ez-Zayat. Ahmed was drowned. Ismail, who was not at the Viceroy's party and not on the train, was naturally accused by rumour of having contrived the accident which made him heir to the throne as being the next oldest male to Ahmed in the direct line of succession. Abdul Halim, the youngest son of Mohamed Ali, but a little younger than Ismail, was also in the overturned coach and saved himself by swimming.

3

The Capitulations

THE Capitulations consisted of a series of treaties concluded between the Sultan of Turkey and most of the European Powers[1] which regulated the trading and living conditions under which European nationals were permitted to reside in the Ottoman dominions. The object of the treaties, from the Ottoman point of view, was to combine the advantages of Western trade with the almost neurotic determination, felt both by the Sublime Porte and by most Ottoman Moslem subjects, to avoid social contacts with, and what they regarded as contamination by, the Christian West. In the same way as with their own Christian subjects, they were, in their dealings with European nationals, prepared to concede a certain measure of self-government in order to preserve their social and cultural integrity. From the European point of view, the object of the treaties was to provide security for life and property, reasonable conditions of trade, and freedom of religious worship and personal status for European nationals living in the Ottoman dominions.

The first of these treaties was that concluded between the French Government and Sultan Suleiman the Lawgiver in 1535. A broadly similar treaty was concluded with the British Goverment in 1583. Over the next hundred years or so treaties on the same lines were concluded with most of the European Powers. They had to be, and usually were, renewed on the accession of each new Sultan, and were sometimes added to and enlarged in scope. The essential clauses in all the treaties provided:

1) For freedom of navigation in Ottoman waters, for freedom of entry to and egress from Ottoman ports, and for freedom of travel in Ottoman territories for European nationals and their merchandise.

2) For fixed customs dues and taxes on merchandise.

3) For consular jurisdiction in all civil suits between Europeans (in this connection the custom grew up that suits between foreigners of different nationalities were tried in the defendant's Consular Court).

4) For the presence of the defendant's consular representative at any criminal trial before an Ottoman Court.

5) For immunity from Ottoman taxes and military conscription for Europeans with less than ten years' continuous residence in the Ottoman dominions.

6) For freedom of religious worship and testamentary dispositions.

7) For the presence of a European's consular representative at any arrest or domiciliary search carried out by the Ottoman authorities against him.

In Egypt during the last quarter of the eighteenth century, the Capitulations were more or less in abeyance as a result of the erosion of Ottoman authority over that province. When European trading was resumed after the French and British invasions, and after the establishment of Mohamed Ali as ruler of Egypt, it followed an entirely different pattern from that prevailing during the eighteenth century (see p. 19). The old monopolistic chartered companies had fallen into desuetude and the arbitrary and capricious tyranny of the Mamluk Beys was succeeded by the no less arbitrary, but infinitely more enlightened and purposeful despotism of Mohamed Ali. Under his regime, most of the immunities and privileges provided for in the Capitulations treaties were not only restored but, in some respects, enlarged. Largely because of this, and in spite of Mohamed Ali's monopolies (which were probably in breach of the strict letter of the Capitulations) European traders in Egypt were in a very favourable position compared both with conditions in Egypt prior to Mohamed Ali and with contemporary conditions in other parts of the Ottoman Empire. Internal security was excellent. Moslem fanaticism was kept in check. There were no *'avanies'*, or periodical forced levies, made upon foreign merchants. And the large jurisdictional immunities conferred by the Capitulations treaties were gradually extended far beyond what was required by these treaties.

For example; in criminal cases these treaties provided that the accused's consul should be present at all trials before the

Ottoman Courts. Under Mohamed Ali this was extended to provide that all European residents charged with non-capital crime should be tried before their own Consular Courts. As the British Consul-General put it in 1833: 'Every European in Egypt, except when charged with a capital crime against the person of an Ottoman subject or against the State, lives under the laws of his own country and the exclusive jurisdiction of his Consul.'[2]

Another foreign privilege in criminal matters, which was only doubtfully justified by the treaties but which, like many other immunities enjoyed by foreigners, grew up by custom during the nineteenth century, was the immunity of foreign-owned or foreign-occupied premises from search, except in the presence of the owner's or occupier's consul. This immunity had originally been restricted to the private houses of foreign residents, but had become extended to their business premises. These, by the middle of the nineteenth century, included 'whole streets of the lowest possible kinds of wine-shops and houses of ill-fame kept by Maltese, Greeks or Frenchmen. According to our assumed treaty privileges . . . a poor, drunken British sailor may be plundered and murdered in one of these dens of infamy, with the Egyptian police looking on from the street without the power to enter or interfere' until they had summoned the owner's consul, by which time the criminal had escaped.[3] This immunity also encouraged the large-scale smuggling which was practised by many foreigners, since it was almost impossible for the police to get their hands on the contraband goods. Because of the lawlessness which prevailed in Alexandria as a result of the influx of undesirable foreigners which took place from about 1850 onwards, the consuls-general themselves requested the Egyptian Government to devise better measures for keeping disreputable foreigners in order. The Egyptian Government responded by drawing up new police regulations providing for the recruitment of Europeans in the police, for the issue of passports to foreigners, and the right to search foreign business establisments. But the British Government, advised by their law officers that the issue of passports and the search of foreign-owned or -occupied business premises were not in accordance with the treaties, refused to agree to the regulations which the foreign consuls had themselves requested. Other governments took the same attitude, these regulations were not put into effect, and the previous abuses continued unchecked.[4]

In civil disputes, the position of European nationals was equally favourable. The treaties provided that civil disputes between foreigners should be adjudicated by the Consular Courts. In the eighteenth century civil disputes between foreigners and Ottoman subjects did not often arise. But, in the nineteenth century, under the changed conditions and with new freedoms and commercial opportunities, they became increasingly frequent. Under Mohamed Ali a practice grew up by which disputes between foreigners and Ottoman subjects in which the foreigner was the defendant were tried, by permission of the Egyptian Government, in the defendant's Consular Court. When the European was the plaintiff they were tried in the Ottoman Courts. In an endeavour to meet European objections to the trial of 'mixed' cases where the defendant was an Ottoman subject, Mohamed Ali followed a precedent set in Constantinople and set up in Alexandria a 'Mixed Tribunal of Commerce' with Egyptian and European judges, to decide cases 'which the Governor of Alexandria finds he cannot settle summarily'. But this did not prove very successful 'due to the want of any defined system of law on which decisions are to be based and the impossibility of inducing the Tribunal to establish a regular system of procedure'. The British Consul-General reported that 'the European members of the Tribunal are so tired out with the procrastination and irregularity which prevail that they can only with difficulty be brought to attend', and that 'in cases affecting Europeans where no Turk of influence is interested the decision is left to the European members, but when redress is sought against an influential Turkish defendant the Turkish members support him unanimously and are generally able to prevent justive from being done'.[5] As a result, when a European suitor had a claim of importance against an Ottoman national, and particularly when he had a claim against the government, the matter tended to be settled by diplomatic pressure, usually under the guise of arbitration.

This method of settlement became particularly prevalent after Said's accession in 1854. Under Abbas, when the process of Europeanisation was halted, commercial contacts between Ottoman subjects and Europeans were comparatively infrequent. But after the accession of Said, with his European

proclivities and his ill-regulated passion for modernisation, the
flood resumed in full spate. Unlike Mohamed Ali, who kept his
modernisation projects firmly in the hands of his government,
financing them himself and employing Europeans as his servants
to carry them out, Said dealt out concessions and contracts,
most of them very carelessly drafted from the point of view of
the government's interest, with a free hand. As a result,
innumerable disputes arose between European concessionaires
and the government, nearly all of which were settled, to the
disadvantage of the government, not through the commercial
Tribunal, or by any other process of law, but by diplomatic
pressure exercised by the concessionaire's consul-general. The
easy 'pickings' to be made in this way encouraged a horde of
European adventurers to come to Egypt concession-hunting,
and also encouraged the raking-up of old and dubious claims,
which would have been resisted by earlier Viceroys, but which
were settled by the pliable and timid Said, who liked to be
pleasant to all Europeans and who dreaded the prospect of
quarrels with European Powers, lest they should make trouble
for him at Constantinople. For example; Galloway, as a result
of the British Consul-General's intervention, received a sum of
£110,000 in respect of a contract alleged to have been promised
to his firm by Mohamed Ali twenty years before for the
construction of the Cairo–Suez railway which had been given
instead (as a result of the pressure of a previous British
Consul-General) to another English concessionaire.

But, on the whole, British consuls-general showed themselves
more judicially-minded than some of their colleagues. Bruce
settled compensation for another British subject, a Maltese
named Giglio, who had claimed £20,000 for some alleged
breach of contract, at £1,000, commenting that Giglio's was
'only one of many of the exorbitant claims brought forward by
individuals against the Government'. He complained of the
'difficulty we experience in obtaining satisfaction for acts of
injustice owing to the systematic exaggeration of losses and to
the unscrupulous means by which demands are often pressed by
agents of other Powers'.[6] He refused to support a claim by a
certain Politis, an Ionian islander, against the Egyptian
Government, for £12,500 on the ground that he was owed
money by Prince al-Hami, Abbas' son, whose estates he was
managing.[7] He did secure some compensation for a Mr Larking,

an Englishman whom Abbas had appointed as his agent in London and whom Said had summarily dismissed.[8] But he refused to support Gisborne, the representative of the Eastern Telegraph Company, in his attempts to secure a monopoly for the electric telegraph lines being laid across Egypt.[9] This refusal may have been partly due to the foreign jealousies which such a monopoly would have been bound to evoke.

But no such considerations prevented some of his colleagues from assisting their nationals to obtain monopolistic concessions and then from demanding on their behalf heavy indemnities as consideration for renouncing them. Rosetti, a nephew of the Rosetti who had been Venetian Consul-General at the end of the eighteenth century, obtained from Said, as a result of the intervention of the French and Austrian consuls-general, compensation of £160,000 for relinquishing a monopoly of the senna trade of Nubia which, he claimed, had been granted to him by Mohamed Ali.[10] Zininia, a Greek merchant who had obtained French nationality and the consul-generalship of Belgium, obtained, as a result of his own efforts and those of the French Consul-General, an indemnity of £130,000 in return for relinquishing a concession entitling him to collect lock dues on the Mahmudieh canal which had been granted to him by Said as compensation for the non-fulfilment of an alleged verbal agreement by Mohamed Ali to give him a monopoly of the transit between Alexandria and Suez.[11] Comte de Castellani, a French subject, received, on the insistence of the French Consul-General, compensation of £26,000 in satisfaction of a probably fraudulent claim alleging the destruction of some silk cultures through exposure to the air by the Egyptian customs.[12] The method by which these, mostly unjustified, claims were settled underlined the desirability of some impartial system of law which could adjudicate claims between Ottoman and foreign nationals, and particularly between the Egyptian Government and foreign nationals. The mistrust of the national Courts felt by the European community was well-justified, but the diplomatic bullying which replaced them as a means of settling 'mixed' disputes was an example of the remedy being worse than the disease. This bullying, which was made possible by the realities of international power politics, by the unscrupulousness of many European nationals and their diplomatic representatives, and by the feebleness of the Viceroy, made Egypt, after the accession of Said, a happy hunting-ground for European adventurers and their Egyptian hangers-on.

The growth of land-ownership by foreigners created special problems of immunity. Under the Capitulation treaties, foreigners were forbidden to own real estate in the Ottoman dominions. This prohibition was waived in Egypt under Mohamed Ali and from about 1830 onwards it became customary for foreigners to own houses and land. In 1856 an Ottoman Firman was promulgated, which regularised the position by allowing foreigners to own land on condition that they conformed to the laws of the country in respect of such ownership and paid the same taxes as were paid by Ottoman subjects. On the authority of this Firman foreigners were able to obtain *hodgas* (title deeds) for real estate acquired by them. But several foreign individuals and companies attempted to invoke capitulatory privileges in their refusal to pay taxes or submit to the ordinary laws of the land in respect of such property.[13] The case was a difficult one since, under the regime which had grown up out of the Capitulations, payment of taxes and enforcement of other laws relating to land-ownership had to be pursued through the Consular Courts and since, in such disputes, the foreigners would be the defendants and the Egyptian Government plaintiffs. Consuls-general were, understandably, not anxious to 'become as a matter of course tax-gatherers for the Ottoman authorities'.[14] The result was that many, if not most, European real property owners were able almost entirely to avoid their financial and other obligations towards the State in respect of their land-holdings. This, in practice, meant that Europeans were exempt from all taxation except customs duties. And many of them evaded even these to a large extent by using capitulatory privileges exempting them from domiciliary search as a cover for wholesale smuggling.

Under cover of these immunities, and under conditions of increasing trade, increasing markets for European goods, increasing opportunities for investment, the European communities in Egypt steadily increased in numbers and prosperity. In 1836 the European population of Egypt was estimated at 14,500. By 1871 it had risen to an estimated 80,000.[15]

Notes

1. In 1860 there were 17 European nations who were represented in Egypt by a consul-general and whose nationals enjoyed the privileges of the Capitulations treaties – Austria-Hungary, Belgium, Denmark, France, Great Britain, Greece, Hanseatic League, Holland, Naples, Portugal, Prussia, Russia, Sardinia, Spain, Sweden, Tuscany, and the United States. Ionian Islanders (until 1863), Gibraltarians and Maltese enjoyed the status of British nationals

2. HMG became increasingly concerned at the extent of criminal jurisdiction exercised by British consuls in Egypt. Under the Foreign Jurisdiction Act an Order in Council was promulgated on 19.6.44 'which clearly and formally defined the magisterial attributions and powers of HM's Consuls in the Levant'. According to this, consuls were required to revert to the strict letter of the Capitulations treaties by which British nationals charged with a criminal offence were to be tried before the local courts in the presence of their consul (Palmerston-Murray, 30.9.47, FO 79/706). This decision met with furious protests from the Consul-General and from the British community (Murray-Palmerston, 8.11.47, *ibid*). It was eventually agreed that the Egyptian Government should be asked to set up the same system as at Constantinople by which 'British subjects accused of a criminal offence are tried before a Turkish Tribunal in the presence and with the concurrence of the British Consul-General. British subjects who are accused of offences against Ottoman subjects may be arrested and taken to prison by the Turkish authorities. Notice of the arrest is given to the Consul-General and a day is appointed for the trial. If the case is of sufficient gravity the Consul-General is present himself. Otherwise his Dragoman attends. On these occasions he acts as judge conjointly with the Ottoman judge and his consent is absolutely necessary to the condemnation of the accused. If there is a disagreement between the Consul-General and the Turkish judge the matter is referred to the British Embassy.' For a few years this system was operated in criminal trials of British subjects in Cairo, but never in Alexandria

3. Green-Clarendon, 15.11.58, FO 78/1401

4. The proposed Regulations, although supported by twelve out of the seventeen consuls-general, were the subject of a protest organised by Walne, the British Consul in Cairo, and supported by most of the 100 or so British residents there, including Mr Shepheard, the hotel owner

5. Bruce-Clarendon, 4.4.56, FO 78/1222

6. Bruce-Clarendon, 28.5.56, *ibid*

7. *ibid*, 10.3.56, *ibid*

8. Bruce-Clarendon, 8.11.55, FO 78/1123. After receiving his compensation he appears to have been re-appointed by Said. See Colquhoun-Russell, 21.7.60, FO 78/1523

9. *ibid*, 6.12.55, *ibid*

10. Sabry, *L'Empire Egyptien sous Ismail*, p 18

11. *ibid*, pp 39–40

12. *ibid*, pp 41–42. A commission of arbitration, presided over by British merchant Robert Thurburn had already rejected the claim

13. One such case was that of Briggs & Co. This firm took over the farming of the estates of Prince Abdul Halim, the youngest son of Mohamed Ali, on a 20-year contract against payment of Halim's debts and the provision of an agreed annual income for him. Briggs & Co requested the British Consul-General's intervention when they were called upon to supply a *corvée* from the estate for government public works. Colquhoun, the Consul-General, took the view that they had agreed to farm the estate 'subject to all the burdens and obligations attaching to them', and refused to assist, commenting that if foreigners were to be allowed to invoke the Capitulations in this way, it would not be long before all the lands in Egypt were farmed out to foreigners in order that their owners might enjoy the benefit of foreign immunities. Colquhoun was supported in his attitude by HMG. But Briggs & Co went to the Viceroy direct and got a payment of £80,000 in return for a relinquishment of the farming concession. See correspondence in FO 78/1522

14. Green-Clarendon, 16.10.58, FO 78/1402

15. Crouchley, *The Economic Development of Modern Egypt*, p 256

4

The Commercial
and Financial Invasion

AT the end of the eighteenth century Egypt was almost entirely an agricultural country. The principal source of revenue was the *miri* or agricultural land tax. Its collection was entrusted to tax-farmers, called *multazimin* who, in return for their services, were granted large tax-free estates (*iltizam*, plural *iltizimat*) with the right of calling upon the peasants for forced labour to cultivate them. In practice the tax-farming, and the estates which went with it, usually became hereditary and were held by the Mamluk beys. These beys lived in their palaces in Cairo and the work of tax-collecting and estate management was left to their *kashefs*, or stewards. Land other than the *iltizimat* was cultivated by village communities. The various families making up these communities held and cultivated their lands by right of custom, but there were no deeds of land-ownership. The *shaikh*, or headman, of the village was responsible for collecting the *miri* assessed on the village as a whole.

Mohamed Ali dispossessed the *multazimin* of their estates, abolished the system of tax-farming and had the *miri* collected directly by the government. The *iltizimat* were either cultivated by Mohamed Ali himself or given to members of his family or to senior officials. He undertook a cadastral survey which established the areas of land of which individual cultivators had the usufruct. He introduced a new and oppressive system in respect of the more profitable export crops by which it was decreed that such crops had to be sold to the government at prices fixed by the government. The government then sold the crop at a profit both to the foreign merchant for export and to the local merchant for re-sale locally. This monopoly system was also applied to many imported articles.

The monopoly system was adopted mainly in order to

provide Mohamed Ali with the money he needed to finance his military and naval expenditure. It was accompanied by improvements in the irrigation system, including the provision of additional summer water by the digging of deep canals and by the multiplication of lifting devices. During the course of his long reign, the cultivated area was increased from about three million *feddans* (a *feddan* is approximately one acre) to about 4,150,000 *feddans*.[1] One of the ways in which this increase was brought about was by the grant of uncultivated lands to rich notables, including foreigners, in full ownership, and free of tax for ten years, with a favourable rate of taxation thereafter, on condition that the land was brought into cultivation. Land so granted was known as *abadieh*, or *ushuri*, land. The increase in the cultivated area was accompanied by an increase in population. In 1800 the population of Egypt was estimated at 2,460,200; in 1847 at 4,476,440.[2] Mohamed Ali made great efforts to develop the valuable export crops – cotton, rice, indigo and silk. His encouragement of cotton cultivation was destined to change the whole of Egypt's economic structure. His silk and indigo experiments were unsuccessful due, in the case of indigo, to competition from India and, in the case of silk, to the unsuitability of the climate. Generally, the increased productivity at which he aimed was defeated by the unpopularity of the monopolies with the cultivators, who did not exert themselves to raise crops from which they derived little or no profit, and by the demands of conscription for the armed services and for public works, which denuded the villages of able-bodied men.

The British Government made a determined and successful stand against the introduction of the monopolies system into Syria after Mohamed Ali's occupation of that country. But they did nothing about the Egyptian monopolies (which served the British merchant community in Egypt well) until after the 1838 Commercial Convention between Egypt and Turkey in 1838. This Convention provided for the abolition of monopolies and for the abolition of all dues except for the regular customs duties at ports of entry and exit throughout the Ottoman Empire. In return the Convention allowed for an increase in the maximum 3 per cent import and export duties provided for in the Capitulations treaties to 5 per cent for imports and 12 per cent for exports. No diplomatic action was taken to enforce the terms of this Convention in Egypt until 1841 – after the European intervention against Mohamed Ali in Syria and his consequent enforced subordination to the Porte.

By that time many of the monopolies had died a natural death. The monopoly on cereals had been abolished in 1838.[3] The monopolised industries had almost been abandoned. The monopoly on Nile transport had been waived. But the cotton monopoly, which was by this time the most important one of all, was still in force. Much of the cotton-growing land belonged to the Viceroy and he could hardly be prevented from selling his own property as he pleased. The monopoly suited many foreign merchants, who were assured of an allocation of the cotton crop in return for the short-term loans which they were in the habit of advancing to Mohamed Ali, and which had become an essential part of his financial system, bridging the gap between government disbursements and the collection of taxes.

The British Consul-General was told that 'HM's Government expect and require that the Convention of 18 August 1838 shall be faithfully and fully executed in Egypt, and Great Britain will not permit the continuance of these monopolies which [Mohamed Ali] proposes to create or prolong. Mohamed Ali will do well not to draw upon himself the active displeasure of Great Britain by attempting either directly or indirectly to restrain the freedom of commerce in Egypt which the 1838 Convention entitled Great Britain to demand and which HMG will certainly enforce.'[4] In face of this threat Mohamed Ali agreed to abolish the cotton monopoly from 1 October 1842.[5] But the British merchants in Egypt were not enthusiastic about the 1838 Convention. Messrs Joyce, Thurburn of Alexandria were not pleased to be told that the exclusive concession for the manufacture and export of nitrate of soda which they had obtained from Mohamed Ali was contrary to the Convention.[6] Another British merchant, Mr J. Peel, told the British Government that the Convention was harmful to British interests since the increase of 2 per cent in the permitted import duty was in fact an extra duty since there were no interior dues in Egypt. Also, Russia, which was not yet a party to the Convention, was importing goods against payment of only 3 per cent duty.[7] This argument was countered by the 'most favoured nation' clause in the Capitulations treaty[8] and eventually Russia associated herself with the Convention. But it was still not possible altogether to enforce it in respect of the cotton monopoly. Barnett, the British Consul-General, reported that Mohamed Ali had at his disposal about two-thirds of the cotton crop, either because he owned the land, or because the government had collected the cotton in taxes, and that this cotton continued to be allocated to merchants as security for loans instead of being sold at public auction, on which Barnett had tried to insist.[9] A little later, Barnett protested against the activities of several of the 'trading' consuls-general – he mentioned particularly those of Belgium, Greece, Sweden and Tuscany – who were members of the monopoly 'ring' and who were defeating the efforts of the 'career' consuls-general of Great Britain, France and Austria to have the 1838 Convention enforced.[10]

The British Government's fight against the cotton monopoly, and the Sennaar gum monopoly, dragged on for several years. In 1848 Murray, the British Consul-General, received a sharp rap over the knuckles from Palmerston for suggesting that British opposition to these monopolies should be abated, since, compared with a more lenient French attitude, it was affecting British influence in Egypt and causing the Egyptian Government to compare Great Britain unfavourably with France. He was told that 'the only purpose for which HMG can wish to have influence over the Pasha is to obtain thereby justice for British subjects and a strict observance of our treaty rights, and if, in order to obtain influence over the mind of the Pasha, HMG were to acquiesce in injustice, they would sacrifice the end for the means. HMG cannot allow the enjoyment of rights secured to British subjects to be defeated by the violence of temper and the irritability of foreign rulers, nor by the timidity or self-interest of their dependents.'[11]

The fight was continued under Abbas. By 1850 the Sennaar gum monopoly was effectively abolished and a British consul was appointed to Khartum to take advantage of the expected opportunities which would result from freedom of British trade with the Sudan.[12] Successive British consuls-general, on instructions from their government, adopted an increasingly hectoring attitude towards the Egyptian Government in matters of trade. Objection was taken to an attempt by the Egyptian Government to prohibit advances by foreign merchants to cultivators on the security of their crops on the ground that this prohibition was in breach of the 1838 Convention.[13] (The Egyptian Government wanted the crops to be unencumbered so that they themselves could seize them if necessary against non-payment of taxes.) Objection was also taken to the prohibition of grain exports in 1853 on the ground of 'extreme hardship to British merchants engaged in a regular trade which is so profitable to Egypt.'[14] The Egyptian Government protested that they had prohibited the export of wheat in order to prevent a famine. But Green, the acting British Consul-General, would have none of it, and suspected Abbas of trying to restore Mohamed Ali's grain monopoly.[15] Eventually Larking, Abbas' agent in London, seems to have convinced HMG that there was a genuine case for limiting the export of wheat from Egypt, in that it was desirable to bring down the internal price, and a compromise was reached by which exports were restricted but not banned.[16]

Gradually, the practice of selling the cotton crop by public auction, as recommended by the British consuls-general, was adopted. By the time of Said's accession in 1854 the old monopoly 'ring' of foreign merchants had been broken. This was advantageous to the Egyptian cultivator and to the European consumer. It was disadvantageous to the Egyptian urban consumer, who could no longer be subsidised at the expense of the foreign consumer, and to the Egyptian Government who, by losing control of the market, were no longer able to use the foreign merchants as a convenient banking system for providing short-term loans on the security of crop allocations.

The ending of the cotton monopoly coincided with, and may have been the cause of, a considerable increase in cotton cultivation. Between 1835 and 1850 annual production had fluctuated between 150,000 and 350,000 *kantars* (a *kantar* is about a hundredweight). During the 1850s it rose to an average of about 500,000 kantars per annum.

The hectoring interventions into Egypt's internal affairs show how the pattern of colonisation was developing. Since the diminution of Mohamed Ali's power as a result of the events of 1840–41, the British Government had begun to use diplomatic pressure towards making Egypt a source of cheap raw materials, and a profitable field for the sale of manufactured goods, without any regard for the interests of the Egyptian Government or for the welfare of the Egyptian people. The Egyptian Government was induced to continue exporting wheat to England at a time of local shortage for the benefit of British merchants and because the wheat harvest in England had been below average.[17] The insistence on cotton being sold at public auction was due to a desire to force down prices for the benefit of the Lancashire cotton manufacturer.[18] The project for a railway was urged, both to speed up the overland route and in order to help the sale of British railway equipment. In the light of contemporary British policy towards Egypt, the British Government's protests against the use of forced labour in the construction of the Suez Canal ring very hollow, particularly as forced labour was used, without British protest, in the construction of the British-sponsored railway.

Mohamed Ali had been no more solicitous of the interests of his subjects than the European governments were. He taxed them mercilessly to pay for his wars and his public works. Revenue increased from an estimated £E810,075 in 1800 to an estimated £4,200,800 in 1847. (£E represents an Egyptian pound, which was approximately equivalent to £1.02.[19]) About four-fifths of this was derived from *miri* (agricultural land tax) and *ferdi* (poll-tax), levied exclusively on the villages,[20] and about one-third was spent on the armed forces.

In Abbas' reign much less was spent on the armed forces and on public works, and in consequence it became possible considerably to lower the rate of taxation. By 1854 the revenue had dropped to just over £E2 million[21] and remained at around this level until about 1856, when it began to rise steeply under the impulses of extensive public works, governmental extravagance and foreign debt service. The reduction of taxation under Abbas and Said was of immediate benefit to the cultivator, but it was achieved in part by a neglect of the irrigation system. A greater benefit to the cultivator was his lessened liability to conscription, which meant that he was able to spend more time in his fields.

More important in the long run than these alleviations was a progressive change in the status of rural landholding. As we have seen, all land in Egypt theoretically belonged to the State with the occupier enjoying the usufruct. Land could not be bought, mortgaged or legally inherited, and the State had the right, which it often exercised, of expropriation without compensation. From about 1829 onwards full ownership in *abadieh* land – uncultivated land granted to magnates on favourable tax conditions provided that it was brought into cultivation – was conceded (tacitly at first, officially in 1859), carrying with it the right to sell, mortgage and inherit. In 1846 the first step was taken towards establishing private ownership of *kharaj* land – cultivated land paying the full *miri* – when a decree was promulgated enabling such land to be mortgaged or sold on the basis of a certificate (*hodga*) issued by the head-man of the village. Such land could still be seized by the State for non-payment of taxes, but could be returned if and when the arrears of tax were paid. In 1854 a new decree, which provided for the registration of all land transfers by the Court (*mahkama*) instead of by the village headman also provided that *kharaj* land could be legally inherited by male issue. In 1858 this limited right of inheritance was changed to provide for inheritance according to Islamic Law i.e. two shares to each son and one share to each daughter. The same decree gave full rights of ownership to any cultivator who had occupied his land for five successive years and had paid his taxes regularly. But the State still reserved to itself the right to confiscate land without compensation. Thus, within almost exactly fifty years, more or less complete private ownership had been established, except in respect of the very extensive estates, consisting originally of the lands confiscated from the *multazimin*, and augmented by subsequent acquisitions and confiscations, which were the property of the Viceroy and his family.

This move towards private ownership was accompanied by a change in the method of taxation. Up to this time of Said's accession the village headman had been responsible for the collection of *miri* on the village lands, and the village was collectively responsible for payment. In 1857 it was decreed that taxes were to be collected by the government from cultivators individually. This involved the issue of what amounted to certificates of ownership in respect of all *kharaj* lands. At the same time it was decreed that all taxes must be paid in cash and not in kind.

This transfer to private ownership and a cash economy was not wholly to the advantage of the cultivator or to the Egyptian economy generally. In practice it meant that much agricultural land began to be alienated from the small cultivator by sale or, later, as a result of the foreclosure of mortgages. Although the average individual holding remained small, and was to become smaller owing to the increasing population and the operation of the Moslem law of inheritance, there developed a tendency towards the growth of large estates as a result of the acquisition of land from small cultivators, who used their new freedom to incur debts on the security of their land, which they eventually had to sell in order to redeem the debt. There were many moneylenders, some of them Europeans, either individuals or so-called banks, who lent money at inflated rates of interest to cultivators with the ultimate object of acquiring their lands. By the end of the century nearly 40 per cent of the cultivated area was owned by some 12,000 landowners, many of them foreigners, with estates of over fifty *feddans* each.

This rather dubious 'liberation' of the small cultivator assisted that process of European colonisation which started with diplomatic pressure on a militarily defeated Egypt to dismantle the monopoly system. It led to the evolution of a *laissez-faire* economy which enabled raw materials and food-stuffs required by European countries, principally cotton and cereals, to be purchased at the cheapest possible price. Once this free market was well on its way to being established, the next stage was to use diplomatic pressure to sell European manufactures to Egypt. We have seen how this operated in the case of the railway. The third stage was to use diplomatic pressure to obtain various public utility concessions. In the operation of these, the European concessionaires were protected by the considerable immunities, derived from the Capitulations, which European foreigners enjoyed in Egypt. The Suez Canal concession was a good example of this. Other examples, of which there were a great many from 1854 onwards, were gas, electricity, water supply, tramways, and light railway concessions. A somewhat disreputable version of this concession-hunting, also illustrated by the Suez Canal concession, was to obtain an unreasonable concession, which was then surrendered in whole or in part against the payment of an indemnity, also extorted by diplomatic pressure. The fourth stage of colonisation was the use of diplomatic pressure to induce the Egyptian Government to accept long-term foreign loans, secured on specific items of the revenue, in order, theoretically, to finance development. These loans were usually contracted on extortionate terms and no attempt was made by the lenders either to ascertain the soundness of what they were intended to finance or to relate the service of the loans to Egypt's ability to repay them. In fact, the proceeds of these loans were used, not for the financing of revenue-producing capital improvements, but for extravagances of all kinds including the payment of indemnities for surrendered foreign concessions, or for the repayment of debts previously incurred. The inevitable result was that more diplomatic pressure had to be employed to induce the Egyptian Government to collect sufficient taxes to service the loans, which service eventually absorbed more than half of Egypt's total revenue. Observers thus had the unsavoury spectacle of the representatives of the Powers, some of whom had expressed humanitarian horror at the use of forced labour for the construction of the Suez Canal, acquiescing in, and even exhorting the Egyptian Government to the flogging of peasants in order to squeeze from them ever-increasing taxes to pay the interest on loans which they had encouraged the Egyptian Government to incur.

Among the forms of diplomatic pressure employed were threats to withdraw consular representation, i.e. breaking off diplomatic relations, and threats to land the crew of a warship, usually conveniently in or near Alexandria harbour, to assist by their presence any negotiations in which their country's consul happened to be engaged. There were also more subtle methods, such as threatening to make trouble for the Viceroy in Constantinople.

In the first and second stages of colonisation England took a leading part. The British Government concluded the 1838 Commercial Convention and took the lead in enforcing its provisions on Egypt. And England took the lion's share of Egypt's cotton and cereal exports. Murray, the British Consul-General, on the instructions of the British Government, used his influence with Abbas to give the Cairo–Alexandria railway contract to Stephenson. Bruce, Murray's successor, induced Said to build the Cairo–Suez railway, which was of no possible use to Egypt's economy. British industrialists had the biggest share in the imports used for constructing and equipping these railways.

In the third stage British nationals took little part. Very few of the public utility concessions were awarded to British firms or individuals. Several of the most lucrative, including the Suez Canal concession, went to French nationals, several others to

Belgians. Perhaps because of this, British consuls-general were apt to assume a high-minded attitude over the indemnity racket.

In the fourth stage, British nationals took a prominent part. Of Egyptian foreign loan indebtedness in 1875, amounting to some £70 million, something like £40 million had been lent by British, or partly British, interests. By that time Great Britain had acquired a major stake in the European colony which Egypt had become, using the word colony in the classical sense as a protected source of raw materials and foodstuffs, a preferential market for exported manufactures, a profitable field for investment, and a privileged place of residence and employment for British nationals.

The reign of Abbas was marked by the dismissal of European officials, by a halt in the progress of modernisation, and by a revival of the old Egyptian habits of fanaticism and xenophobia. The Viceroy, who knew no European language and little of European ways (he had been brought up in the hareem and had never visited Europe), had no European intimates. By calculated inaccessibility he made himself relatively immune to the blandishments and threats of the European consuls-general, apart from Murray, who knew Turkish and who could be used to help him over his difficulties with Constantinople.

When Abbas died – probably murdered by two of his servants[22] – in July 1854, he was succeeded by Mohamed Said, a son of Mohamed Ali, and the eldest living male in the direct line of succession. Said was about thirty-two years of age when he came to the throne. He had been educated in Europe and spoke French with fluency. M. Koenig, an Alsatian, who had been his tutor in childhood and his confidant in youth, became his principal *homme d'affaires* when he ascended the throne. The new Viceroy affected the society of Europeans and was believed to be 'more inclined than his predecessor to introduce improvements into Egypt'.[23] He had been trained by his father as a sailor, but he had never been fond of the sea or of the navy. His preference was for the army, but his military enthusiasm was confined to a childish love of pointless and complicated drills and manoeuvres, a love which he was able to indulge to the full as Viceroy. Normally a good-natured and easy-going man, he was subject to occasional fits of violence and ungovernable rage. He hated unpleasantness, whether with his relatives, with the

European consuls, with his Suzerain, or with concession-hunters, and he was always ready to buy his way out of trouble. He had large, generous and, on the whole, sensible ideas about the government of Egypt. But he had neither the patience nor the capacity to devote himself to detailed administration, and he was too distrustful of his Turkish entourage to delegate his powers. For the first part of his reign he had no regular Council of Ministers, and no responsible heads of departments. So there was no effective barrier between him and the hordes of European place-hunters, concession-seekers and parasites who soon thronged his Court, no effective check on his generosity and his ill-regulated schemes for carrying on his father's work of modernisation. He was not unintelligent. For most of the time he had no illusions about the motives of those who surrounded him. But he was too cowardly to stand up to consular bullying, too indolent to combat unjustifiable claims, and too good-natured to make himself unpleasant to those who made it their business to be pleasant to him. He allowed himself to be imposed on with a wry, cynical acquiescence.

Long before Said came to the throne, speculators in Europe were looking towards Egypt as a potentially profitable field for exploitation. The favourable balance of trade created by the increasing value of Egypt's cotton exports, the almost legendary fertility of Egypt's soil, combined with the exceptional privileges enjoyed by foreigners, seemed to promise almost unique opportunities for European enterprise. Under Mohamed Ali, and under Abbas, these opportunities had, to a large extent, been inhibited, first by Mohamed Ali's determination to keep Egypt's economic development under his own control and, later, by Abbas' dislike of European innovations. During Abbas' reign, the character and probable policy of the Heir Apparent were therefore carefully weighed up by speculators whose mouths were beginning to water at the prospect of Egypt's flesh-pots dangling just out of reach. As soon as the news of Abbas' death reached Europe, scallywags from all quarters began to converge on Egypt as on a new California or Klondyke. 'The most extraordinary projects, the most absurd plans, have been submitted to HH, who seems to me to be mistaken in paying any attention at all to them . . . He is rather too apt to let himself be influenced by the grandiose propositions which are being ceaselessly whispered into his ears.'[24]

The most important of these 'grandiose propositions' was the project for the construction of the Suez Canal, for which Lesseps obtained a concession from Said before the end of 1854. Many other monopolistic, or quasi-monopolistic, concessions were granted during the first few months of Said's reign. The Egyptian Towing Company, of which the moving spirit was Ruyssenaers, the Dutch Consul-General, who was also one of Lesseps' principal collaborators over the Suez Canal, received a fifteen-year exclusive concession for the operation of steam tugs to draw barges on all the internal waterways of Egypt. This concession was vigorously opposed by other foreign interests who used, or intended to use, these waterways, and who threatened to sue the Egyptian Government for indemnities. Eventually Said, faced with the probable alternatives of having to pay an indemnity to the concessionary company if the concession were not implemented, or to others if it were, bought up the whole of the shareholding at a large premium and was thus able to cancel the concession.[25] The Medjidieh Steamship Company, founded in 1856 to provide a line of steamships in the Mediterranean and Red Sea, had a somewhat similar history, being bought up by Said and disbanded five years later.

British policy in Egypt had long been in favour of free trade and the British Government set their faces against the new private monopolies as they had done against the old State monopolies. In 1857 Bruce called attention to the practice growing up in Egypt by which favourites of the Viceroy obtained a monopoly for some particular activity which they then sold to a foreign company set up to exploit it. 'It will fall on England alone to defeat these monopolies and to assert the great principle of "freedom of industry" as she has already asserted "freedom of trade". These companies tend to overpower and supersede the authority of the Viceroy and thereby gradually supplant the Turkish race in Egypt. They have mainly a French character. They prevent the development of the political influence which her material interests would ensure to England were a fair field left for her capital and enterprise.' He told HMG that he had been able to defeat attempts by foreign capitalists (including British ones) to obtain a concession for the operation of the railway. If such a concession were granted, Bruce went on, 'complaints would be made by the company, extravagant demands would be put forward and, if the speculation proved less profitable than expected, advantage would be taken of the dilatoriness and blunders of the government to put them in the wrong, and to throw up the concession with a demand for a heavy indemnity'. Bruce then referred to the 'Lesseps' canal', the Towing Company, and a 'scheme lately put forward by the US Consul-General which would have conferred on the concessionaires a virtual monopoly of the canals of Lower Egypt', as concessions which would involve the Egyptian Government in the supply of forced labour for the benefit of the concessionaires.[26] It had been suggested that the grant of such monopolistic concessions was the only way in which the country could be developed. But Bruce stated that this was not so, and that 'the Viceroy's surplus revenues are quite sufficient to set in movement all the disposable labour in the country and, if directed to well-selected public works, would effect gradually all that Egypt requires'. Bruce quoted the rest of the royal family and most of the leading Turks, as being in general agreement with him and recommended that, as the grant of the concessions was against the interests of the Sultan, the Porte should be asked to make it clear to Said that he had neither power to grant them nor authority to exact forced labour to operate them. 'A firm declaration by the Porte on the policy to be pursued will both meet with the Viceroy's acquiescence and give encouragement to the national and Turkish party over the band of foreign intriguers . . . In their opposition to the canal &c . . . our allies are to be found in the ranks of that party, and it is for our interest that they should carry more weight in the Pasha's council.'[27]

Bruce's attitude was dictated primarily by consideration for British interests. Since the major part of Egypt's imports came from England, and the major part of Egypt's exports went to England, British interests were best served by a policy of free trade and free competition. And this was the British attitude consistently adopted until about 1862. Until then, British consuls-general invariably refused to support requests for exclusive concessions, and demands for indemnities put forward by British subjects in respect of such concessions as they had obtained without consular assistance.

A rather more reputable form of European enterprise (though

later to be abused) was encouraged both by the growth of a
monetary economy generally and by the freedom of access
between Egyptian cultivators and European middlemen resulting from the end of the State monopolies early in Said's reign,
when legislation provided for recognition of private ownership
of land. European banks then began to be established in Egypt
for the purposes of making advances to cultivators on the
security of their crops, granting mortgages for improvements,
and financing trade in general. By the end of 1855 three of
these European banks were in existence. In 1856 a fourth bank,
the Bank of Egypt, incorporated in England and financed by
English capital, was opened. Bruce, giving the project a
modified blessing, pointed out that agricultural credit in Egypt
had to cope with three principal difficulties: the uncertainty of
titles to real property; the unpredictable fluctuations in land
tax; the lack of proper Courts of Justice and a settled system
of law.[28] He was, as it turned out justifiably, suspicious of the
integrity of M. Pasquale, the Bank's principal agent in Egypt.
He was most insistent that the Bank should not attempt to
obtain any privileges over and above those possessed by other
banks in Egypt. He deprecated the choice of name, which
seemed to imply some special official recognition, and expressed
the hope that its existence might help to reduce the current
rates of interest ruling in Egypt.

   The Bank of Egypt was a disappointment. Like all the other
foreign banks, it soon abandoned the commercial purposes for
which it had been founded in favour of the more lucrative
business of lending money to the Egyptian Government. Then,
when it found that it did not get repaid on due dates, it appealed
to the Consulate for help. The Bank's directors got short shrift
from Bruce, who told them that 'in no case short of the most
palpable injustice ought they to apply for Consular assistance'.[29]
In a letter to the Bank's board in London he explained that 'the
Egyptian Government is always in arrears in its payments and
therefore always at the mercy of those with whom it deals.
There is not a merchant in Egypt who has executed commissions
for it who is not entitled, in strict justice, to make protests
against it for non-fulfilment of its obligations, but the custom
has invariably been not to resort to such measures as long as
the Government pays interest and shows its intention to make
gradual arrangements for the discharge of the principal . . . The

Government has no power to raise a loan, nor is it at all desirable that it should so so. It is therefore for the general good that the practice hitherto observed should be followed by the Bank of Egypt; by its departure from this practice it stands in a very unfavourable light compared with other creditors of the Government.' Bruce went on to explain that the Council of Ministers whom Said had just appointed were 'applying themselves seriously to the payment of the Government's debts and have adopted the equitable practice of making pro-rata distributions of the funds at their disposal among the different claimants. In fact, they deal with Egypt as if they were the assignees of a property which is temporarily insolvent, although its assets are ultimately sufficient to meet its liabilities. I could not have insisted on the demand made by the Bank without gross injustice to other creditors, and I know of no reason why I should have attempted to secure on its behalf an undue preference over the other British establishments in this country.'[30]

The state of the Egyptian Treasury as revealed in Bruce's letter was nothing new. Mohamed Ali had been accustomed to borrow from European merchants but, owing to his monopolies, was able to pay them at short-term by awarding crop allocations to cover the advances made. Said could offer no such security and, instead of paying his short-term loans out of the proceeds of taxation, which he needed for more immediate purposes, found it easier to pay the interest and trust to the patience and self-interest of his creditors to get his bills renewed. And since it suited the creditors to keep on good terms with the Viceroy, who had so many and such varied privileges in his gift, they usually were renewed.

But the position steadily got worse. Already, in 1856, the Egyptian Treasury was in arrears in its payment of the Ottoman tribute, which had to be paid in London for the service of the 1854 Anglo-French Ottoman loan.[31] Large sums were being dissipated in the payment of indemnities, in the distribution of presents, in purchases of 'machinery of every shape and size, rails, patent clips, coal, steamers, solid silver epaulets, sword belts and buttons for the troops, steel cannons, iron pavements from London, fantastic looking-glasses of fabulous size and incredible cost from Paris, mules from Spain, barges from Holland, every kind of thing from America, not because the

Viceroy requires them, but because the orders are officially insisted on'.[32] Creditors were beginning to get pressing and Green, the acting British Consul-General, remarked that one of the reasons for Said's constant journeys about the country was to avoid their importunities and those of the foreign consuls.

The revenue in 1857 was estimated by Green at £E4 million, 'one-third greater than that which enabled Mohamed Ali to maintain a fleet and army which threatened the existence of the Porte, and although the *miri* this year has been collected in advance, salaries of officials are unpaid and the amount owing to commercial houses is stated at £800,000'.[33]

The possibility of a foreign loan was first raised in 1857, when the French Crédit Mobilier offered one to Said. Bruce told the Crédit Mobilier representative that he would 'offer all the opposition in my power to any such scheme on the ground that the Viceroy had no power at all to make any such arrangement'. In reporting this conversation to the British Government, he added these prophetic words: 'Nothing could be more fatal to the interest of this country than to concede the power of raising a loan to the Viceroy, as the only guarantee we possess against his recklessness and extravagance is the necessity he is under of providing for his obligations out of his income. His revenue is quite sufficient to meet every legitimate expense and to execute such internal improvements as the interests of Egypt render desirable. But, if he were permitted to borrow on the security of the revenue, no hope would remain of economy or good administration, and the country would descend to his successors with its revenue alienated to foreign speculators.'[34]

By the middle of 1858 Said's indebtedness to foreign merchants had risen to an estimated £1 million, and many of them were in favour of his raising a loan in order to get themselves paid. The Viceroy sent an emissary to Constantinople to ask permission to raise a loan of £2 million. Sherif Pasha, the Foreign Minister, told the acting British Consul-General that there was little prospect of getting permission, and no necessity for a loan anyway. Permission was not, in the event, obtained, but Said soon had recourse to a more insidious, because open-ended, method of obtaining credit. This was by issuing short-dated treasury bonds, a method apparently suggested to him by Lesseps, who was anxious to put Said in funds as a pre-liminary to getting some money out of him for the expenses of the canal. Since Egypt's foreign credit was still reasonably good and since, as yet, the Egyptian Treasury owed no money abroad, these bonds were easily discountable in Europe and opened up a new source of credit which enabled the Viceroy to pay off the more pressing of his local creditors and to embark on new extravagances.

Said's treasury bonds were at first issued at six, twelve and eighteen months and, later, for periods of up to thirty-six months, and bore interest, first at 15 per cent and, later, at 18 per cent per annum. The commercial banks in Egypt, attracted by the high rates of interest, subscribed to them eagerly in preference to the commercial financing, which was the original object of their existence, but which brought them an interest of only between 6 per cent and 7 per cent per annum. The credit seemed good since the bonds were, at first, always redeemed on due date to keep the market sweet for further issues.

By the end of 1859, 'Said's reckless expenditure and the facility with which he allows himself to be pillaged by a set of parasites' had 'not only caused a deficit of £1 million' in the budget, but had 'forestalled all the resources of 1860'. Treasury bonds were being issued payable at two years to an amount of over £1,600,000, salaries of officials were in arrear to the extent of £800,000, and some £52,000 was owed to merchants and tradesmen on open account.[35]

Three months later, the position was even worse. Colquhoun, the new British Consul-General, reported that 'Said's passion for large military works . . . extensive and ill-judged purchases of land and palaces at inflated prices, are being paid for by Government Bonds at 18, 24 and 36 months. The Viceroy found these Bonds much in request at first, and they passed current at a discount of not much above that of government transactions in general, viz. 6 per cent. But when it became plain that large orders had been given to merchants for goods, military stores, rail equipment &c. far above the market price, and that payment was to be made by Government Bonds at long date, the discount rate rose to 18 per cent. It is generally believed that £3–£3½ million worth of Bonds have been issued. Every Government employee is from 14–18 months in arrears of pay.'[36] In these deteriorating circumstances the holders of treasury bonds began to feel a little nervous. In February 1860 a leading British merchant asked Colquhoun whether he thought that, in the event of Said's death, his bonds would be honoured by his successor. Colquhoun replied that a successor might well hesitate to honour debts incurred in so irresponsible a fashion.[37]

There had, for some months, again been talk of a foreign loan, secured on some part of Egypt's revenue, which would enable the uncovered floating debt to be paid off. Towards the end of 1859 Colquhoun had been sounded by Pastré, a local French financier, and Hugh Thurburn, a leading British merchant of Alexandria, about the possibility of an Anglo-French company buying the railways in order to put the Egyptian Treasury in funds. Pastré insinuated that a properly-run railway would render the Suez Canal project superfluous and so improve Anglo-French relationships. But Colquhoun pointed out that the Firman giving permission for the construction of the railway stipulated that it should not be alienated from the Egyptian Government.[38] So the proposal came to nothing. But, early in 1860, French interests went ahead on their own. With the assistance of the French Consul-General, and through the agency of Paolini Bey, a Pole who was one of Said's intimates and hangers-on, a loan of Fcs. 28 million (about £1,200,000) was negotiated with the Paris houses of Charles Lafitte and the Comptoir d'Escompte. The nett amount of this loan, after deduction of commissions, promotion expenses etc., amounted to about Fcs. 20,700,000.[39] It was to be paid to the Egyptian Treasury in five instalments over the second half of 1860, and to be repaid at 6 per cent interest between 1861 and 1865 against non-negotiable treasury bonds deposited in Paris and guaranteed by the customs revenues of Alexandria. A condition of the loan, which did not have the consent of the Porte, was that the Viceroy should not issue any more treasury bonds until it was paid off.[40]

This loan, which was contracted with the connivance and indeed with the encouragement of Thouvenel, the French Foreign Minister, was largely the result of pressure by Said's French creditors, and particularly Lesseps, who was trying to get Said to acknowledge, and make arrangements to pay for, the unsubscribed shares in the Canal Company. It marked the end of the prudent discouragement of the Viceroy's prodigality by the British and French Consuls-General, and the beginning of a competition between French bankers on the one hand and

Anglo-Prussian bankers on the other to lend money to the Egyptian Government.

This first loan was soon spent, on the payment of indemnities promised,[41] on the conferment of *douceurs* on the Viceroy's relatives, and on the settlement of debts, including eleven months' arrears of pay due to the army. By the middle of 1861 the Treasury was again empty and the floating debt, instead of having been reduced, had increased to £7 million. Lesseps was pressing Said to contract for a thirty-year loan to enable him to pay for the unsubscribed Canal shares which he was trying to unload onto him.[42] Moreover, payment of treasury bonds, which hitherto had been met on due dates, was beginning to be delayed. By June 1861 Said was negotiating with the Comptoir d'Escompte for another and larger loan. Once again the Comptoir had the support of the French Government, whose attitude in the matter is illustrated in the diplomatic correspondence between Paris and Cairo. Beauval, the French Consul-General, supporting Said's application, wrote; 'If the Viceroy wants a further loan, would it not be better for him to obtain it from France rather than from any other country? When one is authorised, as a result of arrangements made in the interests of our capitalists, to exercise some measure of control over the finances of the State, one is well on the way to controlling the affairs of the State.'[43] And the French Government, endeavouring to justify their support for a loan which the Viceroy was trying to contract without the authority of the Porte, drew a distinction between 'an inherent act of sovereignty' and 'a simple matter of administration', concluding that the proposed loan was in the latter category, in that the Viceroy was simply 'trying to consolidate and arrange for the payment of existing indebtedness'.[44]

The loan negotiations with the Comptoir failed, mainly because the proposed terms were exorbitant. They wanted $11\frac{1}{2}$–12 per cent interest, a commission of 6 per cent and the nomination of a commission to supervise the Egyptian budget. Beauval protested that it was in the French interest that the Viceroy should borrow from France and that it was the business of the French Government to ensure that the conditions demanded were reasonable. 'If we do not do it, others will.'[45]

There was already a powerful competitor in the market. Hermann and Henry Oppenheim, uncle and nephew, were

German Jewish bankers, originating in Frankfurt, who had strong banking connections both in Prussia and in England, and who had for many years been established in Constantinople and in Alexandria where, in view of their international connections, they could rely on the diplomatic support both of Great Britain and Prussia. In Alexandria the firm of Oppenheim, Chabert et Cie had acquired a somewhat unsavoury reputation as the result of some of their transactions.[46] Although they had not themselves anything like the resources to satisfy Said's needs, they were in a position, by reason of their banking connections in England and Prussia, to negotiate a loan for him. Probably their most important advantage in this connection was their influence in Constantinople, through the firm of Oppenheim, Alberti et Cie, which had been established there since 1854. Through this connection, and with the assistance of the British Embassy, they succeeded, in January 1862, in getting the Porte to agree to the project of a loan which they had offered to Said, and to which the British Consul-General was instructed to give his 'moral support'. The projected loan was for a sum of Fcs. 40 million (later increased to Fcs. 60 million), repayable over thirty years, bearing a nominal 8 per cent and an actual 11 per cent rate of interest, and secured on the land taxes of the Delta. The terms were hardly, if at all, more favourable than those offered by the Comptoir d'Escompte, and Said could not make up his mind between them. But the Oppenheims, supported by the British[47] and the Prussian Consuls-General, maintained that the authorisation for the loan which they had obtained, at Said's request, from the Porte, only applied to the Oppenheim loan and constituted a commitment by Said to take it up. In accordance with the usual practice, they threatened to sue him for an indemnity if he did not do so. Harassed by these pressures, and in any case needing the money, Said signed the contract with the Oppenheims in March 1862.

The actual amount received, after deducting discounts, commissions and so on, was about Fcs. 53,500,000 (£2,150,000) out of a nominal Fcs. 60,000,000 (£2,500,000), and the amount to be repaid over a thirty-year period was about Fcs. 198,000,000.[48] This worked out at 11 per cent interest and amortisation on the nominal amount of the loan and an annual charge of some £264,000 on the Egyptian Treasury. Colquhoun, who helped to negotiate the loan, regarded this as 'very

Mohamed Ali Pasha

Said Pasha

insignificant when money is worth from 12 per cent to 15 per cent'.[49] He had been in favour of a Fcs. 100,000,000 loan repayable over fifteen years, stating that he estimated Egypt's revenue at £3,580,000 p.a. and ordinary government expenditure at £2,600,000 p.a., leaving an annual surplus of £980,000, which would have been more than sufficient to service such a loan. With good management in the future, therefore, the service of the loan actually contracted for should not have proved a serious burden. But such good management was not forthcoming.

The Oppenheims' backers were the Saxe-Meiningen Bank. But, after the contract had been signed, the issue was made in London by the firm of Fruhling & Goschen, partly at eighty-two and a half, and partly at eighty-four and a half. This circumstance perhaps explains the 'moral support' which the British Consul-General was instructed to give to the Oppenheims. Colquhoun, who admitted that the loan was 'a brilliant affair for the contractors', had told Said, while it was being contracted, that 'although British bankers might be interested to a small extent, the conduct of the Egyptian Government has of late been of a nature to deter any British capitalists of note from investing in Egypt'.[50] He may really have believed this at the time. He was presumably undeceived when, in May 1862, Mr Charles Goschen arrived from London on behalf of the firm of Fruhling & Goschen 'to obtain the necessary signatures of the deeds by which the Viceroy engages himself and the revenues of the Delta for the service of the loan'.[51]

During 1861 Said had made some mostly ill-regulated and misconceived attempts at economy. He dismissed a great many European employees on the railway and neglected its maintenance to such an extent that, in the autumn of 1861, the Cairo–Alexandria line was put out of action as a result of embankments being swept away by floods. He also reduced the strength of the army, first to 6,000 and later to 2,500. He auctioned masses of army equipment and disposed of hundreds of horses, camels and dromedaries. He sold, at considerable loss, much of the personal plate and jewellery which he had amassed. But he went on buying lands and palaces, spending some £180,000 in such purchases in a single month, and paying for them with treasury bonds. He went on paying indemnities in settlement of ridiculous and sometimes fraudulent claims.

D

Orders continued to be placed abroad at fantastic prices, in spite of Said's frequently expressed determination to put all such orders out to tender.

In these circumstances of maladministration, there was little prospect of the fulfilment of the hope expressed by Colquhoun that the new loan would be used to pay off old debts and finance some useful public works. In fact, during Said's reign, hardly any useful public works were put in hand. Neither the Cairo–Suez railway, nor the Suez Canal, were of the slightest immediate or ultimate use to the Egyptian economy. The Delta barrage was used as a military encampment and no attempt was made to develop it for its intended purpose. By the time of Said's death at the beginning of 1863 the Egyptian Treasury was heavily in debt and had nothing to show for it. Of the £2,150,000 received from the Oppenheim loan, all but £400,000 had been spent. The sums borrowed had not been used in any way which could conceivably have financed the service of the debts incurred. The foreign loans had not even achieved their intended purpose of liquidating, or even of reducing, the floating debt. Such was the confusion of Egyptian finances that it is almost impossible to arrive at even an approximate estimate of the debts Said left behind him. Apart from a sum of about £8 million, which had to be paid over the next thirty years for the service of the Oppenheim loan, there was still over £1 million owing to the Comptoir d'Escompte, payable over the next three years. The floating debt was probably in the region of £9 million.[52] One of the principal reasons for the indebtedness was the personal extravagance of the Viceroy[53] and the fact that there was no proper distinction between State expenditure and the personal expenditure of the ruler. The first necessity from the point of view of good financial administration was the establishment of a Civil List for the royal family. This was realised in theory and, to a small extent, in practice, under Said's successor. Given this, and given ordinarily good management, there was no reason why the debts left by Said should have constituted a very severe burden on the Egyptian Treasury. With a revenue in the region of £3½ million a year it would have been possible to service the debt and provide for ordinary administrative expenditure. Loans might have been raised on reasonable terms to finance capital expenditure which would generate sufficient revenue to provide for the service of the loans. This would have been a preferable alternative to Mohamed Ali's method of providing for development out of current resources by means of forced labour and oppressive taxation.

It is possible that something of the sort might have been done had Great Britain and France used the authority they undoubtedly possessed. Instead, these Powers, not so much by deliberate policy as by default, allowed Egypt to be exposed to the extravagant ambitions of Ismail, to the exploitation of the Suez Canal Company and other foreign concessionaires, and to the rapacity of French and Anglo-German Jewish moneylenders who, after the manner of their kind, encouraged their client's extravagance in order to possess themselves of his property. The large and international scale of this spoliation gradually transformed the small-scale bullying of the Consuls-General over indemnities, which had been characteristic of the reign of Said, into diplomatic intervention by the Governments of the Powers in the interests of European bondholders. 'Spoiling the Egyptians', which had started as a racket by individual European adventurers supported by some of the more disreputable 'trading' consuls, and had been reprobated by the more respectable of the 'career' consuls, ended by becoming a major source of profit to half the banking houses of Europe, supported by most of the governments of the Great Powers.

Notes

1. Crouchley, *The Economic Development of Egypt*, p 58
2. *ibid*, p 51
3. Campbell-Bowring, 18.1.38, FO 78/342
4. FO-Barnett, 26.8.41, FO 78/451
5. Barnett-Aberdeen, 15.5.42, FO 78/502
6. FO-Barnett, *ibid*
7. *ibid*, 4.2.43, FO 78/451
8. Barnett-Aberdeen, 6.7.43, *ibid*
9. *ibid*, 19.8.43, *ibid*
10. *ibid*, 13.1.44, FO 78/582
11. Palmerston-Murray, 4.2.48, FO 78/756
12. Murray-Palmerston, 5.1.50, FO 78/840
13. FO-Paget, 1.2.53, FO 78/965
14. Clarendon-Green, 30.9.53, *ibid*. On several occasions Mohamed Ali, without protest from HMG, had forbidden the export of cereals from Egypt. The extension of the cotton acreage, the increase in Egypt's population and, on occasion, the incidence of a low Nile, sometimes reduced the cereal crop to below Egypt's domestic requirements. It was occasionally necessary to import cereals
15. Green-Clarendon, 19.9.53, *ibid*. Green quoted figures showing that Great Britain normally took between two-thirds and three-quarters of Egypt's total grain exports. In 1851 Britain had taken 1,146,254 qtrs out of total exports of 1,468,649 qtrs. In 1852 the figures were 563,555 qtrs out of 814,454 qtrs
16. Green-Clarendon, 17.11.53, *ibid*
17. Clarendon-Green, 30.9.53, FO 78/965
18. In the 1830s the price of Egyptian cotton f.o.b. Alexandria varied from a maximum of 18¼ *rials* per *kantar* to a minimum of 13 *rials* (one *rial* = £0.20, one *kantar* = 1 cwt approx). In the 1850s it varied from a maximum of 16¼ *rials* to a minimum of 8½ *rials*. Crouchley, *op cit*, p 263
19. *ibid*, p 259. These figures are only rough estimates. Available budget figures for the period are wildly inaccurate, invariably showing an excess of revenue over expenditure. In fact, the revenue was exacted to meet expenditure and there was never any question of a surplus
20. See, *inter alia*, Murray-Palmerston, 1.1.47, FO 78/707
21. Crouchley, *op cit*, p 275
22. Officially, he died of apoplexy. Bruce discounted the rumour that he had been murdered, but most historians have accepted it as a fact. It appears that there was an abortive attempt to place Abbas' son, al-Hami, on the throne
23. Bruce-Clarendon, 11.7.54, FO 78/1036
24. Sabatier-Ministre, 2.10.54, *Corres. Politique Egypte*, 25
25. Green-Clarendon, 6.11.57, FO 78/1314
26. The scheme put forward by the US Consul-General was a concession for dredging the canals of Lower Egypt to make and keep them fit for navigation. This was not granted by Said, probably because his Council of Ministers resigned in protest against his intention

to do so. Bruce commented that 'the persons who got up the project have not the capital to put it into execution and no doubt, had they obtained it, would have followed the example of the original grantees of the Towing Company and sold it to foreign capitalists. The grantee of the Towing Company obtained £30,000 for his privilege and de Leon's protegé counted on obtaining £45,000. Such charges are an added burden thrown on the trade and population of Egypt for which they receive no compensation whatever . . . As far as I am aware Mr de Leon is the first representative of a principal country who has made himself a party to such speculations and has openly lent the authority of his diplomatic position to force it down the throat of the Viceroy.' Bruce-Clarendon, 30.4.57, FO 78/1313

27. Bruce-Clarendon, 16.4.57 and 29.4.57, FO 78/1313
28. *ibid,* 31.8.55, FO 78/1123
29. *ibid,* 8.4.57, FO 78/1312
30. *ibid.* Three years later the Bank got itself into very hot water as a result of advances made to the *Daira* (estates administration) of al-Hami, Abbas' son. Al-Hami had died heavily in debt and the liquidators of the estate were unable to satisfy all the creditors. The Bank stood to lose something like £150,000, most of which was paid by Said who, with his usual feckless generosity, took over responsibility for his deceased kinsman's debts. Pasquale got the sack and the Bank continued to flourish in a modest way until it went into liquidation just before the first world war. Landes, *Bankers and Pashas,* pp 113 and 138
31. Bruce-Clarendon, 18.9.56, FO 78/1222
32. Green-Malmesbury, 19.6.58, FO 78/1401
33. *ibid,* 1.5.58, *ibid*
34. Bruce-Clarendon, 23.3.57, FO 78/1313
35. Colquhoun-Russell, 5.12.59, FO 78/1568
36. *ibid,* 21.2.60, FO 78/1522
37. *ibid,* 25.2.60, *ibid*
38. *ibid,* 19.11.59, FO 78/1468
39. *ibid,* 13.9.60, FO 78/1523
40. In October 1861 the Comptoir d'Escompte claimed an indemnity on the ground that Said had broken this clause by issuing new Treasury bonds. After the intervention of the French Consul-General they received an indemnity of Fcs. 840,000 (Beauval-Thouvenel, 14.10.61, *Corres. Politique Egypte* 30). It appears that the 'Treasury bonds' in question were in fact '*assignats*' on the Treasury given by government officials in arrears of pay to tradesmen for supplies for their personal use which tradesmen then cashed with the Treasury. See Sabry, *op cit,* p 96. But this is not the whole story. It appears that Said did issue some £600,000 worth of Treasury bonds at 9 per cent 'to cover engagements made long prior to the loan'. At the time of the issue Colquhoun predicted that the Viceroy would have trouble with the Comptoir. Colquhoun-Russell, 26.11.60 and 10.12.60, FO 78/1523
41. Including £130,000 to Zininia, one of Said's Levantine hangers-on, in what Colquhoun described as 'a most preposterous claim'. Colquhoun-Russell, 4.10.60, FO 78/1523
42. Marlowe, *The Making of the Suez Canal,* p 62 35n. In spite of the testimony of most writers on the subject, Said did not commit

himself to taking over these unsubscribed shares. See *ibid,* pp 151–52

43. Beauval-Thouvenel, 18.5.61, *Corres. Politique Egypte* 29
44. Thouvenel-Beauval, 2.8.61, *ibid*
45. Beauval-Thouvenel, 19.8.61, *ibid*
46. In one of them they had managed the estates of al-Hami, Abbas' son, had guaranteed his debts, and had only been saved from bankruptcy by the intervention of the Prussian Consul-General. Subsequently, when al-Hami died in 1861 and the executors sold the estates to pay the dead man's debts, Oppenheim, Chabert et Cie claimed an indemnity on the ground of the management of the estates having been taken away from them, and obtained from the Viceroy a sum of £93,000. Landes, *op cit,* pp 112–116
47. Colquhoun-Russell, 24.1.62, FO 78/1675. Colquhoun told Said that he had a 'moral obligation to take up the German loan instead of contracting with other parties on an almost identical basis, and was laying himself open to an accusation of instability of purpose and perhaps even a claim for heavy damages'
48. Landes, *op cit,* p 117
49. Colquhoun-Russell, 12.10.61, FO 78/1591
50. *ibid,* 24.1.62, FO 78/1675
51. *ibid,* 3.5.62, *ibid*
52. Some of the exaggerated estimates of Said's indebtedness at the time of his death are due to the assumption that he committed himself to taking up the unsubscribed Suez Canal Company shares. In fact, all he was committed to was his original subscription of 64,000 shares, representing a debt of Fcs. 32 million, or about £1,350,000. Landes (*op cit,* p 131) states that the floating debt at the end of Said's reign exceeded £12 million. He does not quote his source, but seems to assume that this included the amount owing on the whole of the 176,000 odd shares which Lesseps was trying to unload onto him. If the unsubscribed shares are deducted, this brings Landes' figure down to about £9½ million. Hamza, in his *Public Debt of Egypt,* estimates the total debt at £12½ million. After deducting the amounts owing on the two foreign loans this brings Hamza's figure for the floating debt down to about £9 million, which agrees with Landes' adjusted figure, and also agrees approximately with Sabry's figure (Sabry, *op cit,* p 106) after making the Suez Canal shareholding adjustment
53. One reason for the extravagance of Said's personal expenditure was his childish habit of ordering, at inflated prices, and usually through his favourites who received large commissions, quantities of 'toys' which took his fancy. There is much in Said's character which reminds one of Mr Toad. After having been shown, to his great gratification, an Armstrong gun on a British warship visiting Alexandria, he ordered twenty-five of these expensive contraptions through his favourite, Bravay who, as the British Consul-General warned him, was certainly not in a position to supply him with the genuine article. When travelling by train it was his custom to drive the engine himself as fast as it would go. He was continually setting out on ambitious journeys and abandoning them almost before he had started. Once he set out for Europe and turned back on the second day because he had been seasick. Once he started off on the pilgrimage to Mecca but gave it up in a rage just after

leaving Suez because he had lost some papers. He converted the irrigation works at the Delta barrage into a military camp, lining the barrage wall with brass cannon. The suspicions aroused in the FO by this were quite groundless: Said was only playing at soldiers. When the pressure of his debts began to become onerous, he reduced his army to practically nothing. He was usually good-humoured, but occasionally got into the most fearful rages, sometimes in the presence of the consuls-general. He had absolutely no discretion and repeated private conversations without reserve to all and sundry. He could be persuaded to promise almost anything by anyone who took the trouble to flatter him, but he could equally be persuaded to break a promise by the next person who came to see him. Like most complaisant people, he had occasional prolonged fits of obstinacy. His only notion of economy was to underpay his servants and officials. He had his virtues. He had some feeling for the Egyptian peasant who, comparatively lightly taxed, more or less immune from the arbitrary seizure of his land, and less subjected than usual to forced labour or military conscription, was better off under Said than he had been for some time, and certainly better off than he was to be under Said's successor

5

Ismail

IN 1835, when E. W. Lane wrote his *Manners and Customs of the Modern Egyptians*, the mode of life which he was describing was characteristic of the inhabitants of Cairo and Alexandria, as well as of the countryside. Contact with the West had not as yet much affected either the appearance of the cities or the daily lives of their inhabitants. In spite of the ruler's modernising tendencies, the Court of Mohamed Ali was still an oriental one. The ruler himself spoke no European language and held his *Divans* (councils) in the traditional oriental fashion, with his advisers, in flowing robes, seated crossed-legged on cushions. The royal palaces, as well as other upper-class buildings, were built in the traditional Turkish mode, with the rooms leading out of a central courtyard and the windows consisting of wooden lattice-work (*mashrubiya*) instead of glass. The food of the upper classes was still cooked and eaten in traditional fashion and without the aid of European tableware and cutlery. The cigar had not begun to replace the water-pipe in polite society and the Prophet's laws regarding abstention from alcohol were still generally observed, at all events in public. There were no European shops or hotels and the streets were still unpaved and unlighted, except for the lanterns carried by nocturnal way-farers. Such Europeans as lived in the two principal cities usually dressed in oriental fashion both for convenience and in order to avoid making themselves conspicuous. One concession to modernity had been made, by order of the ruler; the streets in the commercial quarters had been widened and the *mastabas* (stone platforms or stoeps) outside the shops removed to make room for horse carriages to pass.

Twenty-five years later, in 1860, there had been a tremendous change as a result of the impact of European manners and customs. Edward Stanley Poole, Lane's nephew, in a preface to a new edition of Lane's book published in that year, wrote of the book as 'one that cannot now be re-written. Twenty-five years of steam communication with Egypt have more altered its inhabitants than had the preceding five centuries. They then retained the habits and manners of their remote ancestors; they now are yearly straying from old paths into the new ways of European civilisation.'

Steam communications, the import of European goods, the European education now being received by increasing numbers of upper-class Egyptians, the influence of European business-men and administrators, and, above all perhaps, the influence of the printing press, all played their part in changing the external face of Egypt. But the process only started to gather momentum in 1854 when Mohamed Said succeeded his nephew Abbas on the throne. Said was the first of his line to have been educated on European lines. He spoke French fluently, wore European clothes, was attracted by the external aspects of European manners and customs, and started a fashion for them at his Court and in Egyptian upper-class circles generally. Europeans, many of them adventurers and concession-hunters of doubtful character and antecedents, frequented his Court, where French came to be spoken as freely as Turkish. The *stambouli* (frock coat) replaced the *kaftan* as the formal dress of ministers and high officials. Palaces, government offices and rich men's houses began to be built in the European style. Wooden, brass or iron bedsteads began to replace the old bed-rolls, and rooms began to be cluttered up with ornate furniture in the styles of the First and Second Empire. Glass windows replaced the old *mashrubiya*. Brandy and cigars, instead of sherbet and water-pipes, were offered to distinguished visitors after dinners, which now began to be served with all the cumbersome paraphernalia of European crockery, cutlery and table-linen.

When Ismail succeeded Said in 1863 the process of European-isation was accelerated. There was plenty of money about, owing both to the cotton boom induced by the blockade of the cotton ports by the North during the American Civil War, and to the capital investment which Ismail encouraged and patron-ised. There was a building boom in Cairo and Alexandria. In Alexandria a new garden suburb, inhabited mainly by European cotton magnates, sprang up at Ramle, east of the city, in what had previously been desert. In Cairo a large European-style quarter, Ismailiya, sprang up between the Ezbeqia Gardens, previously marking the western extremity of the city, and the Nile. It consisted of private houses with spacious gardens, hotels, shops and offices, laid out along wide, paved, tree-lined avenues. All this building was encouraged by generous grants of land made by the Government to people who undertook to develop it suitably. South-west of the Esbeqia a vast new palace, Abdin, was built as the official residence of the ruler. Two other large palaces – Qasr-al-Nil and Gezira – were built on the banks of the Nile and on the island of Zamalek respectively. The Ezbeqia Gardens themselves were diminished by the construction of a new, Europeanised quarter on their eastern side. An opera house was constructed after the French style. And, in an age when spas were becoming a fashionable European means of remedying the dietetic excesses of the upper classes, the new spa of Helwan-les-Bains was created out of the desert, twenty miles south of Cairo and connected with the capital by a railway.

What was generally regarded in Europe as the enlightened attitude of the new ruler attracted an increasing number of Europeans to Egypt, both as residents and as visitors. Wealthy holiday-makers were attracted by the agreeable winter climate, by the social life at the Court (for the favoured), the European consulates and in the new hotels, and by the prospect of visiting Egypt's ancient monuments in comfort, which was being opened up by the enterprise of Mr Thomas Cook. Financiers, contractors and speculators were attracted by the boom conditions, by the exceptional privileges available to Europeans, and by the ruler's interest in modernisation. Immigrants, mainly from the over-crowded countries of southern Europe, were attracted by the prospect of employment, of inexpensive living, and of virtual freedom from the law of the land conferred by the Capitulations.

There was plenty of money to be made by enterprising Europeans, in more or less legitimate ways. Many of the smooth confidence tricksters who had frequented Said's Court – adventurers with affable manners and apparently influential connections who talked Said into granting them ill-considered concessions which they then either sold or had revoked against the payment of an indemnity – were still there. But their palmy days were over and most of them had to content themselves with acting as agents and go-betweens for the banking houses and the contracting firms who were exploiting Egypt's boom conditions by lending money, by discounting bills of exchange, by buying land, by importing machinery, by exporting cotton, by building houses, by installing gas-lighting, piped water, harbour-works and cotton-mills. The new adventurers were outwardly of a more respectable type than the indemnity racketeers who had infested Said's Court. They came to Egypt with letters of introduction from members of European governments and even the most respectable consuls were not ashamed to look after their interests. And they were charmed to find in the ruler of Egypt a man who seemed to appreciate the advantages of development, who understood the language of the Stock Exchange, who expressed the most enlightened views with apparent sincerity, and who appeared to agree that what was good for the European speculator was also good for Egypt.

Ismail was in fact an intelligent man. He had been educated in France and spoke French fluently. He had a good head for business and possessed considerable personal charm. He had frequently acted as regent during his predecessor's absences abroad, was acquainted with the business of the various Departments of State and personally directed most of it, treating his ministers as lackeys and issuing orders direct to subordinate officials. He devoted at least equal attention to his own estates and, in spite of his accession promises, made little or no distinction between his own private revenue and expenditure and that of the State. Most of the public works in irrigation and railways expansion put in hand during his reign were for the primary purpose of benefiting his own estates, which were continually being expanded by confiscation or expropriation or by other arbitrary means, which were cultivated entirely by forced labour, and which received absolute priority over irrigation water.

Apart from public works, Ismail spent largely out of State funds on commercial speculations, on military expenditure and on vast bribes paid out in Constantinople and elsewhere. He was recklessly extravagant both in his personal expenditure and in his hospitality. He was for ever building palaces and adding to his already numerous and expensive hareem. Every conceivable occasion – the anniversary of his accession, his return from a trip to Europe or Constantinople, the marriage

of one of the royal princesses, the visit of a European royalty
or celebrity – served as an opportunity for an extravagant and
ostentatious celebration. The fantastic extravaganza laid on to
celebrate the opening of the Suez Canal in 1869 was only one
of an unending series of elaborate fêtes staged mainly for the
delectation and *empressement* of European visitors and guests.
For one ball given by Ismail at his Gezira Palace a bridge of
boats was built over the Nile to convey his guests thither.
When the Prince and Princess of Wales visited Egypt at the
beginning of 1869 the entertainments offered were only slightly
less expensive than those offered for the Canal inauguration
guests a few months later.

But Ismail was no debauchee, no mere playboy. In the midst
of all the entertainments he was usually hard at work inter-
viewing financiers, negotiating with diplomats, sending instructions to his agents in Paris or Constantinople, giving
detailed orders to his officials for the extraction of money from
the peasantry or for the appropriation of land for his estates.
He seems to have regarded his extravagant entertainments
primarily as a public relations exercise for the purpose of
obtaining European support in his negotiations with Constantinople for increased independence, and for impressing
actual and potential creditors with the extent of his wealth. As
his indebtedness increased, so did the extravagance of his
entertainments.

This extravagance, which only accounted for a very small
proportion of Ismail's total expenditure, served its purpose for
as long as, and for no longer than, he was able to pay his debts.
It was his eventual insolvency, and not his misgovernment, his
oppression of the peasantry, and his extravagance which turned
Europe against Ismail, causing European statesmen and
financiers retrospectively to deplore behaviour at which they
had been conniving for years. So long as he paid his debts,
Ismail was able to obtain from Europe most of the public
consideration which his vanity required and most of the
diplomatic support which his policy necessitated. The Powers,
and particularly Great Britain, which had been instrumental in
limiting his grandfather's independence in 1840, raised no
objection to the dubious processes by which Ismail regained
from the Sultan all and more than all, the independence which
Mohamed Ali had forfeited. The British Government conferred

on him successively the Grand Cross of the Bath and the Grand Cross of the Star of India. On a visit to England in 1867, and on a subsequent visit to Paris, he was treated *en roi*. There was hardly a word of criticism in the European press, where Ismail was generally hailed as an enlightened monarch, as remarkable for his administrative ability as for his liberal views.

Ismail was at pains to foster this reputation for enlightenment by a number of gestures designed to impress European, and particularly British, opinion. In 1866, to the accompaniment of much publicity directed towards the European press, he created a Council of Deputies (more commonly known as the Chamber of Notables) which was represented as being in the nature of a parliament on European lines and as the beginning of an evolution towards constitutional monarchy. In fact, the Council had no legislative power, and possessed neither the desire nor the means to exercise any control over, or even to criticise, Ismail's despotic acts. In the same way Ismail made a great parade of his determination to abolish the slave trade in the Sudan and elsewhere in his dominions, and appointed Sir Samuel Baker, the noted British explorer, as Governor of Equatoria, at a salary of £10,000 a year, for this ostensible purpose.

Nobody who mattered, either in Europe or in Egypt, was deceived by these gestures. But, since a great many people were making, or hoping to make, a profit out of Ismail's activities, it suited them that a respectable veil should be drawn over his misdeeds. The financial houses who were lending money to Ismail on exorbitant terms, the contractors who were building his harbour-works, his railways and canals, mostly had friends in high places in England, France and Germany, and were interested in securing Ismail's independence of the Porte and in maintaining his credit on the European money markets. And the rich Europeans resident in Egypt, who benefited in various ways from Ismail's expenditure, were naturally interested in projecting an enlightened and liberal image of Egypt's ruler.

So there was something like a conspiracy of silence. The Egyptians did not dare, the Europeans did not care, to complain of Ismail's misgovernment or of the miseries which this misgovernment was bringing on the Egyptian people.

We have some account of these miseries from the pen of

Lucie Duff Gordon, an aristocratic Scottish lady who went to Egypt for her health, stayed there out of love for the country and its people, and lived in Upper Egypt during the 1860s. Writing at the beginning of 1865, less than two years after Ismail's accession and before his tax-gatherers had taken anything like their full toll, she had this to say: 'The *courbash* has been going on my neighbours' backs and feet all the morning . . . The system of wholesale extortion and spoliation has reached a point beyond which it would be difficult to go . . . I grieve . . . over the daily anguish of the poor *fellahin* who are forced to take the bread from the mouths of their starving families and eat it while toiling for the profit of one man. Egypt is one vast plantation where the master works his slaves without even feeding them.'[1] And two years later, in 1867: 'I cannot describe to you the misery here now; indeed it is wearisome even to think of; every day some new tax. Now every beast – camel, cow, sheep, donkey, horse – is made to pay. The *fellahin* can no longer eat bread; they are living on barley meal mixed with water and raw green stuff, vetches &c . . . and I see all my acquaintances growing seedy and ragged and anxious. The taxation makes life almost impossible. One hundred piastres per *feddan*, a tax on every crop, on every animal first, and again when it is sold in the market; on every man, on charcoal, on butter, on salt.'[2]

In so far as there was any criticism, it was over the difficulties which began to be experienced, from about 1867 onwards, by short-term creditors in getting their bills paid on due dates. But this criticism was mainly directed towards encouraging Ismail to substitute long-term secured for short-term unsecured debt, and trying to get him to understand 'the conditions on which alone a country can maintain its credit on the European exchanges'.[3] These conditions did not include any abatement of Ismail's personal extravagance, any relaxation of his programme of public works, or any element of consideration for Egypt's overtaxed peasantry. What, in the eyes of Europe, was really required to maintain Egypt's credit was better security for money advanced and an even more ruthless system of tax-collecting. As *The Times* put it, 'there is ground to rely on the great resources of the country, and the vigour and good intentions of the Viceroy'.

But, after Ismail had stopped paying his debts, nothing

reported about his behaviour was too bad to be believed. Those who had lauded his sagacity, those who had fallen over each other to solicit contracts, concessions and favours from him, those who had competed for the privilege of lending him money, those who had enjoyed, and abused, his hospitality, all vied with each other in repeating, and even inventing, stories to his discredit: how, in 1859, in order to secure his succession to the throne, he had contrived his elder brother Ahmed's death by arranging for the ferry carrying his railway carriage over the Nile to overturn into the river where Ahmed, a non-swimmer, was drowned; how two of his numerous concubines had been detected in an intrigue, their lovers strangled before their eyes and the concubines themselves flogged to death; how four other unfaithful concubines had been sewn alive into sacks and flung into the Nile; how he had had his faithful Finance Minister and childhood friend murdered in order to divert attention from his own financial misdeeds.

Many of these, and other, discreditable stories, were probably true, although there is no reason at all to suspect Ismail of having contrived his brother Ahmed's death. Ismail had his oriental, as well as his western, side. There was the affable and courteous host at splendid balls and banquets, chatting with diplomats and financiers and paying compliments to fair ladies. There was the royal guest on European tours, behaving impeccably, visiting exhibitions, and exchanging polite small talk with queens and empresses. There was the man of business spending long hours at his desk studying the minutiae of administration and finance. But there was also the oriental despot, cruel, crafty and revengeful, secretive and fearful, enmeshed in the toils of hareem and palace intrigues, having at his secret command the strangling-cord, the dagger and the poisoned cup, and capable of ordering the infliction, and perhaps even watching the execution, of the most atrocious tortures.

But the gravamen of history's charge against Ismail is his maladministration, which led to overtaxation, bankruptcy and foreign occupation, as well as to his own deposition. Let us examine this charge.

It has been estimated[4] that, between 1863, the year of his accession, and 1876, the year of Egypt's bankruptcy and the last year in which Ismail retained any real control of the country's finances, the Egyptian Treasury received, from all sources, a total of some £148,000,000. (This excludes loans raised on the security of Ismail's estates.) This was made up approximately as follows:

Revenue	£94,000,000
Net proceeds of loans	32,000,000
Floating debt	18,000,000
Proceeds of sale of Canal shares	4,000,000
Total	£148,000,000

What did he do with it all? The following estimate has been made:

Administrative expenses	£49,000,000
Tribute to Porte	7,600,000
Service of loans	35,000,000
Suez Canal	16,000,000
Other extraordinary public works	40,400,000
Total	£148,000,000

The revenue in 1862, the year before Said's accession, has been estimated at £4,900,000. This, if maintained during the thirteen years of Ismail's financial administration, would have produced a total of £73,700,000. The excess of £20,300,000 was obtained from increased taxation.

The legitimate cost of ordinary economical administration, as established later by the Anglo-French Dual Control, and including the annual Tribute, amounted to £4,500,000 a year, or £59,500,000 over a thirteen-year period. (The Dual Control figure included the high salaries of a number of European officials; *per contra* it took into account various administrative economies introduced by them. The two items probably balanced each other.) This approximately tallies with Ismail's thirteen-year figure for administration and tribute.

The £32,000,000 net proceeds of loans represented all that the Egyptian Treasury received out of a nominal total of some £53,000,000, on which interest and sinking fund had to be paid, and of which some £35,000,000, or more than all that had been received, was paid during the thirteen-year period. In spite of this, the capital of the debt, after excluding some

£18,000,000 of floating debt, amounted, in 1876, to some £52,000,000, or about £20,000,000 more than the Treasury had ever received.

The net expenditure of some £12,000,000 on the Suez Canal gave Egypt a corresponding asset in the shape of Preference Shares entitling the Treasury to 15 per cent of the Canal Company's net profits. In 1880 these were sold by the Dual Control for about £3,000,000, leaving a net loss of some £9,000,000 on the Suez Canal speculation, representing some two years' ordinary revenue.

The amounts spent on extraordinary public works, excluding the Suez Canal, are estimated to have consisted of:

Irrigation canals	£12,000,000
Bridges	2,150,000
Sugar mills	6,100,000
Alexandria harbour	2,542,000
Suez docks	1,400,000
Alexandria waterworks	300,000
Railways	13,361,000
Telegraphs	853,000
Lighthouses	188,000
Miscellaneous	906,000
Total	£40,400,000

A very large part of this expenditure – irrigation canals, sugar mills, some of the railway expenditure – was incurred primarily for the benefit of Ismail's private estates. All, or nearly all, of it was inflated owing to the high prices paid for the work done (there was no proper system of tendering, no proper supervision of the contractors employed). The benefits accruing to the Egyptian people from the public works expenditure as a whole – the only tangible assets to set against Egypt's indebtedness – were almost grotesquely inadequate by comparison with the weight of the burden imposed by this indebtedness.

An unascertainable amount of the ordinary revenue and the proceeds of the foreign loans and other borrowings was spent on bribes at Constantinople and elsewhere and on Ismail's African campaigns. The floating debt of some £18,000,000 consisted largely of unsecured treasury bills and partly of unpaid accounts from tradesmen for supplies and for services rendered and salaries owing to government officials

It is easy to demonstrate, and to castigate, the greed, and indeed the fraudulence in some cases, of Ismail's European creditors. But it is impossible (although it has been tried) to acquit Ismail of the grossest financial maladministration. Taxation nearly doubled, a burden of indebtedness carrying an annual charge greater than the entire revenue at the beginning of his reign, an empty Treasury, unpaid officials and a horde of clamorous creditors, with nothing to show for it but a 15 per cent share in the profits of the Canal Company – later estimated at a capital value of £3,000,000, 8,400 miles of canals, 900 miles of railway, 5,200 miles of telegraph, 15 lighthouses, 64 sugar-mills, 430 bridges, a modern harbour at Alexandria, a white elephant of a dockyard at Suez, and a piped water supply at Alexandria for the principal benefit of its European inhabitants – all built by European contractors at exorbitant prices and largely by means of forced labour.

Why did Ismail do it? He understood administration and, after a fashion, finance. He had managed his own estates competently before coming to the throne. He started his reign with the genuine intention of checking and controlling the foreign influences which his predecessor had encouraged. His dealings over the Suez Canal, his speculative business combinations with local European financiers and entrepreneurs, were embarked upon with the object of asserting his own control over Egypt's economic expansion and of putting an end to Said's laxity and *laissez faire*. But the Europeans whom he sought to make the agents of his will were too clever for him. He hoped, by appealing to their cupidity, to make them do his will. Instead, they exploited his ambitions, his vanity, and his necessities, to make him do theirs. He thought to make them his dupes; they made him their dupe. 'It was they who managed to ensure that almost every one of Ismail's major initiatives contributed to their own enrichment.'[5] Although by no means a fool, Ismail was not nearly so clever, not nearly so sophisticated, as he thought he was. He was ambitious for absolute power in his own country, for independence of his suzerain, for the creation of an African Empire, for the respect of the European Powers. In his pursuit of these things he lost his throne, and such power, independence, dominions and respect as he had been able temporarily and precariously to achieve with the aid of merciless taxation and borrowed money. Perhaps part of the explanation is provided by Ali Pasha, at various times during Ismail's reign Grand Vizier and Foreign Minister of the Ottoman Empire, who knew Ismail well, opposed him consistently and, almost alone of contemporary Turkish ministers, never accepted his bribes: 'Ismail Pasha is the victim of whoever knows how to exploit his vanity, his pretensions to magnificence and, above all, his fears; for he is afraid of everything; he is afraid of European opinion and has tried to bribe it; he is afraid of his hareem and tries to purchase the good opinion of his wives, his slaves and his eunuchs by means of costly presents . . . Convinced that everyone is venal, he is surrounded by a horde of people whose greed confirms him in his view. He tries to satisfy everyone with money and that is the reason for his excessive taxation and for his ruinous loans.'[6]

There was something, but not much, on the credit side. Apart from the railways, canals and other public works which have been enumerated, the cultivable area of Egypt increased from 4,052,000 to 5,425,000 acres during the course of his reign. The value of exports rose from £4,454,000 a year to £13,810,000 (mostly for the benefit of European creditors). The increase in the cultivated area was due partly to the new irrigation canals dug during Ismail's reign, partly to the increased demand for cotton which arose as a result of the American Civil War. The increase in exports was due almost entirely to increased cotton exports arising from this increased demand. Although the boom in cotton prices ended with the end of the war, the increased demand persisted and, at the end of Ismail's reign, the annual value of cotton exports was about £9 million compared with about £2 million at the beginning. Henceforward cotton was to be the dominant item in Egypt's economy, eventually enabling its debts to be paid and its future development to be financed. Ismail's contribution to this was to provide the public works in the way of railways and harbour works which enabled the cotton to be moved, and to encourage the capital investment which enabled its cultivation, ginning, packing, shipping etc. to be financed. Indirectly, his oppressive taxation may have contributed by forcing the cultivator to concentrate his efforts on raising a burdensome but lucrative crop. This concentration on cotton did not, however, diminish the production of other agricultural products. The annual average exports of wheat, beans, barley, maize, rice and sugar at the end of Ismail's reign as compared with the beginning rose from about £1 million to about £2.6 million a year.[7]

The increased cultivated acreage and the increased agricu-tural production provide some long-term justification fo Ismail's development policies, since they provided the basis for Egypt's subsequent financial and economic rehabilitation. They also, combined with a population increase of something like 30 per cent during his reign, seem to contradict the stories which were sometimes circulated of rural depopulation caused by excessive taxation, conscription, forced labour, etc. On the other hand, it seems likely that much of the increased cultivable area and agricultural production was attributable to the royal and other large estates, whose owners had the means adequately to exploit them, rather than to the peasant cultivators. This likelihood is borne out by the fact that the proportion of large to small holdings steadily increased during Ismail's reign. It has been estimated[8] that the area of small holdings decreased from 3,750,000 *feddans* to 3,425,000 *feddans* while the area of large estates increased from 636,000 *feddans* to 1,300,000 *feddans*. In any case, the increased agricultural production was, in the short term, of no benefit to, and merely involved increased labour for, the majority of Egypt's rural population. Annual imports to a value of about £4.5 million at the end of Ismail's reign consisted of manufactured goods consumed almost entirely by a small, and largely urban and European section of the population. Apart from these the increased agricultural exports merely provided foreign exchange for the benefit of European creditors.

There was some genuine and beneficent progress in educa-tion, for which nothing had been done by Ismail's two imme-diate predecessors. With the assistance of European experts – including Dor Bey, a Swiss, and Rogers Bey, an Englishman – a system of primary, secondary and higher education was drawn up and a start made in implementing it. For the first time secular, as well as Quranic, education was given in the primary schools. Educational missions to Europe were revived. A start was made in female education. By the end of Ismail's reign some £150,000 a year was being devoted to education from

State funds at a time when State education had barely started in England. The Awqaf (Moslem religious endowments) and European missions were encouraged in their educational efforts, the latter mainly by grants of land. The various higher educational establishments set up by Mohamed Ali – medical, veterinary, law, agriculture and military and naval schools – were reactivated. In education, as in public works, Ismail's administration did something to provide Egypt with the infrastructure necessary for a modern State.

The following chapters will describe the course of Ismail's financial and commercial speculations, his African adventures, and his expensive negotiations for independence of Constantinople. They will describe how, in his pursuit of these things, he was led ever more deeply into debt and ever more deeply into the clutches of European bankers, and, eventually, into those of European governments. They will describe how Ismail's improvidence, and the rapacity of his creditors, hastened and completed the process of European colonisation which Bonaparte's invasion had begun.

Notes

1. Lucie Duff Gordon, *Letters from Egypt*, pp 208–9
2. Lucie Duff Gordon, *Last Letters from Egypt*, pp 108–9
3. *The Times*
4. These, and the following, estimates, are taken from various sources, including: The Cave Report Parliamentary Papers Commons, 1876, LXXXIII, 99; Crouchley, *The Economic Development of Modern Egypt*; Douin, *Regne du Khedive Ismail*; Owen, *Cotton and the Egyptian Economy*; Crabites, *Ismail, the Maligned Khedive*; Hamza, *The Public Debt of Egypt*; Mulhall, article on 'Egyptian Finance' in *Contemporary Review*, London, October 1882; Marlowe, *The Making of the Suez Canal*
5. Owen, *op cit*, p 159
6. Douin, *op cit*, Vol II, p 362
7. Owen, *op cit*, p 171
8. *ibid*, p 148

6

Ismail the Speculator

ISMAIL succeeded to the throne at the age of thirty-two on the death of his uncle Said in January 1963. He was the eldest surviving son of Ibrahim and the oldest living male in the direct line from Mohamed Ali. While heir apparent, he had won golden opinions from the foreign consuls. He had avoided intrigues and spent his time successfully and economically in cultivating his estates. The British Consul-General described him as 'the only one of his family who appears to have anything like order in his private affairs, and is not a spendthrift'.[1] His conduct when acting as Regent during Said's absences abroad had 'been marked with great prudence, activity and concilia-tion'.[2] This favourable impression was confirmed by an address which he delivered at a reception given soon after his accession to high officials and foreign consuls. 'I am determined to devote all the perseverance and energy of which I am capable to the prosperity of the country which I have been called upon to govern. The basis of all good administration is financial regularity and economy. I will do everything in my power to achieve this, and, as earnest of this, I am going to separate my personal finances from those of the State and fix for myself a Civil List which I shall strictly adhere to. This will enable me to devote all the resources of the country to the development of agriculture. At the same time I am determined to abolish the corvée system which is the principal barrier to this development.'[3]

The British Government appears to have been most favour-ably impressed. When Colquhoun informed them of attempts made by Beauval, the French Consul-General, to bully Ismail with threats of lowering the consular flag and landing marines as the result of an alleged assault on a French sailor by some Egyptian soldiers, he was told that 'HMG desire that you should act with energy in upholding Ismail Pasha and that specifically you should support him in resisting unjust demands, holding out to him the moral and friendly assistance of England in representing these injustices to the French and other Governments.'[4]

Ismail, although a good man of business, was, above all, a speculator. And, unfortunately for him and for Egypt, his accession coincided with what appeared to be a remarkably good opportunity for speculation. The American Civil War was on, the Southern cotton ports were blockaded and there was a consequent unprecedented demand for Egyptian cotton in European markets. During Said's reign the average annual export of cotton from Egypt to England had been in the region of 500,000 cwts, fetching an average price at Liverpool of about seven pence a pound. In 1862–63 1,200,000 cwts were exported to England, fetching an average price of twenty-two pence a pound. In 1863–64 1,750,000 cwts were exported at an average price of twenty-nine pence a pound. In 1864–65 the quantity exported to England increased to over 2,000,000 cwts, but the average price dropped to twenty pence a pound.[5] There was therefore plenty of money about in Egypt, plenty of credit available, and plenty of revenue to be collected. It was no time, in Ismail's view, for a prudent policy of retrenchment. He was determined to make use of the buoyant circumstances, and of the presence of the European bankers and speculators who proliferated in Egypt, to pursue an ambitious policy of expansion and development, both as regards his own estates and his Viceregal dominions.

Broadly, Ismail's idea was to encourage a selected group of European bankers to join with monied Egyptians, including himself, in the formation of development companies, to which something like monopoly concessions would be granted. In return for these concessions, and for commissions on orders placed in Europe by these companies, which would be given to the various European directors in their private capacities, Ismail would be able to borrow money on open account from the banks and merchant houses controlled by these directors, and repay the money in due course from the profits which he would derive as a shareholder in respect of his private borrowings, and from the increased revenue derived from development in respect of Treasury borrowings. (In spite of the promise given at the beginning of his reign, he never established a proper distinction between his personal finances and those of the State and much of his personal expenditure, over and above a nominal Civil List, came from State funds.) At the same time, the State interest, and his own personal shareholding, would, he hoped, ensure his being able to exercise control of the activities of these companies. Also, by this method of obtaining credit on open account he hoped to avoid both the rigidity of fixed date Treasury bills and the necessity of the Porte's consent and the probable hypothecation of revenues and foreign interference in general which would be involved in a foreign loan.

Ismail's principal henchman and adviser in these plans was Nubar Bey, a nephew of Boghos Yusef, who had for many years been Mohamed Ali's Minister of Foreign Affairs and Commerce. Nubar had served a long apprenticeship in the Egyptian service. He had been an interpreter under Mohamed Ali and Chief Interpreter under Abbas. He had for a time been Director of the Transit Administration under Said, and had later been Said's secretary, employed by him on a number of confidential missions. Under Ismail he was made a Pasha and became, at various times, Minister of Public Works, Minister of Foreign Affairs and Commerce, and Minister of Justice. From time to time he fell out of favour, and once he had to go into exile. But for most of Ismail's reign he exercised great influence.

The two most notorious of Ismail's development companies – the Egyptian Trading and Commercial Company and the Societé Agricole et Industrielle d'Egypte – were formed during the first few months of his reign. Henry Oppenheim and Edouard Dervieu, the two leading Alexandria bankers, were on the board of directors of both companies. By this time, the firm of Oppenheim, Chabert, who had been the contractors for Said's second foreign loan, had gone into liquidation and been succeeded by the firm of Oppenheim, Neveu et Cie, consisting of Hermann Oppenheim and his nephew Henry. Henry was established in Alexandria and managed the Egyptian end of the business, while Hermann settled in Paris and acquired French nationality, thus gaining for himself French diplomatic support in addition to the Prussian and British support which he already enjoyed. Ismail wanted to cultivate the Oppenheims because of their access to the European money markets. Edouard Dervieu was head of a French private bank in Alexandria, Dervieu & Cie, which had been founded a few years previously. He was a great favourite with Ismail, who persuaded him to increase his bank's capital from three to ten million francs, with a view to enabling it to increase its lending powers, which he wished to use.

The Egyptian Trading and Commercial Company – usually known as the 'Trading' – was an English-registered company, and most of the original capital was raised in London with the assistance of Henry Oppenheim. It was to have been called the Sudan Company, and had as its original object the development of the latent resources of the Sudan and Upper Egypt. In the event, no attempt at such development was ever made, and the Company confined its activities almost entirely to advancing money to cultivators in Lower Egypt on the security of their cotton crops. This was encouraged and assisted by the Egyptian Government which, in effect, instructed their *Mudirs* (Provincial Governors) to act as the 'Trading's' agents.[6] Fortified with this patronage, with cotton prices rising, and with more and more cotton being planted, they did a brisk trade at first. Later, in 1865, when the cotton boom was beginning to break, the Trading found itself in difficulties as a result of having over-extended its credit facilities, and the Egyptian Government took over its debts against an issue of 7 per cent Treasury bonds.[7] But, for the time being, it served Ismail's purpose in that he was able to use Oppenheim, Dervieu, and the other European directors as a source of credit in return for the privileges extended to them.

The Societé Agricole had an even more discreditable history. It was originally founded by an Austrian engineer named Lucovitch with the object of importing mechanical pumps and hiring them under contract to cultivators for irrigation purposes, and particularly for the irrigation of cotton, which requires summer water when the Nile is low. Lucovitch required capital and turned to Oppenheim, Dervieu, Ruyssenaers (the Dutch Consul-General, who had a finger of most of Egypt's dubious financial pies at this time) and others for it. These men, apparently with Ismail's connivance, and in the same way as had been done with the Trading, changed the original purpose of the Agricole and converted it into an organisation for speculating in urban real estate. One of the reasons for this was that Dervieu and his associates had plans of their own for importing irrigation engines on commission and did not want competition from the Agricole. Another reason was that they found it convenient to 'milk' the Agricole by using their authority as directors to buy from themselves in their private capacities, at a substantial profit to themselves, contracts which they had obtained for urban building as a result of their connections with the Viceroy. Lucovitch, who seems to have been an honest man, was bought out, and the Agricole, which relied for its profits almost entirely on the proceeds of contracts with the Egyptian Ministry of Public Works which it had bought at inflated prices from its own directors, the original grantees, soon found itself in difficulties. These became acute in 1866 when Nubar, who was closely associated with Dervieu and his friends, was transferred from the Ministry of Public Works to that of Foreign Affairs. Eventually, in 1869, as a result of diplomatic pressure from France and Great Britain, the Egyptian Government took over the whole of the Agricole's shares at a discount of between 20 per cent and 30 per cent.[8] As in the case of the Trading, the Egyptian Government – which meant the Egyptian cultivators – had to pay for Ismail's folly and for the dishonesty of the directors. But, as in the case of the Trading, Ismail's immediate purpose was achieved in that he was able to use Oppenheim, Dervieu and their associates as sources of credit in return for favours received.

A third attempt by Ismail at company promotion was less successful from his immediate point of view in that he was unable to attract much European capital. At the beginning of his reign he revived the defunct Medjidieh Steamship Company, the assets of which had been bought up by Said, and gave a thirty-year concession to a new company, to be named the Egyptian Steam Navigation Company, for steam navigation under the Egyptian flag in the Mediterranean and Red Sea, and on the Nile. He sold to the company, on favourable terms, the old Medjidieh ships which were laid up, and guaranteed 6 per cent interest on the company's shares. In spite of this, the shares were not fully subscribed. The history of the company, in the incapacity and dishonesty of its management, was similar to that of the Trading and the Agricole. In 1866 it was reconstituted and renamed the Azizieh Steamship Company. In 1870 the Egyptian Government agreed to pay its debts and to buy its shares over a period of seven years, paying 7 per cent interest in the meantime, at a total cost of some £2,150,000.[9] It was then operated under the name of the Khedivial Mail Line.

Since there was only a small foreign shareholding, this transaction was accomplished without the accompaniment of diplomatic pressure, but with results at least as favourable to its
shareholders as in the cases of the Trading and the Agricole.
In all three cases, dishonesty was rewarded, and incapacity
indemnified, at the expense of the Egyptian taxpayer, who
derived no benefit whatever from the operations of the companies concerned.

But Ismail's most important, and probably his most disastrous, speculation was in connection with the Suez Canal
Company. He was anxious to get the Canal into his own hands
and out of those of Lesseps. As a first step, he agreed with
Lesseps, at the beginning of his reign, to take up the whole of
the unsubscribed shares (which Said had refused to do)
amounting, together with the 64,000 shares Said had taken up,
to 177,642 Ordinary shares out of the total issue of 400,000.
Ismail, or rather the Egyptian Treasury, thus became easily
the largest single shareholder. The next step was to remove
what, owing to the British attitude, were the two insuperable
obstacles to the grant of the Sultan's Firman – the use of forced
labour and the grant of land to the Company over and above
that required for the Canal's construction and maintenance.
There followed a long and complicated wrangle between
Ismail (represented by Nubar) and the Canal Company in
which Ismail tried to wrest control of the Company from
Lesseps and have the terms of the concession amended so as to
remove Turkish and British objections. But Lesseps succeeded
in avoiding the traps set for him and, at the beginning of 1864,
both sides agreed that Napoleon III should act as arbitrator
between the Egyptian Government and the Company in order
to decide what compensation, if any, should be paid by the
government to the Company as indemnity for such amendments
to the concession in respect of forced labour and land grants as
would enable to Sultan to grant his Firman. Ismail agreed to
this arbitration in the mistaken belief that his friends in France,
chief among whom was the Duc de Morny, Napoleon III's
illegitimate half-brother, Président du Corps Legislatif, and a
great power in the land, would be able to use the arbitration
to discredit Lesseps and to get the objectionable features in the
concession cancelled at no great cost to the Egyptian Government. But Lesseps remained well in control of the situation and

the result of the arbitration was entirely favourable to the Company. The Emperor's award provided that the labour contract should be cancelled, that 60,000 hectares out of about 80,000 hectares of land granted to the company under the concession should be returned to the Egyptian Government, and that the Egyptian Government should pay an indemnity of 84 million francs to the Company as compensation for these lost privileges. It so happened that 84 million francs represented the approximate par value of the Egyptian Government's Ordinary shareholding, and it is probable that Lesseps hoped Ismail would be forced to hand over his shares to the company in payment of the compensation awarded.

There followed some eighteen months of negotiation on minor points in Constantinople and in Paris, at the end of which two Conventions were concluded between the Egyptian Government and the Company, amending the concessions in accordance with the terms of the arbitration award and arranging for the payment of the compensation awarded and of the balance still owing on the shares. Immediately after the signature of these Conventions, in March 1866, the Sultan issued his Firman. The long diplomatic battle was over and Lesseps had won an almost total victory after more than ten years of incessant intrigue, propaganda and financial chicanery. Although the company had, *pro forma*, fought against British and Turkish insistence on the retrocession of lands and the abolition of forced labour, the compensation awarded against the withdrawal of these privileges was much more valuable than the privileges themselves. The Company had no ready money with which to develop the surplus lands. As for the forced labour, once excavation had got down to water level, hand labour was impracticable anyway and it was necessary to use expensive dredging and excavating machinery. The compensation money was very welcome, and indeed necessary, as a means of purchasing this.

The issue of the Sultan's Firman removed all diplomatic difficulties from Lesseps' path. But the financial difficulties remained and dogged him until the completion of the Canal in 1869, and for many years after that. The financial operation remained very much on a hand-to-mouth basis and, even when the Canal was nearing completion, bankruptcy was never far off. It was staved off principally by means of financial subsidies from the Egyptian Government. Ismail, accepting defeat in his battle with Lesseps for the control of the Company, and impressed by the influence Lesseps was apparently able to command with the French Government, made a tacit bargain with him by which he gave Lesseps most of what he wanted in the matter of the Canal in return for Lesseps' supposed influence with the French Government in the perennial negotiations and intrigues in which Ismail was involved in Constantinople. This complaisance involved a good deal of expenditure by the Egyptian Government, and contributed substantially to Ismail's increasing financial difficulties.

Ismail also speculated with his own estates. At first, these speculations were successful. He took full advantage of the cotton boom, and used his position as ruler to secure priority in irrigation water, rail transport facilities, shipping and so on for his own cotton. In 1863–64, after a cattle murrain had killed off many of the country's cattle, which were used for turning irrigation water-wheels and for ploughing, he imported for his own account a large number of steam-driven pumps and ploughs, some for use on his own estates, others for re-sale. Later, after the cotton boom had subsided, his efforts were less successful. Having purchased his brother Mustafa Fazil's estates in Middle Egypt with borrowed money, he tried to re-coup himself for his decreased profits on cotton by the development of sugar cultivation on these estates. Sugar, like cotton, requires summer water, and Ismail had a new 190-mile irrigation canal – the Ibrahimieh – dug, with State funds and forced labour, from Asyut to Biba to provide summer water for the Middle Egypt estates acquired from his brother and others. He had the railway extended from Cairo to Asyut mainly in order to provide rapid transport for his sugar. He had nineteen sugar-crushing factories built, mainly out of the proceeds of his various *Daira* loans. Most of these factories were badly located, badly constructed, and inordinately expensive. This, together with the extortionate terms on which the money to finance them had been procured, nullified any profits which Ismail might have been able to make from the greatly increased sugar production. And the increased forced labour and the expense to the State involved in the railway and canal construction added to the burdens which Ismail was already imposing on the Egyptian peasantry But the orders for machinery and plant were very profitable to a number of European contractors.

Notes

1. Colquhoun-Russell, 5.3.61, FO 78/1590
2. *ibid*
3. Sabry, *op cit,* p 106
4. Russell-Colquhoun, 19.3.63, FO 78/1753
5. Landes, *Bankers and Pashas,* p 240
6. Colquhoun-Russell, 4.8.63, FO 78/1755
7. Landes, *op cit*, p 240
8. Fo· a good account of the Agricole's career see Douin, *op cit*, Vol I, pp 241–47
9. *ibid*, pp 250–57

Ismail's African Empire

EGYPT's empire-building in Africa started with the invasion of the Sudan by Mohamed Ali in 1820. The object of this invasion was to tap for the benefit of Egypt the supposed wealth of the Sudan – manpower for the Egyptian army and for domestic slavery, gold, cattle, ivory, gum and various agricultural products. As a result of the invasion, Egyptian rule was established over most of the northern Sudan. The town of Khartum, at the junction of the Blue and White Niles, was founded as an administrative capital. Under the terms of the 1841 settlement Mohamed Ali was invested with the 'governments of Nubia, Darfur, Kordofan and Sennaar' for life by the Ottoman Sultan, although these territories had never been regarded as part of the Ottoman Empire, and although Darfur was an independent Sultanate, which was not conquered by the Egyptian forces until some twenty-five years later. Subsequently, in 1846, Mohamed Ali obtained from the Sultan a lease of the two Red Sea ports of Suakin and Massawa which were part of the Ottoman Pashalik of the Hijaz. But, in 1849, on Abbas' accession, this lease was not renewed and the two ports reverted to direct Ottoman rule.

Economically, the conquest of the Sudan did not bring to Mohamed Ali the results for which he had hoped. The gold deposits were disappointing. There was little agricultural development, owing partly to the nature of the soil and climate, partly to the temperament of the Sudanese, who were less docile and less industrious than the Egyptian *fellahin*. The experiment of recruiting Sudanese into the Egyptian army was not entirely successful. As a result of the strict collection of taxes the Sudan generally paid its way, but it was not a source of profit.

Militarily, the Egyptian administration in Mohamed Ali's time did not succeed in extending its rule much beyond the

Ismail Pasha

François Champollion

mainly Arab districts of the northern and central Sudan which had been occupied and garrisoned during the initial campaign of conquest. To the west, the Sultanate of Darfur remained independent. To the east, advances into the districts of Taka (Kassala) and Fung involved the Egyptians in continual skirmishing with the Abyssinians along the seven hundred miles of foothills extending from the Red Sea to the Sobat River, which formed the undefined and uncharted borderline between Abyssinia and the Sudan. To the south, the difficulties of navigation through the reedy swamps of the Upper Nile, and the hostility of the riverine tribes, inhibited the extension of Egyptian authority towards the still unknown lands of Central Africa, that great reservoir of manpower and elephants which provided the raw material for the trade in slaves and ivory.

This trade was carried on by Arab, and by some foreign, merchants established in the northern Sudan, who built their trading stations, recruited private armies, maintained flotillas of boats, organised slave and elephant hunts, and generally acted as independent robber barons, in the regions of the Upper Nile and the Bahr-al-Ghazal. As these penetrated southwards, towards the Great Lakes, they found themselves in competition with Arab traders, similarly engaged, from Mombasa and Zanzibar on the east coast of Africa. Slaves and ivory always went together. The one was not profitable without the other and, as European and, particularly, British disapproval of the slave trade manifested itself, trading in ivory became a cover for trading in slaves. The Egyptian authorities connived at the slave trade, although they did not directly engage in it. There was an immense domestic market for black slaves both in the northern Sudan and in Egypt; there was also a large export market in Arabia and in most of the rest of the Ottoman Empire. It was a major source of revenue, since the taxable capacity of the Sudan was largely derived either from the trade in, or from the employment of, slaves. It was a principal source of profit for most of the magnates of the northern Sudan upon whose goodwill the Egyptian Government relied.

Under Abbas and Said, Egyptian interest in the Sudan declined. Said, after a visit to the Sudan in the winter of 1856–57, seems to have considered abandoning it altogether. But he did not do so and, in deference to the views of the European Powers who, in 1857, induced the Sultan (on paper)

E

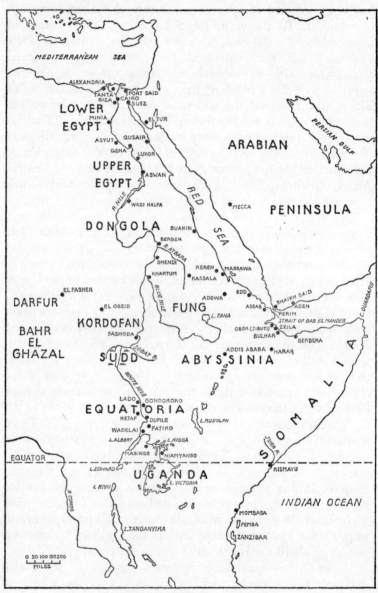

ISMAIL'S AFRICAN EMPIRE

to outlaw the slave trade in the Ottoman dominions, made some attempt to put down the slave trade in the Sudan by establishing a control post at Fashoda on the White Nile.

Ismail had large ideas about the extension and development of the Egyptian dominions in the Sudan and the conscious ambition of creating an Egyptian empire in Africa to replace that which Mohamed Ali had lost in Asia twenty years before. His grand strategy seems to have been somewhat as follows:

to secure a defensible and short frontier with Abyssinia by occupying all the foothills between the Sobat River and the Red Sea and, in the process, to establish Egyptian rule over the mainly Moslem tribes inhabiting these foothills so that they should serve as a buffer between the Sudan proper and the mainly Christian inhabitants of the central highlands of Abyssinia;

to include within Egyptian territory the source of the Blue Nile in Lake Tana;

to seal off Abyssinia from the sea and to secure control of its overseas trade by occupying the coast and immediate hinterland of the Red Sea between Massawa and the Straits of Bab-al-Mandeb and of the Gulf of Aden between the Straits of Bab-al-Mandeb and Cape Guardafui;

to extend effective Egyptian rule southwards up the White Nile towards the Great Lakes with a view to including the whole of the Nile basin in Egyptian territory;

to open up an alternative and shorter route to the Great Lakes by occupying the Somali coast and hinterland south of Cape Guardafui as far as the Juba River and to establish an Egyptian-controlled route between the Indian Ocean and the Great Lakes which would complete the encirclement of Abyssinia and avoid sole dependence on the long and precarious Nile route between Egypt and the Great Lakes;

to protect the long Nile route from the west by establishing Egyptian rule over Bahr-al-Ghazal and Darfur.

This programme of expansion, although the financial, military and administrative means at Ismail's disposal were at all times inadequate for its efficient execution and maintenance, did not remain wholly chimerical and was not motivated entirely by megalomania.

Abyssinia had always been a troublesome neighbour and, at the time of Ismail's accession, was particularly so under the rule of the Emperor Theodore, whose ambitions embraced the extension of Abyssinian rule to the whole of the Sudan east of the Nile. Abyssinia was to Egypt what the North-West Frontier was to India, and it was not unreasonable to try to pursue a similar policy of containment.

In the coastal areas, between Massawa and Cape Guardafui, there were other expansionist ambitions to be taken into account. The near prospect of the opening of the Suez Canal, and the development of European interests and colonies all round the Indian Ocean, meant that the Red Sea would soon become a great international highway. The French were concerned to obtain footholds there as ports of call and coaling stations for their own vessels and in order to offset the British hegemony conferred by their possession of Aden. The British, concerned to protect this hegemony, occupied the island of Perim, in the Straits of Bab-al-Mandeb, in 1857. Once European stations were established on this coast, overseas trade with Abyssinia would be diverted through them, and a European influence developed in Abyssinia which might well be used as a means of intrigue and pressure against Egypt.

Ismail's ambitions in the direction of the Great Lakes were even more readily comprehensible. Since it was clear that the exploration and opening-up of Central Africa then proceeding would result in the annexation of the areas around the Great Lakes by some Power or other, it was not unreasonable for Ismail to regard Egypt as having a prior claim to, and a prior need for, possession of the headwaters of the river on which the economy and indeed the existence of Egypt were dependent. In the international atmosphere of the time, one did not need to be unduly suspicious to believe that possession of these head-waters by a foreign Power would be used by that Power as a means of putting pressure upon Egypt. In this context, the attempt to open an alternative access to the Great Lakes by way of the east coast, and the buttressing of the Nile route to the Lakes by the occupation of Darfur are also readily com-prehensible.

Given Egypt's material weakness, this grand strategy could only be embarked upon with some prospect of success if British benevolence were secured. The British controlled the Red Sea and the Gulf of Aden and, by their virtual protectorate over the Sultanate of Zanzibar, also controlled the approaches to the

Great Lakes from the Indian Ocean. Since one of the principal British preoccupations in this area was the suppression of the slave trade, Ismail determined to purchase British benevolence by co-operation with them in the work of suppression.

In spite of the fact that Ismail made genuine and, for Egypt, very costly, efforts in the direction of suppressing the slave trade in Egypt itself, in the Sudan, and in the Red Sea, this British benevolence was only manifested to a very limited extent. British reservations were due to a justified belief that Egypt's resources were inadequate to support Ismail's programme of Empire-building; to a reluctance, inspired by the Missionary Societies, to encourage Moslem colonisation and Islamic proselytism in the area of the Great Lakes, where Christian missionaries were already settled; to a reluctance to see Egypt encroaching on the territories of the Sultan of Zanzibar; and to a reluctance, inspired principally by the Government of India, to seal off Abyssinia from the possibility of British-Indian trading via the ports on the African coast of the Gulf of Aden (this reluctance was later overcome when it became desirable to recognise Egypt's authority over this coast as a means of preventing other Powers from establishing themselves there). There was also some doubt, inspired principally by the anti-slavery associations, about the sincerity or efficiency of Ismail's efforts to suppress the slave trade. There does not seem to be any substance in the suspicion, expressed by several writers (e.g. Sabry) that British reluctance to give whole-hearted support to Ismail was due to any British territorial designs on Central Africa. These designs only materialised after Great Britain had assumed responsibility for the defence and administration of Egypt, when they became anxious, for the same reasons as Ismail, to prevent any foreign Power from establishing itself around the headwaters of the Nile.

Ismail's African adventures can best be considered under the two heads of (I) Abyssinia and the Red Sea and Somali coasts; and (II) the Upper Nile.

(I) *Abyssinia and the Red Sea and Somali Coasts*

The large, ill-defined and mountainous area of Abyssinia had for long been of interest to European countries both from the missionary and from the commercial points of view. The existence of an ancient Christian civilisation in the heart of Africa, surrounded by Moslem and pagan tribes, aroused such chivalrous instincts as still remained in Christian Europe and provided a favourable base for missionary activity, both Roman Catholic and, from about the end of the eighteenth century, Protestant. The European consuls who were, intermittently, appointed to Abyssinia were principally concerned with looking after the missionaries and with investigating the prospects of, and trying to develop, trade.

Authority in Abyssinia was usually divided and disputed between some three or more powerful territorial chiefs. From time to time one of these would establish a temporary ascendancy over the others which enabled him to be regarded as King of Abyssinia. This periodical and temporary unity was usually accompanied by a phase of attempted expansion at the expense of Abyssinia's Moslem and pagan neighbours, and followed, when Abyssinia once more became fragmented, by a countermovement of retraction under the pressure of these neighbours. Thus the tide of endemic border warfare ebbed and flowed around Abyssinia's long and undefined frontiers.

In 1820 Henry Salt, the British Consul-General in Egypt, and previously Consul in Abyssinia, had warned Mohamed Ali against any attempt to invade Abyssinia in the course of his attempted conquest of the Sudan. Mohamed Ali took heed of this warning, but the Egyptian occupation of the Sudan led to an endemic state of tension between Egypt and Abyssinia along the disputed borderlands.

The lease of Massawa by Mohamed Ali in 1846 caused some perturbation both in London and Paris, since Massawa was the principal port of access to and egress from Abyssinia, and since its possession by Egypt seemed likely to be used both as a *point d'appui* for territorial encroachment into Abyssinia and as a means of impeding European trading and other communications. Probably as a result of this lease, although it expired and was not renewed in 1849, the British Government, in 1848, appointed a Consul in Abyssinia with the principal object of developing British trade. The Consul, Plowden, who was normally resident at Massawa, impressed on HMG the necessity for Abyssinia to obtain some access to the sea if trade with Europe was to be developed. Suzerainty over the whole of the coast from Suakin to Cape Guardafui was claimed by the Ottoman Sultan. Plowden contested this claim and tried to induce HMG to do so with Constantinople. In this he was supported by similar representations made by the French Consul to his Government. But neither the British nor the French Governments were prepared to question Ottoman suzerainty over the coastal area. The reason for this was probably a realisation that this suzerainty prevented a free-for-all competiton among the European Powers. In miniature, it was the same policy as that adopted by the Powers towards Ottoman possessions elsewhere. Plowden and the French Consul also intervened, more successfully, in favour of a Roman Catholic mission to the Christian inhabitants of Bogos, the country round Keren claimed by the Egyptians, which was raided by them from the Sudan in 1854. Their intervention resulted in an Egyptian withdrawal and the payment of an indemnity to the inhabitants.

Plowden was in favour of a powerful central authority in Abyssinia which would be able to provide better internal security and prosecute more effectively Abyssinia's claims for access to the sea. From about 1852 it became apparent that such an authority was in process of being created. Kassa, a soldier of fortune from southern Abyssinia, by a series of campaigns against his rival territorial chiefs, proceeded to make himself master of the whole of Abyssinia. In February 1855 he was crowned as King of Abyssinia, taking the title of Theodore.

Theodore proved to be a cruel and capricious tyrant. After trying, in vain, to secure British and French support for his territorial claims which included not only access to the sea, but possession of the whole of the Sudan east of the Nile, he arrested the British Consul Cameron, who had succeeded Plowden, and several British missionaries. He also arrested Rassam, an emissary sent to negotiate for Cameron's release. These acts brought HMG reluctantly to the decision that a British force must be sent into Abyssinia to secure the release of the captives and put an end to Theodore's rule.

By this time the nearest coastal approach to Abyssinia, by way of Massawa, was once more in Egyptian hands as a result of the 1866 Firman which had ceded to Egypt the two Red Sea *Qaimaqamat* of Massawa and Suakin. Egypt's position in the Sudan and on the Red Sea coast was always threatened by a strong and united Abyssinia, and Ismail was anxious to make common cause with England in the invasion of that country. He was also anxious to avoid the establishment of a permanent British presence on the Red Sea coast, and possibly in Abyssinia itself, which he feared might be the result of an all-British punitive expedition against Theodore. But HMG, while needing the use of the Egyptian base at Massawa, were adamant against any Egyptian alliance, partly because this would have united Christian sentiment in Abyssinia against an invasion, and partly because, while determined to depose Theodore, they had no intention of forwarding Egyptian territorial ambitions at the expense of Abyssinia.

To the accompaniment of delicate negotiations designed to secure Egyptian passive co-operation without incurring the liability of identification with a Moslem ally, a British-Indian force of about 14,000 combatant troops, under the command of Sir Robert Napier (afterwards Lord Napier of Magdala), landed at Massawa towards the end of 1867 and, at the end of January 1868, set out on the invasion of Abyssinia. The advent of the British force precipitated the manifestation of those centrifugal tendencies which were endemic in Abyssinian affairs and Theodore's adherents melted away as the British advanced. By the end of March, Napier's force, without having had to do any fighting, arrived at the fortress of Magdala, where Theodore had taken up a defensive position with his few remaining adherents and with his European captives, or hostages. After some confused negotiations designed to secure the release of the captives, the British attacked on 9 April. The Abyssinians were defeated, Theodore was killed, and the fortress of Magdala was captured. By the end of April, after having rescued the captives and destroyed the fortress, the British force was on its way back to the coast. Within a few more weeks it had sailed from Massawa and Abyssinia was left in a state of civil war. From this, the Ras (chief) of Tigre, in the north of Abyssinia, through whose territory Napier had marched on his way to and from Magdala, eventually emerged as master of all Abyssinia and was crowned as King in January 1872, taking the name of John. Although Napier had scrupulously avoided taking sides in the internecine struggles which were beginning to develop in anticipation of Theodore's fall, the future King John, anxious to secure British benevolence as an insurance against Egypt, had gone out of his way to cultivate friendly relations with Napier.

Egyptian expansion was pursued with energy in the Red Sea and Gulf of Aden from 1866 onwards, after the cession of Massawa and Suakin had given Egypt a footing in the area. An Egyptian Governorate covering the 'East Coast of Africa' from Suez to Cape Guardafui was created. An Egyptian naval squadron was sent to cruise in the Red Sea and the Gulf of Aden and, in 1870, the Egyptian Government officially made it clear that they regarded Massawa and Suakin and their dependencies as comprising the whole of the African coastline between Suez and Cape Guardafui.[1]

Several factors combined to cause HMG to take a favourable view of this claim. Themselves in possession of Aden (since 1838) and Perim (since 1857), their principal interests on this coast were to prevent the establishment of rival bases by other European Powers; to suppress the slave trade carried on with slaves exported from Abyssinia via the ports on this coast; and to facilitate trade between Aden and Abyssinia via Berbera. All these matters could probably be arranged without much expense or trouble with a weak and friendly Egypt in possession of the coast.

There had been numerous European attempts to establish themselves on this coast since the British occupation of Aden and since the development of the steamship and the possibility of a Suez Canal had enhanced the potential importance of the Red Sea route. In 1840 the French Societé Nantes-Bordelaise had acquired by purchase from a local chief a title to the port of Edd, between Massawa and the Straits of Bab-al-Mandeb. The ostensible object of this purchase, which was never exploited, was to develop trade between France and Abyssinia. At about the same time, the British Resident at Aden, alarmed by these French activities, made an agreement with the Sultan of Tajura, on the African coast of the Gulf of Aden, providing for the use of that port for trade with Abyssinia and for the lease of the Musha Islands in the Gulf of Tajura. A few years later, the British made a similar arrangement with the Ruler of Zeila, on the Gulf of Aden east of Tajura, which provided for the lease of the island of Aubat, off Zeila. Neither of these acquisitions was exploited. In 1862 the captain of a French warship, *Somme*, sent to the area to avenge the murder of M. Lambert, French

Consul at Aden, who had been killed by tribesmen on the African coast, signed a treaty with a local chief for the acquisition by France of Obok, on the Gulf of Tajura. In 1868–69 a French commercial company made a contract for the purchase of, and endeavoured to occupy Shaikh Said, on the south-west tip of the Arabian Peninsula, overlooking the Straits of Bab-al Mandeb and the British-occupied island of Perim. This trans-action was frustrated by the Porte which, moved by HMG, sent troops from the Yemen to occupy the district. In 1870 an Italian shipping company purchased from the local ruler a site on the Bay of Assab, on the African coast of the Red Sea, a little north of the Straits of Bab-al-Mandeb.

None of these purchases or leases were recognised either by the Porte or by the Egyptian Government which, after 1866, maintained that all the territories involved, except Shaikh Said, were under Ottoman suzerainty and Egyptian administration and could not be alienated by the action of local chiefs. From 1870 onwards the Egyptian Government took steps to make their administration effective by establishing garrisons and mediating between the tribes along the whole coastal area between Massawa and Cape Guardafui. The Egyptian occupa-tion of Berbera, in 1873, brought about a direct confrontation with the British in Aden.

Berbera was the principal port on the Somali coast and a great entrepot for trade with the Harrar district of eastern Abyssinia. It was almost opposite Aden, which depended for its supplies of meat on exports from Abyssinia via Berbera. The British Resident at Aden was accustomed to send a warship to Berbera during the time of the great annual fair to keep the peace between the tribes and to check any attempt to ship slaves. In 1854, after the murder by local tribesmen of a British naval Lieutenant who had been sent there on a mission in connection with the slave trade, Berbera was blockaded for several months. There was some question of appointing a British Resident there. This was not done, but thereafter the British in Aden kept a close interest in Berbera and its occupa-tion by Egypt could hardly fail to raise the whole question of the status of this part of the coast in the minds of the British Government. At about the same time HMG received informa-tion that the French Government regarded the Egyptian occupation as part of an Anglo-Egyptian plot to annex the whole of East Africa and were considering sending a military expedition to activate their concession at Obok.[2] Ismail proposed to Vivian, the acting British Consul-General in Egypt, that HMG should recognise Egyptian sovereignty, under Ottoman suzerainty, of the African coasts of the Red Sea and the Gulf of Aden, and thus deny the validity of all territorial concessions made to foreign Powers in the area by local chiefs.[3] Sir Henry Elliot, the British Ambassador in Constantinople, recommended that this proposal should be accepted as a means both of keeping foreign European influence out of the area and of providing for better control of the slave trade.[4] HMG disagreed on the grounds that recognition of Ottoman suzerainty might call in question the British title to Aden and that British renunciation of their titles to concessions would not automatically lead to a renunciation of similar French and Italian titles.[5] Ismail's proposal was therefore not accepted. The French expedition to Obok did not materialise and no attempt was made either by the British, French or Italians to activate the other concessions. HMG, although they had rejected Ismail's proposal for formal recognition, accepted the position *de facto* and made no attempt to interfere with it. In September 1874, about a year after the Egyptian occupation of Berbera, Colonel Stanton, the British Consul-General in Egypt, reported that 'the establishment on the Somali coast of a regular administration capable of suppressing the tribal quarrels which, up to the present, have prevented any development of trade in this area, would seem to offer better guarantees of friendship with Aden than those offered by existing commercial treaties with the shaikhs of Berbera, Zeila and Tajura.' There was likewise no British objection to the Egyptian occupation of Harrar, a district in the hinterland of Berbera and Zeila, which was successfully accomplished by the Egyptians with a small military expedition which left Zeila in September 1875.

From the time of the Egyptian occupation of Berbera onwards, there was close co-operation between the British and Egyptian navies in the area over the suppression of the slave trade. In January 1877 McKillop Pasha, a British naval officer in the Egyptian service, was sent by Ismail to make an inspection of all the east African ports, from Suez to Berbera inclusive, with a view to taking measures to suppress this trade. On 4 August 1877 a Slave Trade Convention was signed between the

British and Egyptian Governments. Article IV of this Convention, dealing particularly with the Red Sea and the Gulf of Aden, provided; 'In order to render more efficacious the suppression of the traffic in negro or Abyssinian slaves in the Red Sea, the Egyptian Government agrees that British warships may board, search and, if necessary, detain, with a view to handing over to the nearest or most convenient Egyptian authority, any Egyptian vessel found to be engaged in the traffic of negro or Abyssinian slaves, as well as any vessel which may reasonably be suspected of having been, or about to be, engaged in this traffic. This right may be exercised in the Red Sea, the Gulf of Aden, along the Arabian coast and the east coast of Africa and in the territorial waters of Egypt and its dependencies.'

At the beginning of 1878, at the instance of HMG, and on their nomination, Captain Malcolm RN was seconded to the Egyptian service and appointed Director-General of the Service for the Suppression of the Slave Trade in the Red Sea, with his HQ at Massawa. It soon became obvious that any really determined attempt to put down the slave trade on land would arouse powerful local animosities with which the Egyptian Government were not equipped to deal. This was pointed out by Gordon, who had recently been appointed Governor-General of the Sudan, and who criticised Malcolm for his heavy-handed zeal. Malcolm resigned in disgust a few weeks after his appointment, his principal contribution having been to estimate that the annual number of slaves shipped from Africa to Arabia via the Red Sea and the Gulf of Aden amounted to between 1,500 and 1,700, and not some 30,000 as had previously been estimated.[6]

On 7 September 1877, immediately after the signature of the Slave Trade Convention, the *de facto* British recognition of the Egyptian position on the Somali coast was converted into *de jure* recognition by means of a Convention in which HMG recognised Ismail's sovereignty under Ottoman suzerainty over the whole of the African coast of the Gulf of Aden as far east as Ras Hafun (Cape Guardafui) on the following conditions: that Bulhar and Berbera be regarded as free ports and that no dues be levied on the 10,000 cows and 60,000 sheep exported annually from Berbera to Aden; that no part of the territory be ceded to any foreign Power; and that HMG should have the right to maintain consuls in any of the ports or other parts of the territory. By this Convention the particular interests of Aden in Berbera were safeguarded at the expense of a *de jure* recognition of a *de facto* situation. The terms of the Convention were less satisfactory to Egypt, in that an important item of revenue was foregone in the interests of Aden. But, by that time, Ismail was prepared to go to great lengths in order to try to secure HMG's benevolence over his financial troubles.

Meanwhile, Egypt had run into serious difficulties and humiliations further north, in the hinterland of Massawa. In 1871 Munziger, a Swiss adventurer who had previously been French Consul at Massawa, entered Ismail's service and was appointed Governor of Massawa. Profiting by the weakness of Abyssinia, which was still engulfed in civil war, Munziger embarked on an aggressive frontier policy. He reoccupied Bogos in 1872 and made preparations for further advances. John, who had just been crowned King of Abyssinia, complained bitterly about Egyptian aggression and sent his *homme de confiance*, Kirkham, an English adventurer, to Europe to obtain the support of the Powers. None of the Powers were anxious to interfere in so complex and profitless a dispute and Kirkham returned to Abyssinia empty-handed.

Force of arms succeeded where diplomacy had failed. In September 1875, as a result of reports of Abyssinian troop movements in the direction of Massawa, the Egyptian Government sent a small force of about 3,000 troops to Massawa under the command of a Danish officer named Arendroop. At the same time Munziger, with an even smaller force, set out from Massawa to Tajura with a view to going from there to Shoa in southern Abyssinia to join forces with Ras Menelik who was in revolt against King John. Both expeditions came to grief. Munziger's force was ambushed and killed almost to a man, including Munziger himself, soon after they had left Tajura. Arendroop's force, advancing with what appears to be almost incredible foolhardiness through the mountains towards Adowa, where the King had his HQ, was also ambushed and almost annihilated.

As a result of these two disasters the Egyptian Government prepared an expeditionary force of 30,000 men, under the command of Ratib Pasha, and with an American General, Loring, as Chief of Staff, to proceed to Massawa and march into

Abyssinia in order 'first to re-establish Egyptian prestige and
then to obtain from the King of Abyssinia such guarantees as
may be sufficient to secure the future tranquillity of the frontier
districts'.[7] Ismail assured the British Agent that Ratib Pasha
had received 'the most positive instructions' not to advance
beyond Adowa. Later, he told him that although the expedition
might cost £1 million, 'it was necessary if Egypt was to retain
her African empire'.[8]

This more ambitious expedition was defeated at Gura, on
the road between Massawa and Adowa, by a large Abyssinian
army led by King John in person in a battle which lasted for the
three days of 6, 7 and 8 March 1876. Ratib was able to retire on
Massawa with the remainder of his army, most of which was
soon after evacuated back to Egypt. A garrison of 2,000 troops
was left to guard Massawa and the British Agent in Egypt was
informed that any idea of a further expedition to Abyssinia had
been abandoned.[9] Peace negotiations were entrusted to Gordon,
who had just been appointed Governor-General of the Sudan.
Nothing came of these negotiations, nor of subsequent negotiations conducted by Gordon in 1879. By that time civil war had
broken out between King John and Ras Menelik of Shoa who,
after King John's death in 1889, was eventually to become King
of Abyssinia. Meanwhile, the Egyptian positions at Massawa,
on the Somali coast, and in Harrar, remained *in statu quo*. But
there was no further question of Egyptian expansion.

II. *The Upper Nile*

At the beginning of Ismail's reign the southernmost limit of
effective Egyptian authority on the White Nile was at Kawa,
about 150 miles south of Khartum, and the river terminal of a
trade route running westwards into Kordofan. South of this
point, trade – which was mostly trade in slaves – with the
Upper Nile and the Bahr-al-Ghazal was carried on by Khartum
merchants, some of them Europeans, who used the river as a
principal means of communication between Khartoum and the
great slave and elephant hunting grounds of the south.

Under pressure from the European Powers, attempts were
made by Said and Ismail to put down the slave trade by policing
the river and by trying to control the Khartum slave merchants.

Foreign merchants were gradually eliminated from the trade and the Egyptian frontier was extended up the White Nile to as far as Gondokoro on about latitude 5 N. The new frontier post was linked with Khartum only by a tenuous line of communication through the reedy swamps of the Sudd and through densely-forested and fever-ridden country inhabited by mainly hostile tribes. This extension of the frontier, and the policing of the river, did not greatly diminish the activities of the slave traders, but it did remove their principal transport route away from the river westward to the overland caravan routes through Bahr-al-Ghazal and Darfur.

Between 1856 and 1863 the Great Lakes and the sources of the White Nile had been discovered by Speke, Grant and Baker, and the geography of this previously unknown area, although not mapped in detail, had become generally known. The discoveries of the explorers indicated that south and west of Lake Victoria there was relatively stable government, but that between Lake Victoria and Gondokoro there was a 'no man's land' of chaos, which inhibited economic development and legitimate trade, and encouraged bloodshed and the depredations of the slave traders. In 1864 the Royal Geographical Society, which had sponsored much of the exploration in the region of the Great Lakes, recommended to the British Government that Ismail should be encouraged to occupy this 'no man's land' in order to bring some effective administration to it.[10] Ismail was not unwilling and, in March 1869, invited Sir Samuel Baker, the English explorer who had discovered Lake Albert and travelled extensively throughout the region, to enter the Egyptian service and lead an expedition to annex to Egypt the country between Gondokoro and Lake Victoria, and to suppress the slave trade and encourage legitimate commerce there.

Baker established his headquarters at Gondokoro and, with a military expedition, advanced southward from there, opening the river up to navigation, pacifying the country, and setting up a chain of military posts, linked by sure means of communication, which was intended to stretch between Gondokoro and Lake Victoria.

Baker's expedition was not a success. He penetrated southward as far as Masindi, between Lake Albert and Lake Victoria, set up a number of posts between there and Gondokoro, and declared the annexation to Egypt of the country as far as the northern limits of the territory ruled by King M'tesa of Uganda, which extended a little north of Lake Victoria. But his expedition had no permanent result, except for the southward extension of the Egyptian frontier to Fatiko, about half-way between Gondokoro and Lake Victoria, where a permanent garrison was established.

Baker, by his heavy-handed methods and by his anxiety to achieve quick results, incurred the hostility of the local inhabitants, and his expedition had little effect on the slave trade, except to accelerate the process of driving it westward from the Nile to the overland caravan routes. He failed to set up any settled administration which might have facilitated the growth of economic and social alternatives to the slave trade. His experience underlined the extreme difficulties of trying to administer a province so far distant from and so tenuously linked with Cairo and Khartum.

Since 1865 Ismail had been making plans to speed up communication between Cairo and Khartum by building a railway southward across the desert from Wadi Halfa, by-passing the Nile cataracts. There were also alternative plans for a railway across the eastern desert linking Khartum and Suakin. Neither of these came to anything owing to financial difficulties and both were abandoned in 1875 after a start had been made on the Wadi Halfa line. An even more serious obstacle than the cataract and desert barriers between Cairo and Khartum was the reedy and all-but-impassable Sudd between Khartum and Gondokoro. It was apparent that the easiest method of communication between Egypt and Gondokoro and points south was via the coast of East Africa. During the course of Baker's expedition, when he was believed to be in difficulties, plans were made in Cairo for a relief expedition to be sent via the East African coast under Colonel Purdy, one of the American officers in Ismail's service. Baker's safe return to Gondokoro at the beginning of 1873 obviated the necessity for this, but the possibility of using this route was kept in mind.

Baker, who was on a four-year contract with the Egyptian Government, expiring in April 1873, returned to Cairo in July of that year. He made exaggerated claims for the success of his expedition, but Ismail told Vivian, the acting British Consul-General, that 'his operations had given rise to a general feeling of hostility and dislike' towards the Egyptian Government and that, even between Khartum and Gondokoro, the route was unsafe. Tribes there, previously friendly, were giving trouble. He did not believe Baker's claim that orderly government had been set up south of Gondokoro or that the slave trade had been suppressed.[11] In the course of the same conversation, Ismail assured Vivian of his sincerity in wishing to abolish the slave trade 'which demoralised and corrupted all concerned in it', offered his mediation with the Sultan of Zanzibar in efforts being made by HMG to induce him to co-operate in anti-slavery measures on the East African coast, and complained of what he referred to as the British Government's pro-Abyssinian attitude.

A few days later, at the end of August 1873, Ismail informed Vivian that he wanted to invite Colonel Charles Gordon to succeed Baker as Governor of the region south of Gondokoro, which had been named the Province of Equatoria. He expressed the hope that the British Government would see in this proposed appointment proof of his determination to organise the new province thoroughly and suppress the slave trade.[12] Gordon was already something of a public figure in England as a result of his Chinese exploits ten years previously. HMG replied, rather unenthusiastically, that there was no objection to Gordon's taking service with the Egyptian Government, if he were willing to do so, that the War Office would release him for the purpose, but that the terms of his appointment should be negotiated direct between Gordon and the Egyptian Government and that HMG could take no responsibility in the matter.[13] Gordon was duly appointed and departed for the Sudan in February 1874. He was entrusted by Ismail with powers equal to those given to Baker, but was 'instructed to avoid as far as possible any hostile demonstration against the tribes, as it is [Ismail's] wish to conciliate the people, to open a legal trade with them, and to put an end to the constant quarrels between the traders. Colonel Gordon is further instructed to act with the utmost rigour against all slave dealers and to do all in his power to suppress the slave trade.'[14] On his arrival at Gondokoro, Gordon transferred his headquarters from there to Lado, on the opposite bank of the river, and 'infused new life into the flagging administration. He did what he could to soften the effect of Baker's harshness . . . Stage by stage . . . he extended the Egyptian sway towards the Great Lakes. He set up a chain of military posts between Rejaf and Dufile where clear water could carry his boats to Lake Albert. He then brought Unyoro, and a part of Uganda between Lakes Albert and Ibrahim (Kioga) within the sphere of Egyptian influence, planting his farthest garrison at Niamyango on the Somerset Nile sixty miles from Lake Victoria.'[15]

Gordon soon became convinced that the extension of Egyptian administration southward necessitated the opening of regular communication with the east coast. As a result of a request sent by him in January 1875 the Egyptian Government prepared an expedition under the command of McKillop Pasha, a British naval officer in the Egyptian service. He was instructed to land at the mouth of the Juba River, north of Mombasa, and set up a base there to enable Gordon to establish a line of communication with him after reaching Lake Victoria. McKillop's expedition landed at Kismayu, at the mouth of the Juba River, in October 1875. HMG, advised of this landing by Kirk, British Consul at Zanzibar, immediately protested to the Egyptian Government against an invasion of territory belonging to the Sultanate of Zanzibar which was, to all intents and purposes although not formally, a British protectorate. The McKillop expedition was ordered by the Egyptian Government to withdraw, which it did at the beginning of 1876, after Ismail had protested to Stanton, the British Consul-General, telling him that the million or so pounds he had spent, with British encouragement, in the colonisation of Equatoria would be entirely wasted if he were not allowed to establish regular communication between his new province and the east coast of Africa.[16]

Partly as a result of the fiasco of the McKillop expedition, Gordon abandoned his plans for an extension of the Egyptian frontier to Lake Victoria. In September 1876 he set up a post as far south as Niamyongo, at the south end of Lake Kioga and only about sixty miles from the northern shore of Lake Victoria. Any further advance would have brought him into conflict with M'tesa, the King of Uganda, with whom he was already in contact and who seemed likely to resist any Egyptian attempt to annex part of his kingdom. Gordon therefore decided to fix the southern frontier of Equatoria Province at Niamyongo.

Having made this decision, Gordon departed for England on

leave. He had not, any more than Baker, succeeded in putting down the slave trade, but he had done rather more than Baker in setting-up a settled administration in Equatoria and in reconciling the inhabitants to Egyptian rule. Ismail was anxious to retain his services and, in order to do so, appointed him in February 1877 as Governor-General of the entire Sudan, after Gordon had told him that nothing less than the authority conferred by this post would enable him to take effective measures for dealing with the slave trade.

By this time, the area under Egyptian administration in the Sudan had been enlarged by the addition of Bahr-al-Ghazal and Darfur. Over the years, Zubair Rahmat, one of the principal Khartum slave traders, and a man of great power and prestige, had made himself virtual ruler of the Bahr-al-Ghazal area. In 1870 the Egyptian Government determined to take Bahr-al-Ghazal under their direct administration. A military expedition commanded by Shaikh Mohamed al-Hilali, another slave trader, set off from Khartum under orders to annex Bahr-al-Ghazal. After some inconclusive negotiations with Zubair, fighting broke out, in the course of which Hilali's force was defeated by Zubair and Hilali killed. The Egyptian Government, recognising the *fait accompli*, made Bahr-al-Ghazal an Egyptian province and appointed Zubair as Governor. Three years later, in 1873, the Sultanate of Darfur, which had been at continual odds with Egypt since the Egyptian occupation of Kordofan fifty years before, and through whose territory passed the caravan routes between Bahr-al-Ghazal and Khartum, and Bahr-al-Ghazal and Egypt, was invaded simultaneously by Zubair from the south and by Ismail Ayub, the Governor-General of the Sudan, from the east. Mainly as a result of Zubair's efforts, the Sultan of Darfur was defeated and killed and his capital, al-Fasher, occupied in November 1874. Darfur was then made into an Egyptian province. Zubair, who considered that he should have been given the Governorship of Darfur as well as that of Bahr-al-Ghazal, proceeded to Cairo to negotiate with Ismail, leaving his son Sulaiman in charge of Bahr-al-Ghazal.

As has been observed, the establishment of effective Egyptian authority on the banks of the Upper Nile had had the effect of driving the slave traders westward on to the caravan routes through Bahr-al-Ghazal and Darfur. The Egyptian annexation of these districts therefore involved the assumption by Egypt of responsibility for suppressing this trade. This responsibility was emphasised by the conclusion of the Slave Trade Convention between England and Egypt in August 1877. This Convention, apart from the powers of search and arrest conferred on the British Navy in the Red Sea, also committed Egypt to taking all possible steps to suppress the trade throughout Egyptian dominions.

Such was the position of affairs when Gordon arrived in Khartum to take up his appointment in May 1877. In his letter of appointment Gordon had been given jurisdiction over the whole of the territory of the Egyptian Sudan, including the Red Sea Provinces, and had been assigned the principal tasks of suppressing the slave trade as completely as possible, and of achieving as rapidly as possible the integration of the Sudan with Egypt. HMG warmly approved Gordon's appointment and told Ismail that they recognised 'in this spontaneous act a sincere desire on his part to put an end to the slave trade and to those slave-hunting expeditions which are being organised on a vast scale, no doubt in violation of HH's orders, on Egyptian territory'.[17] But HMG went on to warn Ismail that they would not approve of any attempt by him to extend his territories in Central Africa, so long as slave-hunting and slave-trading were still being practised in the Provinces which he had just annexed. In the event, during Gordon's period of office between 1877 and 1879, the Egyptian frontier in Equatoria was pulled back to Dufile, just north of Lake Albert, and the whole country between there and Lake Victoria, including Lake Albert, was evacuated, leaving a 'no man's land' extending for some 700 miles between Egyptian territory and the dominions of King M'tesa.

During his three years as Governor-General Gordon's activities were devoted almost entirely to the suppression of the slave trade in Darfur and Bahr-al-Ghazal. In attempting to fulfil this part of his assignment he neglected his other principal duty of building up a viable, efficient and effective administration. He ignored economic and financial matters almost entirely. He was even more capricious than most of his Egyptian predecessors in the appointment and dismissal of officials. He spent most of his time touring his vast 'parish' on camel-back, leaving routine administration in Khartum to look after itself. He caused resentment by appointing a number of not always well qualified foreigners to important posts in the administration.

Gordon's concentration on the suppression of the slave trade, unaccompanied as it was by any attempt to develop legitimate trade, undermined the Egyptian position in the Sudan by alienating the sympathies of almost all the Moslem population. It thus paved the way for the subsequent Mahdist rebellion, which was to sweep Egypt out of the Sudan. 'In Islam there had never been any great moral gulf between the slave and the free; the slave was rather an indentured servant than a social outcast. Islam knew no colour bar or racial discrimination between a slave and his master . . . The suppression of the Trade was one of Ismail's objectives because his dominions were slowly progressing towards a way of life in which slavery was becoming an anachronism. The abolition of an out-of-date social institution was only one part of his instructions to his Governor-General, but it was one requiring deliberate, considered treatment and the pursuit of that exercise of tact which Marshal Lyautey afterwards devised and practised in Morocco – *"la politique de la tache d'huile"*. Gordon had not the temperament which would enable him to understand the causes of slavery, its position in Islam, and how the slave trade could be brought to an end. It followed that his indignant hatred of the Trade drove him to the indiscriminate repression of the slave traders. Neither the traders nor the owners of slaves in the Sudan could see reason in the arbitrary repression practised by the Governor-General. The keeping of slaves was no offence against their religion and they knew that without slaves they could not get their work done.'[18]

HMG's attitude towards the slave trade 'reflected the dominant feeling of the British at the time – that slavery was a moral issue. They thought of a slave as being in fundamental contrast to a free man, and that none but the free could maintain a free world. The feeling was overlaid with mawkishness and a certain hypocrisy, but it was there.'[19] British public opinion was also affected by reports of the appalling cruelty which accompanied the capture and transport of negro slaves, reminiscent of the horrors of the West African slave traffic, which had been abolished over half-a-century before. Successive British Governments were driven by this feeling to use the influence which they had acquired in East Africa and in the Ottoman Empire to enforce upon local rulers demands which were excessive, impracticable and unrealistic. Ismail tried to comply with these demands because he needed British official benevolence in his negotiations with the Porte for independence and, later, over his financial difficulties. Gordon did more or less what the British Government wanted, not because he was a British agent, ready and eager to betray Ismail in the interest of British policy, but because, as a fervent Evangelical Christian, he shared to the full current British prejudices against slavery, and because Ismail, who employed him, was not prepared to risk British official displeasure by checking his ardour.

Gordon's war against the slavers brought him into conflict with Sulaiman Zubair, son of Zubair Rahmat, the titular Governor and uncrowned king of Bahr-al-Ghazal. After long and complicated manoeuvres aimed at breaking up the great slave trading organisations conducted by Sulaiman and others, Gordon sent one of his lieutenants, Romolo Gessi, into Bahr-al-Ghazal with a military expedition to reduce them to submission and to destroy their trading stations. To a large extent, Gessi succeeded in doing this and, in July 1879, brought his campaign to an end by capturing Sulaiman Zubair and having him shot.

In June 1879, just before this had happened, Gordon, hearing of Ismail's deposition, and out of loyalty to the master whom he seems to have liked and respected, resigned his post as Governor-General and returned to England.

Notes

1. Sherif-Stanton, 1.6.70, FO 78/3186
2. Decazes-de Cazaux, 8.12.73, quoted on pp 281–82 of Douin, *op cit*, Vol III, *2me partie*
3. Vivian-Granville, 22.9.73, FO 78/3187
4. Elliot-Granville, 13.11.73, FO 78/3187
5. Granville-Stanton, 29.6.74, FO 78/3187
6. Vivian-Derby, 22.3.78, FO 84/1511
7. Stanton-Derby, 18.12.75, FO 78/2404
8. *ibid*, 29.12.75, *ibid*
9. Vivian-Derby, 23.1.77, FO 78/2631
10. Memorandum by President and Council of RGS in FO 78/1839
11. Vivian-Granville, 22.8.73, FO 78/2284
12. *ibid*, 30.8.73, *ibid*
13. Granville-Vivian, 29.7.73, *ibid*
14. Stanton-Granville, 21.2.74, FO 78/2342
15. Hill, *Egypt in the Sudan, 1820–1881*, p 139
16. Stanton-Derby, 9.1.76, FO 78/3189
17. Derby-Vivian, 18.2.77, FO 84/1472
18. Hill, *op cit*, p 146
19. *ibid*, pp 145–46

8

Ismail's Quest
for Independence

THE desire for independence of Constantinople manifested by
Ismail and his predecessors was not merely a matter of personal
ambition. Egypt derived no benefit whatever from the Ottoman
connection, which had been perpetuated by the Powers, without
any reference to Egyptian interests, as a device for preserving
the balance of power between themselves. The attempts by the
Powers, and by Great Britain in particular, to impose such
Ottoman 'reforms' as the *Hatti Sherif* of Gulhané and the
Tanzimat on Egypt, in the alleged interests of the inhabitants of
Egypt, were particularly hypocritical. Such reforms as had been
imposed by the Powers on an unwilling Porte were by no
means observed in the Ottoman dominions outside Egypt,
where the state of public security was certainly worse, and the
standards of justice and the condition of the masses no better,
than they were in Egypt. And the Powers, who were responsible
for perpetuating the Ottoman connection, were not consistent
in supporting it. When it suited them, as it suited Great
Britain over the railway, and France over the Canal, and as it
suited Great Britain and France from time to time over foreign
loans, they encouraged successive Viceroys to ignore the terms
of the connection to which they themselves had subscribed in
1841. And, in the matter of the Capitulations, they supported
either the letter of the Ottoman treaties or the practices in
Egypt sanctioned by '*droit acquis*' as happened to suit their
nationals best in the particular point under dispute.

The annual tribute, the continual demands for military
assistance in Turkey's numerous and usually unsuccessful wars,
and the bribes and subventions exacted by the Sultan[1] and his
ministers, represented a serious drain on the Egyptian Treasury
and manpower for which Egypt received no return whatever.

The chaotic and ruinous regime of the Capitulations derived from the Ottoman connection, which also imposed serious economic disabilities. Commercial relations with foreign Powers could not be negotiated without the consent of the Porte, which wished to use Egypt as a dumping-ground for its surplus products, e.g. tobacco, and as a means of supplying Turkey with the Egyptian products which it needed, e.g. grain. The law of hereditary succession imposed in 1841 almost compelled successive Viceroys to make the sort of extravagant provisions which they did for their personal heirs.

Even in the negative sense, the Ottoman connection was quite ineffective in preventing Viceroys from doing stupid and extravagant things. It merely made these things even more expensive by making it necessary for the Viceroy to bribe the Sultan and his Ministers into agreeing to them. In the matter of Ismail's foreign loans, the Ministers of the Porte addressed solemn remonstrances to the Viceroy, preaching the virtues of economy and good financial management, as a preliminary to allowing themselves to be bribed into giving their consent to them. In any case, such advice coming from the Porte was a case of Satan rebuking sin, since the Sultan was pursuing precisely the same improvident path as Ismail and was to reach the inevitable end of bankruptcy even sooner than Ismail did.

From the beginning of his reign, Ismail set himself out to regain by bribery and diplomacy all, and more than all, that his grandfather had been compelled by the European Powers to relinquish in 1841. His first aim was to achieve the right of succession by primogeniture to the throne of Egypt. The Ottoman mode of succession by the eldest living male in the direct line – by which the Ottoman Sultanate was itself transmitted – had been imposed on Mohamed Ali in 1841. It avoided the possibility of a minor coming to the throne, with all the dangers and disadvantages of a regency in what was still an absolute monarchy. But it had many disadvantages. It almost compelled the ruler to make adequate provision for his own children, often by nefarious means. It was productive of manifold intrigues – by the ruler against the heir presumptive, and by the heir presumptive against the ruler. Often, it acted as a powerful incentive to assassination. Ten years earlier Abbas had tried, unsuccessfully, to get the order of succession changed in favour of his son, al-Hami. In Ismail's case, under the Ottoman law of succession, the heir presumptive was his younger brother Mustafa Fazil. Nearest to him was Abdul Halim, Mohamed Ali's youngest son, a year or two younger than Mustafa Fazil. Abdul Halim lived in Egypt, where he owned considerable estates and a palace at Shubra, just north of Cairo. Mustafa Fazil also had estates in Egypt, but lived in Constantinople. At the time of Ismail's accession he was one of the Ministers in the Ottoman Government. Not unnaturally, he used all his influence to oppose Ismail's efforts to change the order of succession. In this he was supported by Kiamil Pasha, Grand Vizier at the time.

Ismail was on bad terms both with Mustafa Fazil and with Abdul Halim, accusing them, probably correctly, of stirring up prejudice against him at Constantinople and of intriguing against him generally. He was determined to put an end to what he regarded as an intolerable situation by having them both disinherited and by acquiring their estates in Egypt. The process of disinheritance involved a long and complicated process of bribery and intrigue at Constantinople. Eventually, on 27 May 1866, he obtained from Sultan Abdul Aziz a Firman by which the order of succession to the throne of Egypt was changed to provide for the succession of the Viceroy's eldest son instead of the eldest surviving male in the direct line of descent from Mohamed Ali, as provided in the 1841 settlement. The Firman also provided for the cession to Egypt of the *Qaimaqamat* of Massawa and Suakin, of which Ismail had been granted the life tenure in 1865, and authorised an increase in the permitted strength of the Egyptian army from 18,000 to 30,000, of which 12,000 had to be kept at the disposal of the Sultan. In return for these privileges, the annual tribute was increased from 130,000 purses (£598,000) to 150,000 (£690,000) a year. The formal consent of the Powers to this Firman, deemed necessary since they had underwritten the 1841 settlement, was obtained without much difficulty.

By the time the Firman had been obtained, Ismail had already arranged for the purchase of Abdul Halim's estates in Egypt, in return for undertaking to give him a suitable annual allowance. The negotiation was assisted by the fact that Abdul Halim was heavily in debt. Soon afterwards, he was charged with conspiring against Ismail, and expelled from Egypt. He spent the rest of his life in Constantinople. Ismail also acquired by purchase Mustafa Fazil's estates, thus depriving his brother of any plausible excuse for returning to Egypt. Mustafa Fazil died in Constantinople in 1875, leaving Abdul Halim as the principal claimant to the throne in the event of a revocation of the 1866 Firman.

A year later, after more bribery and diplomacy, Ismail obtained another instalment of independence. On 8 June 1867 a Firman was promulgated which conferred on Ismail the title of Khedive and so lifted him a grade above the other Pashas and Walis of the Ottoman Empire and officially recognised his superior position as compared with them. It authorised him to conclude arrangements with foreign Powers over 'special matters dealing exclusively with Customs, Postal Conventions, and transit and police regulations applicable to foreigners, it being understood that all treaties concluded by the Porte with foreign Powers were also applicable to Egypt'; and in matters of internal administration, 'and consequently the financial, material and other interests of Egypt, which are the responsibility of the Egyptian Government'. It authorised him 'to make such regulations as are necessary for the safeguarding of these interests'.[2] This last was taken by Ismail, but not recognised by the Porte, as conferring authority to raise foreign loans without specific sanction from the Sultan. The promulgation of this Firman involved prior discussions with the British and French Governments, who raised no objections. Ismail was still *bien vu* in London, in Paris, and in Europe generally.

During 1869 Ismail needed all the support he could get from Europe over his relationships with the Porte. In February of that year, Fuad Pasha, the Reis Effendi (Foreign Minister), died, and his portfolio was taken over by Ali Pasha, the Grand Vizier, a declared opponent of Ismail's pretensions. Ali Pasha was intent on Ismail's deposition, and on a revocation of the 1866 and 1867 Firmans, with a view to enabling Mustafa Fazil, who had occupied many high posts in the Ottoman service and who had just been made Minister without Portfolio, to succeed him and thus ensure the effective subordination of Egypt to Turkey. Having incited the weak-minded Sultan Abdul Aziz against Ismail, Ali Pasha submitted to the Khedive a formal list of complaints and asked for his explanation. He alleged that Ismail was acting in defiance of the 1841 settlement, which

remained in force except in so far as it had been modified by
the 1866 and 1867 Firmans, and implied that, unless Ismail
could give a satisfactory explanation, the Sultan would be free
to act as the 1841 settlement provided, i.e. by deposing him.
The specific grounds of complaint were: that Ismail had,
without the Sultan's consent, withdrawn the force he had, at the
Sultan's order, sent to Candia to help put down a rebellion
there; that, although not authorised to negotiate treaties of
commerce with foreign Powers, Nubar Pasha had, since 1867,
been negotiating such a treaty under the guise of 'judicial
reforms'; that various taxes had been imposed in Egypt in
defiance of the terms of the 1841 settlement; that two ironclads
and various other munitions had been ordered by Ismail in
excess of the proper needs of his armed forces; and that Ismail
had acted improperly in issuing direct invitations to European
sovereigns for the Canal inauguration festivities to take place
later that year. As Ismail's explanations were not considered
satisfactory, Ali Pasha presented him with five demands, which
amounted to an ultimatum. Ismail was ordered: to reduce his
army immediately to the level of 30,000 permitted by the 1866
Firman; to sell, or to transfer to the Porte at cost price, the
ironclads and other munitions on order; to submit the Egyptian
budget annually to the Porte for approval; to abandon all
direct negotiations with European Powers; and to contract no
more foreign loans without the Sultan's permission.

On 5 September 1869, after consulting the Consuls-General,
Ismail sent a telegraphic reply to Ali Pasha, accepting the first,
second and fourth demands, but rejecting the third and fifth.
This reply was communicated by Ali Pasha to the European
Ambassadors at the Porte, who expressed the vew that the
demand for the submission of the budget was unjustified and
that the only real remaining point at issue was the question of
the Sultan's authority for foreign loans, as conveyed in the
fifth demand. After talking to the Ambassadors, Ali Pasha sent
Ismail a telegram explaining that the demand for submission
of the budget was simply a request for information and not an
attempt to control Egypt's internal affairs, but maintaining his
demand over foreign loans. Discussing the matter with the
Ambassadors, Ali Pasha used some prophetic words: 'We do
not want one day to see Europe, in the name of a horde of
foreign creditors, impose upon Egypt, as she has already

imposed on Tunisia, the obligation of accepting foreign control over her financial administration.'[3]

The Ambassadors took the view that Ismail's claim to contract foreign loans without the Sultan's permission was unjustified by the terms of the 1867 Firman and undesirable from the point of view of the general interests of Europe, of Turkey and of Egypt. Both Sir Henry Elliot, the British Ambassador, and M. Bouré, the French Ambassador, wrote to their governments in this sense.[4] But these two governments worked upon by Nubar, who had been scurrying busily between London and Paris, took a diametrically opposite view. Clarendon, the British Foreign Secretary, while deploring Ismail's tactlessness in having embroiled himself with the Porte, told Elliot that 'the Porte should not insist on the necessity of their agreeing to foreign loans, still less should they insist on the submission to them of the annual Egyptian budget'.[5] The Prince de la Tour d'Auvergne, the French Foreign Minister, drew Bouré's attention to the clause in the 1867 Firman providing that financial matters connected with internal administration were confided to the Egyptian Government, and expressed the view that 'the faculty of freely contracting loans came within this provision', adding that the 1868 loan (see Chapter Nine) had been raised without the Porte's permission and that, in any case, if Ismail were prevented from raising money by foreign loans, he would do so on current account and by means of Treasury Bonds, as he was in fact doing.[6] The British and French Ambassadors were therefore compelled to try to persuade Ali Pasha to abandon his demand and to make his peace with Ismail on the basis of such concessions as the Khedive had already made. But Ali Pasha stood firm and made it clear to the Ambassadors that he regarded the question as on of the reality or otherwise of Ottoman suzerainty over Egypt, and that he would rather resign than give way.

It was the 1839–41 crisis over again, on a smaller scale, and the reactions of the British and French Governments tended to be similar, although far less drastic. Although the appearance of a united front was maintained, and although there were no open recriminations, the British Government, faced with Ismail's and with Ali Pasha's obstinacy, tended to veer towards support of the Porte, while the French Government tended to veer towards support for Ismail. Ali Pasha did his best to encourage this divergence, which had served Turkey so well thirty years before. But, in 1869, both the British and French Governments were determined that matters should not get out of hand. Various lifelines in the shape of conciliatory formulas were thrown out. The French Government proposed, and Ismail agreed, that matters should be left as they were, that a distinction should be made between loans required for specific public works and those required for general purposes, and that Ismail should ask the Sultan's permission for the latter only. It was pointed out to the Porte that the question was, for the time being, academic, since Ismail was bound, by the terms of the 1868 loan, not to raise another foreign loan for four years. But Ali Pasha would have none of it and sent a telegram to Musurus Pasha, the Ottoman Ambassador in London, telling him that the Sultan had decided to revoke the 1867 Firman unless Ismail agreed, within a matter of days, to accede to the Porte's demand over foreign loans.[7] The British Government deprecated this threat and Sir Henry Elliot produced a suggestion that, in order to settle the affair, the Sultan should promulgate another Firman clarifying the 1867 Firman and making it clear that the right to contract foreign loans had not been conceded. If Ismail accepted this, the matter would be settled and faces saved all round.

This was the position of affairs when the Suez Canal opening ceremonies took place in Egypt in November 1869. In the intervals of the festivities, Sir Henry Elliot, who was present, sought to persuade Ismail to accept such a Firman provided that it was worded so as to avoid affronting him. At the same time, the French Government, reluctantly, came round to the British view about the issue of a clarifying Firman, provided that it was confined to the question of foreign loans and did not seek to restrict Ismail's prerogatives in any other way. Telegrams in identical terms and to this effect were sent to Constantinople from London and Paris, warning the Porte that they would not be supported if they attempted to enlarge the scope of the Firman.[8]

The Firman was promulgated on 26 November and sent to Egypt by the hand of Server Effendi, an emissary who was known to be on good terms with Ismail. Couched in conciliatory terms, it accepted the explanations Ismail had already given about his army, his armaments and his relations with the

Powers, and stated that all taxes in Egypt were collected in the Sultan's name without any restriction on the forms or amounts of such taxes. Coming to the ostensible point at issue, the Firman laid down that 'foreign loans which hypothecated for long periods the country's revenues must not be contracted for until they have been submitted to the Ottoman Government and without My permission having been obtained for the reservation from the revenues of the sums necessary for the service of the loan'.[9]

Elliot, who had remained in Egypt after the opening ceremonies, succeeded in persuading Ismail to have the Firman read publicly, in accordance with protocol, and to send a suitable reply accepting it. This reply,[10] which indicated, in the politest terms, that Ismail was not satisfied, was dated 9 December 1869 and sent to Constantinople by the hand of Server Effendi. The immediate crisis was over.

But the settlement of the crisis had left relations between suzerain and vassal in a very unfriendly state. The delivery of the two ironclads, which Ismail had ordered and which the Porte insisted should be transferred to them, was delayed pending arrangements for their being paid for by the Porte. There were rumours of large orders for arms being placed by Ismail in England and the United States. At the beginning of 1870 Ismail engaged twenty-one American army officers as instructors. Measures were put in hand for fortifying the Egyptian coast of the Mediterranean. There were rumours of an Egyptian rapprochement with Russia. A revolt against Turkish rule in the Asir district of the Hijaz was attributed to Egyptian incitement. All these things inflamed the minds of the Sultan and his Ministers against Ismail, whom they suspected of being on the point of declaring his independence. Every opportunity was taken of complaining to the Ambassadors of the Powers about Ismail's activities. Objection was taken to the 1870 *Daira* loan (see Chapter Nine) as being in defiance of the 1869 Firman. The matter of the ironclads was satisfactorily arranged, but a visit paid by Ismail to Constantinople in 1870 to renew his homage to the Sultan was not very successful.

But Ismail had no intention of asserting his independence by force. Instead, he was determined to secure his liberty of action by bribery. In June 1871 he sent Abraham Bey, Nubar's brother-in-law, to Constantinople with the mission of improving the general atmosphere. This mission was facilitated by the death of Ali Pasha in September 1871. The death of this great Minister, who held the offices of Grand Vizier, Reis Effendi and Minister of the Interior, enabled the vain and venal Sultan Abdul Aziz, for the first time, to exercise some real control over his Empire. It also enabled Ismail to work effectively on his cupidity for the attainment of his desired ends. In September 1872, after a liberal distribution of presents and bribes by Abraham Bey, and after another visit by Ismail to Constantinople, the Sultan issued a Firman, which cancelled the restrictive Firman of 1869, and an explanatory Hatt which specifically 'renewed and confirmed the permission to borrow the necessary sums in the name of the Egyptian Government without seeking permission whenever the prosperity of the country called for the contracting of a foreign loan.[11]

In this way, the ostensible point at issue in the 1869 crisis was resolved in Ismail's favour. The Firman and Hatt had been negotiated direct with the Sultan without the intervention or, it appears, even the knowledge of Midhat Pasha, the Grand Vizier, who consulted the Ambassadors of the Powers about the propriety of recognising these instruments. The Ambassadors took the view that it would be undesirable to question the personal authority of the Sultan, and Ismail was allowed to gain his point. But this was only one more instalment of the complete autonomy at which he was aiming.

There followed nine months of intensive bribery which was rewarded, in June 1873, by the promulgation of a Firman conferring on Ismail virtually everything which he was seeking. This Firman,[12] apart from confirming all the privileges granted in the 1866, 1867 and 1872 Firmans, provided: (i) for the succession in the event of the failure of a male heir by conferring it on the Khedive's next eldest brother; (ii) for the reigning Khedive to make his own arrangements for a Regency Council against the succession of a minor heir; (iii) for the removal of all restrictions on the size of the Egyptian armed forces, with the single exception that the Khedive was not permitted to build or order ironclads without the Sultan's permission; (iv) for the fullest autonomy in the internal affairs of Egypt; (v) for the Khedive to be able to 'renew and to contract, provided that nothing was done contrary to existing treaties to which the Porte was a party, Conventions with agents of foreign Powers for Customs and commerce and for all matters concerning foreigners and the internal and other affairs of the country, with the object of developing commerce and industry and of regulating relations between foreigners and the Egyptian Government and people; (vi) for the investment of the Khedive with 'the complete and entire control of the financial affairs of the country and the full facility of contracting, without authorisation from the Porte, in the name of the Egyptian Government, for foreign loans at any time when he shall consider this necessary'.

In the space of two-and-a-half years, as a result of his own and of Abraham Bey's diplomacy, assisted by the distribution of bribes estimated as something over £1 million, Ismail had succeeded in converting the atmosphere at Constantinople to one of almost unlimited complaisance towards himself. He had also succeeded in enlarging his own powers to an extent which conferred on him independence in everything but name. He had, in effect, anticipated the concept of 'Dominion status'. He had been able to do this partly because, after the death of Al Pasha, the feeble Sultan Abdul Aziz had no Ministers honest and firm enough to resist Ismail's intrigues, and partly because none of the Powers were prepared to resist his pretensions.

But Ismail's victory was a precarious one. Its maintenance depended, *inter alia*, on the continued complaisance both of the Sultan and of the Powers. It was also a two-edged one, in that the autonomy which he had gained might eventually be used by his creditors to assert their own control over Egypt without the possible measure of protection which Turkish suzerainty might have afforded. In the event, this is exactly what happened. But, even before that, and within a few months of the promulgation of the 1873 Firman, the practical limitations on Ismail's autonomy were revealingly displayed. Towards the end of 1873 the Porte, pushed by the Powers, ordered Ismail to send troops to occupy the Suez Canal in order to compel the Canal Company to apply the tonnage dues fixed by an International Conference at Constantinople. Ismail, knowing that the Powers were behind the Porte, had no choice but to obey.

F

Notes

1. Sultan Abdul Majid died in 1861 and was succeeded by his brother Abdul Aziz, who reigned until 1875 when he was deposed and afterwards committed suicide
2. Douin, *op cit*, Vol I, p 440
3. Douin, *op cit*, Vol II, p 385
4. *ibid*, pp 385–6
5. *ibid*, p 382
6. *ibid*, p 379
7. *ibid*, pp 407–8
8. *ibid*, p 485
9. *ibid*, pp 486–87
10. *ibid*, pp 490–91
11. For texts of Firman and Hatt see *ibid*, pp 661–62 and 665
12. For text see *ibid*, pp 723–27

The Rake's Progress

FROM about the beginning of 1864, the Oppenheims started trying to persuade Ismail to pay off his existing floating debt by means of a long-term loan as a preliminary to borrowing more money on open account. Neither the Oppenheims nor Ismail's other creditors wanted him to get out of debt. Lending money to him was a profitable business. Moreover, there were additional profits to be made out of commissions payable on foreign orders, which could only be placed as long as Ismail and the Egyptian Treasury were in receipt of borrowed money. The foreign loan was simply a way of getting short-term indebtedness settled whenever it was beginning to glut the market with Egyptian paper. To the Oppenheims, whose European connections enabled them to raise large sums of long-term money on the European money-markets, a foreign loan had the additional attraction of the profits attaching to the contractors' commission. But this source of profit was not available to some of Ismail's other creditors, such as Dervieu, who were, at first, opposed to a foreign loan, which would tend to weaken the profitable links forged between Ismail and themselves. But, by the middle of 1864, Ismail's borrowing from Dervieu had reached the limit of his bank's resources. Other creditors, too, were becoming clamorous and a foreign loan seemed to be the only remaining resource.

Ismail was reluctant to abandon the system of financing which he had devised and resort to a foreign loan. It 'was the one form of debt which the Viceroy disliked. It was open and subject to the approval of his suzerain in Constantinople. It meant disagreeable bargaining. It placed his credit on the block, as it were, to be scrutinized and priced in the market-place. More important, public loans imposed punctuality – when a rentier clipped his coupon, he wanted to collect right away. And finally, there was the little spark of pride that remained;

like the fallen woman who clings to the last appearance of virtue, Ismail cherished the illusion that he had not added to the nation's debt.'[1]

But, in July 1864, when the French Emperor's Canal Company arbitration award condemned him to pay Fcs. 84 million indemnity to the Company, and when it became apparent that his plans for taking over the Company had miscarried, Ismail realised that a foreign loan was necessary. There were many lenders ready and anxious to oblige him. Apart from the Oppenheims, who had been involved in Ismail's plans for taking over the Canal Company,[2] there was the new Anglo-Egyptian Bank, a French group represented in Egypt by Sabatier, the ex-French Consul-General who had been dismissed from the foreign service for his lack of adequate support for the Canal Company, and Bravay, one of Said's favourites and still a hanger-on at the Court, who gave himself out to be an agent of Rothschilds.

The Anglo-Egyptian Bank, which had been founded in 1862 with a capital of Fcs. 40 million, was an Anglo-French combination of which Pastré, an Alexandrian French banker whose own bank had been absorbed by the Anglo-Egyptian, was the Egypt manager. This bank, which was to play an important part in Egyptian financial affairs,[3] was another link in the chain of Anglo-French financial co-operation in Egypt, started by Hermann Oppenheim's assumption of French nationality, which replaced the previous Anglo-French rivalry. The co-operation, like the rivalry, was never absolute, but was sufficiently close to deprive Ismail of the possibility of British diplomatic support against French exigencies and *vice versa*.

The Oppenheims, who had the powerful advantage of their Constantinople connections, which helped to obtain Ottoman consent to the loan, got the contract in October 1864 after a good deal of haggling. The nominal amount of the loan was £5,704,200, repayable over fifteen years at 7 per cent interest and 3.87 per cent amortization. It was issued on the London market in April 1865 at 93 through Fruhling & Goschen. After deduction of discount, commission etc., Ismail received just under £5,000,000, of which some £3,500,000 went immediately towards settling his short-term indebtedness to Oppenheim, Dervieu and his other Alexandrian creditors. The service of the debt amounted to about £620,000 a year over the next fifteen years, secured on the revenues of Dakhalia, Sharqia and Behera.[4] Together with the service of the 1862 loan, this amounted to an annual charge on the revenue of £924,000. (By this time the Comptoir d'Escompte loan had almost been paid off.) *Facile descensus Averni.* The long slide towards bankruptcy had begun. From this time on, the process of indebtedness followed a regular pattern: short-term indebtedness redeemed in part from the proceeds of a long-term secured loan, the service of which hypothecated part of the revenue, followed by more short-term indebtedness, partly redeemed in due course by another foreign loan on more onerous terms, which hypothecated another *tranche* of revenue. *Et ainsi de suite* until so much revenue had been hypothecated that the proceeds of the next foreign loan had to be used, not to redeem floating debt, which grew and grew, but to supplement such unhypothecated revenue as remained.

During the next three years – 1865–67 – three more foreign loans were negotiated for theoretically sound and unobjectionable purposes. One, secured on the railway revenue, was to raise capital for the equipment and extension of the railway system. The other two, secured on the revenues of the *Dairas* – royal estates – were for the purpose of purchasing the large estates of Mustafa Fazil and Abdul Halim who, until the promulgation of the 1866 Firman, were next in line of succession to the throne, and who were barred from the succession as a result of that Firman.

The railway loan was first negotiated in Paris between Nubar and Hermann Oppenheim in October 1865. But the terms of this loan, for £3 million, were so exorbitant that Ismail refused to agree to them. The contract was rescinded by mutual consent and, in January 1866, a new contract was signed for a loan of £3 million repayable over six years from January 1869 at 7 per cent interest and 8.55 per cent amortisation. The loan was secured on the railway revenues and issued on the Paris market at 92. After deduction of contractors' commission etc. this provided the Treasury with a net sum of about £2,640,000 against a charge on the railway revenue of some £710,000 a year for six years as from 1869. These terms were not quite so favourable as appeared on first sight, since only half of the £2,640,000 receivable was to be paid in cash; the other half was to be paid in railway equipment, on which the Oppenheims reserved for themselves a commission of 5 per cent.[5]

The negotiation of this loan marked the end of the previous intimate financial relationship between Ismail and Nubar. This came about as a result of Nubar's maladroit bargaining in Paris over the railway loan, which followed hard upon the failure of his Suez Canal negotiations. In January 1866 he was removed from the office of Minister of Public Works and became Foreign Minister. In his new office he continued to be responsible for relations with the Suez Canal Company, and with Constantinople and the European Powers. He soon became deeply absorbed in negotiations with the Powers over judicial reform. But he never resumed his previous intimate complicity with Ismail and, ten years later, became bitterly estranged from him.

The first *Daira* loan was for a nominal sum of £3,387,300 and was intended primarily for the purchase of Abdul Halim's estates, which Nubar had arranged, for a sum of £1,300,000.[6] The money was to be raised, as to one-half in London by the Anglo-Egyptian Bank, and as to one-half in Paris by Pastré, the Egypt Manager of the Bank, who also had banking interests in France. According to the contract, which was signed in March 1866, the nominal amount of the loan was to be repaid over fifteen years, at 7 per cent interest and 3.27 per cent amortisation, and was secured on the revenues of the Viceregal estates – the *Daira Khassa* which provided Ismail's civil list and the *Daira Sanieh* which represented his personal property.[7] The flotation, which coincided with a financial crisis in Egypt caused by the Austro-Prussian war, was a failure. The loan was floated at 92, less 3 per cent for the contractors, in March 1866. The Anglo-Egyptian Bank were unable to place £1,400,000 out of their share of the flotation and Pastré eventually arranged for the Crédit Foncier to take over this unsubscribed portion for £900,000, equivalent to a price of 69½. In the result Ismail received some £2,660,000 out of the nominal amount of £3,387,300, on which he had to pay some £369,000 a year interest and amortisation over the next fifteen years. In addition, as a result of the intervention of the French Consul-General, the Anglo-Egyptian Bank received an indemnity of £50,000, and a two-year contract for the supply of coal which was expected to yield them a profit of £100,000, to compensate them for losses alleged to have been incurred as a result of their mismanagement of their share of the flotation.[8]

The second *Daira* loan was contracted for in 1867 and was for the ostensible purpose of paying for the purchase of Mustafa Fazil's estates. These had already been purchased by Ismail for £2,100,000 payable over two years at 9 per cent interest.[9] The loan was for a nominal amount of £2,080,000, repayable at 9 per cent interest and 3.4 per cent amortisation over fifteen years, and secured, like the first *Daira* loan, on the revenues of the *Daira Khassa* and the *Daira Sanieh*. It was contracted for by the Oppenheims and floated by the Imperial Ottoman Bank at 90 in December 1867. The amount received by Ismail, after deduction of discount, commission etc., was about £1,700,000. But this was only paid partly in cash, the balance being paid in short-term treasury bonds, bought up by the contractors at a discount and paid into the subscription at par, thus providing the contractors with a handsome additional profit. The annual service of the debt amounted to some £257,000 over the next fifteen years.[10]

During the 1866 financial crisis the foreign banks in Egypt requested and received the support of the Consuls-General, who represented to Ismail the importance of settling some of the outstanding floating debt, 'particularly as there was some reason to fear that one or more of these establishments might suspend payment'.[11] As a result, the Egyptian Government 'resorted to a forced loan collection on land under cultivation, nominally repayable in four years'. This loan, which was at a rate of twenty piastres (twenty new pence) a *feddan*, produced a sum of £1 million, which enabled the Viceroy to meet some of his more pressing engagements.[12] The 'loan' was never repaid and simply became an extra tax.

At the same time new short-term indebtedness was being incurred, piling up the pressure towards another foreign loan in order to liquidate it. There was no attempt to confine current expenditure to such revenue as was left after the service of fixed obligation loans. And now that the cotton boom was over, the revenue was less buoyant. It fell from a peak of £E6,972,000 in 1864 to £E5,356,000 in 1865, £E5,058,000 in 1866, and £E4,129,000 in 1867.[13] But Ismail was still spending mostly borrowed money with a careless hand. Anxious to ingratiate himself with the Sultan, he had, at his request, sent a force of six battalions to the Hijaz in November 1864, and was main-

taining a large and increasing force in Candia, to help put down
rebellions against the Porte in these two Provinces. On annual
visits to Constantinople he was spending large sums in bribes
and entertainments.

In 1866, after the Sultan's Firman for the construction of the
Suez Canal had at last been granted, Ismail re-purchased from
the Canal Company, at a cost of Fcs. 10 million, 10,000 hectares
of land, known as the Wadi lands, along the Zagazig canal in
the eastern Delta, which Said had sold to the Company for
Fcs. 2 million; took over the Fresh Water Canal from the
Company against payment to the Company of Fcs. 10 million
as provided in the Emperor's arbitration award; and accelerated
the rate of payment of the indemnities laid down in the rest of the
award so as to provide for their liquidation by the end of 1869.

In 1867 there were expensive visits by Ismail to Paris and
London and expensive negotiations in Constantinople which
resulted in the issue of the 1867 Firman granting Ismail the
title of Khedive and enlarging the scope of his autonomy.

By the beginning of 1868 the resources of short-term borrowing were again almost exhausted and a new foreign loan had
become necessary. A contract was signed in February with a
French group, but it was discovered that the French representative in Egypt dealing with the matter had no power to act and
the contract was cancelled. In April the Treasury, in order to
find ready money, issued £650,000 worth of thirty-month
bonds at a discount of 30 per cent. At about the same time
Ismail dismissed Ragheb Pasha, his Finance Minister, and
appointed in his place Ismail Sadiq, the son of his own foster-
mother, a childhood friend and playmate, and lately manager of
his estates. Ismail Sadiq, who became well known throughout
Egypt as the *Mufattish* (meaning Inspector, his title when
managing the royal estates), was able, energetic and unscrupulous, as well as loyal to Ismail, and was meant to use
these qualities for squeezing as much revenue as possible from
the country. In this task he succeeded only too well.

But his first business was to arrange for a new foreign loan.
After Ismail had gone through the formality of obtaining the
consent of the Chamber of Notables, the entirely subservient
body which he had instituted in 1866 as a concession to foreign
critics who were accusing him of despotism,[14] and after some
brisk competition between the Societé Générale, who were

supported by the French Consul-General, and the Oppenheims, a contract was signed with the Oppenheims in May for a nominal amount of £11,890,000. The conditions of the loan, which was floated by the Imperial Ottoman Bank and the Societé Générale, indicated the extent to which Ismail's credit had deteriorated. (Although the Oppenheims and the Societé Générale had been in competition over the contract, the Société Générale, the losers, were admitted to a share in the flotation.) The loan, which was for the ostensible purpose of paying off the floating debt, was repayable over thirty years at 7 per cent interest and 1 per cent amortisation. The issue was made at 75 and the actual amount received, after allowing for discount, commission, etc., was £7,193,334. But not all of this was in cash, since it was provided in the contract that Egyptian treasury bonds, which were at a considerable discount, could be paid into the subscription at par. In the result, the total amount of cash received was about £5,500,000. The service of the debt, which was secured on the customs revenue and certain specific taxes, amounted to some £950,000 a year over the next thirty years.[15] A condition of the loan was that no more foreign loans secured on the State revenues were to be incurred for the next five years.

This loan did not receive the sanction of the Porte. (Neither had the railway loan, nor the two *Daira* loans, but they were regarded as being in a special category.) The wind at Constantinople was veering away from Ismail, mainly as a result of the increasing influence of Ali Pasha, the Grand Vizier, who was a determined enemy of Ismail's ambitions. Being a relatively honest man, he was immune from Ismail's bribery and, until his death in 1872, consistently opposed the freedom which Ismail claimed to contract for foreign loans without permission from the Sultan.[16]

The proceeds of the 1868 loan enabled some of the more pressing floating debts to be paid. But the familiar process of incurring new floating debt was continued, supplemented by the increments of revenue which the Mufattish was extracting from the countryside. In 1868 the revenue rose to £E5,011,000, in 1969 to £E5,255,000, and in 1870 to £E5,389,000.[17]

The basis of the Egyptian revenue was the *miri*, or agricultural land tax. Cultivated land was divided into two categories – *kharaj*, which paid the full rate of *miri*, and *ushuri* which paid a reduced rate of about one-third. During Ismail's reign there were about 4.8 million *feddans* of *kharaj* and 1.25 million *feddans* of *ushuri* land. The *miri* on both classes of land had been increased by 25 per cent at the beginning of Ismail's reign, and the average rate towards the end of the reign was about £1.20 a *feddan* for *kharaj* and £0.37 per *feddan* for *ushuri* land. Since cultivated land produced a gross income of between £8 and £15 per *feddan* a year, these rates were not, in themselves, particularly onerous. The *miri* was estimated to produce an annual revenue of about £E4.5 million. The comparative lightness of the tax, combined with Egypt's agricultural prosperity, made it possible for the government to collect the *miri* in advance by one or even two years.[18] This practice, which was habitually followed, made it all the more necessary for the Mufattish to seek new sources of revenue. During his career as Finance Minister, between 1868 and 1876, old taxes were increased and a proliferation of new taxes imposed. In 1868 the *miri* on *kharaj* land was increased by one-sixth; in 1870 a water-tax amounting to 10 per cent of the *miri* was imposed on all agricultural land. In 1873 a stamp-tax of one piastre (about 1p) per *feddan* and a 'war tax' of five piastres a *feddan* was imposed. In 1878 it was estimated that the annual revenue from all agricultural land taxes had risen over the previous ten years from £E4.5 million to about £E7,350,000, of which £E6,750,000 was paid on *kharaj* and £E600,000 on *ushuri* lands. In addition to the agricultural land taxes, poll tax, house tax, date palm tax, flour mill tax, oil mill tax, boat tax, shop tax, *octrois* of various kinds, and even a burial tax, were imposed and collected with the aid of the *kurbash* and *bastinado* and systematically pilfered on the way between the taxpayer and the Treasury. But, in spite of this pilferage, the revenue, under the inexorable demands of the European bondholders at one end and the *bastinado*-wielding tax-collector at the other, steadily increased, rising to £E5,711,000 in 1871, £E7,293,000 in 1872, and to a peak of £E10,542,468 in 1875.[19]

1869 was a particularly extravagant and improvident year. In April Ismail signed a Convention with the Suez Canal Company agreeing to pay them Fcs. 30 million (£1,200,000) for the revocation of certain 'rights' (which the Company did not possess) and for the purchase of various buildings and installations (for which the Company had no further use). This

Fcs. 30 million was paid by surrendering for twenty-five years the coupons on the Egyptian Government's Suez Canal Company Ordinary shareholding, which entitled them to 5 per cent interest and dividends over that period, and by surrendering for these twenty-five years the voting rights conferred by their shareholding. By offering these coupons to the other shareholders the Canal Company were able to raise the Fcs. 30 million in cash from them.[20] After concluding this 'bargain' Ismail set off for Europe, distributing invitations for the festivities which were to accompany the formal opening of the Suez Canal in November. These festivities were on a fantastically lavish and extravagant scale, and cost the Egyptian Treasury some £2 million.

Deprived by the conditions of the 1868 loan of recourse to another foreign loan, Ismail continued to find finance mainly by means of Treasury bonds issued locally at discounts of up to 18 per cent a year for the longer-dated bonds. So long as the coupons on the foreign debt were paid regularly, Ismail's credit on the European money markets remained reasonably good, and local banks eagerly took up these bonds, which they were able to discount with their European correspondents at 10 per cent, thus ensuring to themselves a handsome profit, while providing for the Egyptian Treasury, at very considerable cost, a regular flow of borrowed money.

In 1870 Ismail contracted another loan on the security of his private estates, which he held to be exempted both from the five-year ban on foreign loans imposed under the conditions of the 1868 loan and from the terms of the 1869 Firman (Chapter Eight). He contracted a loan for a nominal sum of £7,142,860 at 7 per cent interest and 2.35 per cent amortisation repayable over twenty years with the Banque Franco-Egyptienne, which had recently been founded in Egypt by a consortium of European financiers headed by a M. Bishoffsheim. Ostensibly, the loan was for the purpose of equipping Ismail's Middle Egypt estates with sugar refineries and other equipment. The service of the loan, like that of the previous two *Daira* loans, was secured on the revenues of the *Daira Khassa* and the *Daira Sanieh*. The loan, which was floated in London and Paris, was not very enthusiastically subscribed, partly because the Porte officially protested to the British and French Governments against its having been floated in defiance of the 1869 Firman. Only two-thirds of the loan was subscribed at 78 and the rest had to be raised at a greater discount still. The amount received by Ismail, after deduction of discounts, commission etc. was about £5,000,000. The service of the loan amounted to about £669,000 a year for the next twenty years. As a result of the Ottoman protest Ismail was advised firmly, if rather belatedly, by the British Government not to enter into any financial arrangements whatever incompatible with the Sultan's Firman.[21]

Towards the end of 1870 Ismail arranged with his old friends, the Oppenheims, to borrow £1.5 million on the London market against six, seven, and eight months' Treasury bonds guaranteed on the railway revenues (already hypothecated in part to the service of the 1865 railway loan which had not yet been paid off). The Oppenheims received 4 per cent commission on this transaction, which they offered to waive in return for a concession for the operation of the railways.[22] The negotiations for this concession failed[23] and the Oppenheims presumably got their commission. In May 1871, since the Treasury was unable to pay the £1.5 million worth of bonds on their due dates, the issue was replaced, also through the Oppenheims, by an issue of £2 million worth of bonds, half at seven months and half at twenty-seven months.[24] Arrangements were also made with the Oppenheims for them to take up, at 8 per cent discount, £6.5 million worth of Treasury bonds falling due between September 1871 and March 1873 in exchange for bonds at two years' maturity issued at 12 per cent discount.[25] It was clear that the Oppenheims were carrying Ismail over until the stipulated five years after the 1868 loan had elapsed when, if he could get over the Ottoman objection, he would be in a position to contract for another large foreign loan which, in view of the accommodation provided in the meantime, would have to be contracted with the Oppenheims.

In 1871, the Mufattish, in his endeavours to raise money, produced a device which stands out as a masterpiece of improvidence even by the standards of Ismailian finance. This aimed at the extiction of the estimated £27 million worth of floating debt. Known as the *Muqabala* (compensation), it was an arrangement offered by the government to the landowners of Egypt providing that any land on which an additional six years' *miri* was paid within a stated time should be exempt in perpetuity from one-half of the *miri* payable on it. Payment could either be made in one sum, or in annuities spread over twelve years, exemption to start from the date on which the six years' *miri* had been paid in full.[26] With the aid of a certain amount of persuasion, between £E7 and £E8 million in cash and engagements to pay some £E1,530,000 in twelve annuities were obtained out of the £27 million which had been the original object of the operation. The security, which was nothing more than the promise of the Egyptian Government to pay, was not a very valuable one.

The proceeds of the *Muqabala*, although disappointing, together with the short-term money borrowed from the Oppenheims, were sufficient to tide the Treasury over until 1872. By that time, the floating debt had again become pressing. In another year, the five-year ban on foreign loans would have expired, but there were still the probable objections of the Porte and the Powers to be reckoned with.

While Ismail was negotiating for the 1872 Firman (see Chapter Eight), the Oppenheims let it be known that a substantial loan would be available if the Ottoman objection were removed. At the same time, they arranged in London and Paris for another advance of £4 million against eighteen-month Treasury bonds bearing interest at 18 per cent a year, plus 1 per cent commission for themselves.

After the promulgation of the 1872 Firman and Hatt, Ismail borrowed £3 million from the bankers of Constantinople and £2 million from the bankers of Alexandria on the security of the *Muqabala* annuities.[27] Before leaving for Constantinople in 1873 to apply the finishing touches to Abraham Bey's diplomacy, Ismail gave instructions to the Mufattish to negotiate a new loan through the Oppenheims. The intention was that it should be large enough to mop up the entire floating debt, which was estimated at £28 million. A contract was signed for a loan for a nominal amount of £32 million at 7 per cent interest and 1 per cent amortisation repayable over thirty years. Subscriptions were opened in London, Paris, Alexandria, Amsterdam, Brussels, Antwerp, Geneva and Constantinople, and were divided into two parts of £16 million each. The first £16 million, for which Egyptian Treasury bonds could be subscribed at par in lieu of cash, was issued at 84¼; the second £16 million, for which only cash could be subscribed, was issued at 70. The amount received was £11,750,000 in cash plus £9,000,000 in Treasury bonds. The service of the loan, which was secured on railway receipts, *Muqabala* annuities, salt tax and general revenues, amounted to £2,565,670 a year over the next thirty years.[28]

After this immense loan had been contracted for, the annual service of the foreign funded debt amounted to some £5 million a year, excluding some £1.5 million a year for the service of the *Daira* loans, out of a total revenue of about £9 million a year. The actual amount received, either in cash or in redeemed Treasury bonds, had been about £37,400,000, excluding some £9,360,000 from the *Daira* loans. The total amount to be repaid, over periods ranging from five to thirty years, was about £139,767,000, excluding some £27,760,000 on the *Daira* loans.

On top of all this, there was the floating debt, costing something like 18 per cent a year in interest and renewal charges. Of the £11.5 million received in cash from the 1873 loan, about £5 million was devoted to paying off floating debt in addition to the £9 million worth of redeemed bonds included in the subscription.[29] This must have reduced the floating debt to about £14 million.

The Egyptian budget for the financial year September 1874 to September 1875 gives a picture of Egypt's official finances at that time. The total revenue was stated at 2,108,493 purses (£E10,542,465). Of this, 839,500 purses (£E4,197,500) was estimated to come from the *miri*, 36,934 purses (£E184,670) from the tax on date palms, 82,346 purses (£E411,730) from various taxes on commerce and industry, 98,517 purses (£E492,584) from *octrois*, 314,858 purses (£E1,572,290) from the proceeds of the *Muqabala*, 124,737 purses (£E623,685) from customs duties, 193,207 purses (£E966,035) from railway receipts, 140,523 purses (£E296,170) from the salt tax, and 32,313 purses (£E161,565) from lock fees.

The Khedive and his family, who owned about one-fifth of all the cultivable land,[30] paid no taxes at all. The prosperous foreign communities paid practically no taxes, and most Egyptian notables paid very little, both because of widespread evasion and because they owned most of the privileged *ushuri* lands. Nearly all these taxes therefore were collected from the poorer cultivators.

Of the expenditure shown in the budget, which was greatly

understated at 2,105,295 purses (£E10,526,475), 982,151 purses (£E4,910,755) was shown for the service of the fixed debt, and 290,625 purses (£E1,453,125) as interest on the floating debt. After allowing for tribute payments amounting to £E750,000, this left about £E3,750,000 for the general expenses of administration. In fact, expenditure was much greater than this and was met by a progressive increase in the floating debt.[31]

In the budget no account was taken of the income, expenditure and indebtedness of the royal *Dairas*. The income of these *Dairas*, all of which was at the disposal of the Khedive and his relatives, was burdened with charges on funded and floating debt amounting to about £E1.5 million a year. In their large capital expenditure for the acquisition of new lands and for the installation of expensive plant, and in the payment of their debts, the *Dairas* were largely subsidised out of the State revenues, as was the Khedive's personal expenditure.

The service of the 1873 loan greatly increased the difficulty of providing for the payment of the foreign debt coupons. During the second half of 1875 these difficulties came to a head. By September there were rumours that the half-yearly coupon payments due on 1 December and amounting to about £3,250,000 could not be met. The Treasury's only remaining unpledged assets were their 177,000 odd Suez Canal Company Ordinary shares, worth some £3,500,000 at current market price. Negotiations were in train with the Crédit Foncier, which held some £7 million worth of Egyptian Treasury bonds, for the floating of a long-term loan, secured by the Suez Canal shares, for the liquidation of part of the floating debt. Another French group, Societé Générale, with which Lesseps was connected, obtained an option through their agents in Egypt, Dervieu et Cie, for the outright purchase of the Canal shares for Fcs. 92 million. But Societé Générale was unable to find the money as a result of Crédit Foncier's opposition, which had the French Government behind it. The British Government, tipped off by Henry Oppenheim about the Societé Générale option, unwilling to see such a large block of Suez Canal shares fall into French hands, and apparently unaware that Societé Générale were unable to find the money, made an offer of £4 million sterling for the shares, which Ismail promptly accepted. The receipt of this sum, provided for HMG by

Rothschilds at $2\frac{1}{2}$ per cent interest, relieved for the time being Ismail's financial anxieties. The December coupon was duly met and 1873 loan stock, which had become the accepted barometer of Egyptian credit, and which had fallen to as low as 54, rose again to 72.[32]

The news of HMG's purchase was badly received in France, where government and public opinion were always sensitive to any apparently unfriendly British move against French interests in Egypt. In this case there were two particular reasons for French anger. The negotiations for the purchase had been kept secret from the French Government, who had also been told by Lord Derby, the Foreign Secretary, that purchase of the shares by a French interest would be regarded as an unfriendly act. The purchase also wrecked, for the time being, Crédit Foncier's hopes of getting some adequate security for their imprudently large holding of Egyptian Treasury bonds. Ismail, who was being harassed by Crédit Foncier about this holding, and who was always ready to try to exploit for his own advantage any differences between Great Britain and France (he had learnt by bitter experience that he could not withstand them when they were united), told Stanton, the British Consul-General, that he was 'anxious to engage the services of two gentlemen to superintend, under the Minister of Finance, the receipts and revenues of the country'.[33] Nubar, who had returned to Egypt and to office as Foreign Minister a few weeks before (he had left Egypt for a short time in 1874 as the result of a disagreement with Ismail), assured Stanton that the Khedive realised the implications of his request and appreciated 'the absolute necessity of putting the fullest information as to the finances of the country before the gentlemen who may be selected'. A few days later, Nubar told Stanton that 'the Egyptian Government really wished to procure the services of gentlemen competent, not only to direct the specified Departments of the Ministry of Finance, but also to advise the government on all financial matters'. 'We do not want clerks,' Nubar told Stanton, 'these we can find ourselves, but gentlemen of standing (or at least one of them) competent to give us sound advice on the financial administration of the country.'[34]

HMG, on receipt of the Khedive's request, 'determined that the preferable course to adopt in the first instance . . . will be to send out a special envoy to confer with the Khedive and his

Government as to the financial position and administration of
Egypt'.[35] The envoy selected was the Rt Hon Stephen Cave MP,
the Paymaster-General in Disraeli's Government. Mr Cave
arrived in Egypt on 17 December 1875, accompanied by
Colonel Stokes RE, who was HMG's principal adviser on all
matters connected with the Suez Canal, by one official from the
War Office and by two from the Foreign Office.

Up to the time of the Cave Mission, HMG took very little
interest in the growth of Egypt's indebtedness. During Said's
reign Bruce, as we have seen, expressed strong views about the
danger of alienating Egypt's revenues to 'foreign speculators'.
Nevertheless HMG, spurred by French competition, instructed
Colquhoun, Bruce's successor, to give 'moral support' to the
Oppenheims in their negotiations for the 1862 loan. But there
was no such diplomatic support for the Oppenheims in their
later money-lending activities in Egypt, of which HMG seem
to have been only cursorily informed. Generally, Disraeli's
first administration, lasting from 1866 to 1868, in which Lord
Stanley was Foreign Secretary, took very little interest in
Egyptian finances. They raised no objection to the enlargement
of Ismail's privileges under the terms of the 1866 and 1867
Firmans, or to the 1868 loan, although this was almost certainly
ultra vires. (By this time the element of Anglo-French competition over foreign loans had almost disappeared and British
and French interests were almost equally involved in the
Oppenheims' operations.)

In 1869, when a Liberal Government, with Gladstone as
Prime Minister and Lord Clarendon as Foreign Secretary, was
in office, British official interest in Egypt revived, mainly
owing to the imminent opening of the Suez Canal. The British
Ambassador in Constantinople took a leading part in the
settlement of the 1869 crisis between Ismail and the Porte,
when the principal ostensible point at issue was Ismail's right
to incur foreign loans, and when the real point at issue was the
extent of Ismail's subordination to the Sultan. But HMG
showed none of that Palmerstonian determination to take sides
with Turkey and reduce Egypt to submission. And, in 1872,
when Ismail obtained from the Sultan a Firman giving him
permission to contract foreign loans as he pleased, the British
Ambassador gave no encouragement to Midhat Pasha, the Grand
Vizier, when he suggested that the Firman might be annulled.

The first sign of HMG's detailed interest in Egypt's financial affairs was in July 1869. Lord Clarendon, the Foreign Secretary, wrote to Stanton in connection with Ismail's differences with the Porte: 'One of the grievances which the Porte alleges against the Viceroy is the embarrassment which is likely to result in Egypt from his financial administration and the large amount of loans lately contracted by his government. It is evident during late years that the Egyptian Government have incurred great liabilities in the shape of loans, that the terms on which these loans have been effected have comprised high rates of interest, and that the conditions involve repayment within a limited number of years. A portion of these loans have very probably been applied by the Viceroy in carrying out the complicated pecuniary transactions in which Egypt has been involved on account of the Suez Canal, and a portion may also have been raised to enable the Viceroy to meet the large outlay he was called upon for by the Porte during the late insurrection in Candia. The necessity for other portions is not so obvious. They may have been contracted and applied for productive purposes or they may have been squandered away for expenses of a private nature or even for expenses on public objects which there was no occasion to incur, such as military or naval armaments . . . HMG would wish to be furnished with the fullest information, not only generally as to the financial position of Egypt, but specifically as regards the several loans, the purposes for which they were contracted, the conditions under which they were raised, and the manner in which they were appropriated.' Clarendon went on to specify that he particularly wanted details about expenditure on behalf of the Suez Canal Company, and information about 'not only loans properly so called, but also the issue of other securities charge-able on the revenues of Egypt and the public *Dairas*. The most important point is whether the resources of the country are adequate to meet the charges for loans . . . and to provide for their redemption at the accepted dates.'[36] The last sentence of this despatch makes it clear that HMG's interest was concen-trated on the anxieties of the bondholders, many of whom were British.

Stanton's reply was rather unduly optimistic: 'The public revenue of Egypt, according to the latest published returns, was £E7,518,000, and the expenditure, independent of the

amounts required to pay the service of the loans, is returned at
£E3,255,200, leaving a balance of £E4,263,200 to be applied
to unforeseen expenses and the service of the Government debt.
This is exclusive of the revenues of the Viceroy's private
estates, which are estimated at £E2 million p.a. The liabilities
of the State and *Dairas* amount to £E31,321,000 and the
service of the funded debt to £E3,230,000 . . . It may reasonably be supposed that the 1864 loan was contracted for the
purpose of liquidating the floating debt contracted by Said
Pasha. The proceeds of the railway loan were applied to the
improvement and extension of the railways, and the 1868 loan
was contracted for the purpose of reducing the very large
amount of Treasury bonds then in circulation and to reduce the
exorbitant rate of discount at which government bonds were at
that time negotiated . . . It is impossible to doubt that large
sums have been wasted in unnecessary extravagance . . .
Egyptian Government expenses on behalf of the Suez Canal
Company alone have amounted to nearly £E8 million . . . The
Cretan expedition cost £E1 million. Large sums have been
spent on public works for agriculture which will eventually
prove productive. 800 miles of railway have been opened; the
cultivated land has been increased by about 300,000 acres.
There have been great improvements in Cairo and Alexandria
and a graving dock has been constructed at Suez.' Stanton
added that about £E2 million was said to have been spent in
Constantinople to obtain the 1866 and 1867 Firmans. 'Not-
withstanding the heavy amount at which the Egyptian debt
stands, the finances will shortly be relieved. In 1872 the
Medjidieh Bonds will be liquidated,[37] and in 1874 the railway
loan will be paid off. In 1879 the 1864 loan will be liquidated
and the Halim Pasha loan . . . By 1882 all the *Daira* loans will
have been redeemed and the annual payments on account of the
funded debt reduced from £E3,230,500 to £E1,217,383 p.a.'
Stanton went on to tell Clarendon that it was almost impossible
to obtain an exact statement of the other liabilities of the
Egyptian Government, i.e. the floating debt, but estimated
outstanding Treasury bonds at £E4/£E5 million 'of which
£E3 million are at long date issued before the 1868 loan and
the rest recently issued at 3/12 months'. Stanton summed up as
follows: 'The financial position does not appear to be such as
to warrant the apprehensions expressed by the Porte. The

State burden is undoubtedly heavy and taxation has been largely increased during the last few years but . . . the extra-ordinary expenses forced on the Government during the same period have been excessive . . . In proportion as the foreign debts are redeemed corresponding reductions may be made in taxation; at present, out of a total revenue of £E9,500,000,[38] £E3,230,595 is required for debt service, and £E3,250,200 for the expenses of administration, leaving over £E3 million to meet the Khedive's private expenditure, the gradual absorp-tion of the floating debt &c. This balance should be amply sufficient, but the expenses this year will greatly exceed revenue and the expenditure for the opening of the Suez Canal will amount to about £E2 million.' Stanton concluded by esti-mating the total Egyptian debt at £E31,321,049, made up of:

State debt	£E21,644,900
Daira debt	5,035,040
Medjidieh Bonds	141,109
Outstanding Treasury bonds from 3 months to 3 years	5,500,000
Total	£E31,321,049[39]

This report seems to have satisfied HMG (or rather the bondholders) for the time being. But, a few months later, they expressed anxiety about the Bishoffsheim *Daira* loan after Stanton had told them that 'the ostensible and avowed object of the loan is to enable HH to establish several new sugar factories in Upper Egypt; it being clearly demonstrated that the cultivation and manufacture of sugar is profitable. It is argued that the loan is purely a private matter and that the 1868 contract is not infringed but . . . considering the very close connection between HH's public and private revenues, the Khedive was at least morally bound not to contract a new loan even for his private account.'[40] HMG, obviously briefed by the bondholders, replied; 'The effect in England is highly prejudicial to the Khedive, having regard to HH's engagement not to contract further public loans for five years, and those British subjects who lent money on the faith of that engagement are now both irritated and alarmed, as they cannot draw any dis-tinction between the public revenues of Egypt and the private revenues of the Khedive.'[41]

It may be that the real cause of HMG's and the bondholders' irritation was that the loan had been managed not by any of the established banking houses in which there was a British interest, but by interlopers in the shape of the Banque Franco-Egyptienne. At all events, there was no British objection to the improvident conditions of the *Muqabala*, which were reported without comment by the acting British Consul-General[42] and received without reply by HMG. This complaisance was in spite of the fact that, as early as the autumn of 1870, Stanton had reported that the Egyptian Government had arranged with the Oppenheims to borrow £1.5 million in London at 12 per cent to provide for the payment of foreign loan coupons falling due in October, November and December, and that the rate of discount on Egyptian Government Treasury bonds had risen to between 15 per cent and 18 per cent according to the length of the bonds. HMG's reaction to this information was to instruct Stanton to warn Ismail against 'engaging in any financial arrangement inconsistent with the Firmans of the Porte'.[43]

The next serious official warning which HMG received about the deteriorating state of Egyptian finances was given to them by the Hon H. C. Vivian, who acted as Consul-General in the summer of 1873 during Stanton's absence on leave. Writing just after the floating of the 1873 loan, he told them about 'the financial position of Egypt as connected with the new loan issued at $84\frac{1}{2}$ and its reception in foreign markets, which is said not to be very flattering'. He referred to an article in the *Economist* newspaper appearing on 3 July which stated that Egypt was on the verge of bankruptcy, listed Egypt's debts as amounting to £63 million – made up of £19 million funded debt, £28 million floating debt, and £15.5 million *Daira* debt – and expressed the opinion that Egypt's continued solvency depended on a funding of floating debt obligations on which she was paying interest at the rate of 12 per cent. Vivian went on: 'The annual charge on the debt is estimated at £6.3 million and the revenue at £7,312,000. Deducting the Viceroy's debt in consideration of his income not being included in the revenue,[44] we reduce the debt to £48 million with an annual charge of £4.8 million which, with the addition of the tribute, which amounts to about £0.5 million,[45] leaves a margin of about £2 million for the expenses of government.' He added

that Sherif Pasha, the Foreign Minister, estimated the debt at
£50 million, the debt service at £5 million, and the revenue
at £7 million, and that the Government contemplated measures
for increasing the revenue considerably. 'I should not be
surprised,' commented Vivian, 'if the Viceroy made the first
use of the powers granted to him by the new Firman to make
some alteration in the customs dues, probably an equalisation
in the import and export dues, which now stand at 8 per cent
and 1 per cent. It is evident that things cannot go on as they
are, and that if the Viceroy's Government continues to borrow
at the present rate, a crash must inevitably come. The Viceroy's
personal expenditure is most extravagant and I suspect that the
annual tribute to the Porte by no means represents the drain
on his resources at Constantinople.'[46]

A few days later Vivian told HMG that the peasants in
Upper Egypt were reported to be starving because their lands
had been taken from them and their labour remained unpaid.[47]
In October he reported that there had been a crisis in the local
money market 'arising from the scarcity of coin and the
difficulty of obtaining the liquidation of bonds and other
Government securities, the value of which has much depreciated.
The crisis has arisen partly from the Government's having
recently and suddenly sent £½ million out of the country to
meet bonds falling due abroad and partly to unsound speculation . . . If the country could be cleansed of men who, with a
nominal or inadequate capital, speculate heavily in paper and
on the heavy interest they exact from the Viceroy and his
Government on advances to meet their pressing necessities, it
might provide a healthier system of credit, while it would
certainly be of great advantage to the Government, which
would no longer be encouraged to mortgage such securities as
they can offer at a ruinous loss and add to the already heavy
floating debt . . . The Government are straining their credit
beyond what it will legitimately bear and, failing to obtain
funds on moderate terms, they are obliged to have recourse to
ruinous expedients.'[48]

A week later, Vivian told HMG: 'Every available source of
credit is claimed by the Government, including the second half
of the new loan, which has not yet been floated, and of which
the success is very doubtful. The Viceroy's *Daira* is not in the
budget, although it is notoriously mixed up with the Govern-

ment accounts, and it is the *Daira* bonds which are at such a heavy discount.' He drew attention to the fact that the Viceroy drew £½ million a year from the State revenues 'beyond what he receives from his present estates' and remarked that his only idea of economy consisted in the sacking of junior employees. He concluded: 'Egyptian Government credit is now pledged to the utmost limit, almost every available source is mortgaged, and great financial embarrassment can only be avoided by wise and economical administration, by the abandonment of all extravagant projects, and by the paying off of present debts and releasing the securities of the country before any fresh loan is incurred.'[49]

None of this seems to have had much effect on HMG. They were not yet interested in purchasing the Egyptian Government's Suez Canal Company Ordinary shareholding, although the possibility of this had been suggested by Ismail to Stanton as early as 1870. (The India Office had been in favour, but the Foreign Office was uninterested.) When, towards the end of 1875, these shares were purchased by HMG for £4 million, thus enabling the Egyptian Government to meet the foreign debt coupons falling due at the end of the year, they were purchased, not to help the Egyptian Treasury or the bondholders, but as a 'defensive investment' to prevent the possibility of their being acquired by French interests.

At the time of the purchase of the shares HMG were, of course, well aware of the state of Egyptian finances. Their attitude, at the time of the Khedive's request for financial experts, was that the prime necessity was to ensure effective control of revenue and expenditure. Ismail's idea was that the two British experts asked for should be employed by and under the control of the Egyptian Government – that is to say, himself. HMG considered that this would not ensure effective control and that, in the interest of the bondholders, supervision should be exercised by British experts responsible to themselves. That was the thinking behind the appointment of the Cave Mission, and the point at issue during the complicated negotiations which followed. The Khedive had always been anxious to employ foreign experts in all his Departments of State, but had always insisted that they should be responsible to himself and not take orders from or report to their own governments. The British and French Governments had tended to regard such experts as being, at least in part, agents of their own governments and that, if their work was to be effective, they had to be protected from pressures which the despotic tendencies of the Khedive would otherwise impose on them. This could be interpreted as a desire to use these experts as a means of imposing British or French policies. Ismail did so regard it, and his replacement of French by American officers as instructors in 1870 was due partly to a desire to divest himself of this political pressure. (It was also due to a departure of some of the French officers owing to the demands of the Franco-Prussian war.) In spite of HMG's assurance that the Cave Mission 'must not be taken to imply any desire to interfere in the internal affairs of Egypt', Ismail was well aware of the dangers involved in his request to HMG, which was made as part of the dangerous game of playing England off against France and so avoiding the interference of both in Egypt's affairs.

As far as England was concerned, this interference was mostly being manifested over Ismail's expansionist designs in the Sudan and in the Horn of Africa. As far as the French were concerned, it was being manifested in the affairs of the Suez Canal Company, in the French resistance to the Egyptian Government proposals to set up 'mixed courts' with the object of putting an end to the virtual legal immunity enjoyed by European foreigners in Egypt, and in the increasing French pressure for a funding of the floating debt, which was principally held by French nationals and, particularly, by Crédit Foncier, in which the French Government had a direct interest. In 1875 the weight of French interference was the greater of the two, and Ismail wished to exploit the British purchase of the Canal shares and to drive a wedge between British and French interests in Egypt by using British interests to offset French interference. It was a dangerous game and it failed, mainly because the point at issue, which was financial, had become an international one, in which the British and French Governments, instead of acting independently and competitively in accordance with their respective conceptions of their national interests, acted in comparative unison as agents for the creditors of the Egyptian Government, who acknowledged no national allegiance and who were only interested in the security of the money which they had advanced.

Notes

1. Landes, *Bankers and Pashas*, p 209
2. See Marlowe, *The Making of the Suez Canal*, p 211
3. It existed as an independent entity for over sixty years, after which it was taken over by Barclays
4. See *inter alia* Landes, *op cit*, pp 339–40, and Crouchley, *op cit*, p 119
5. See Sabry, *op cit*, p 132, and Landes, *op cit*, p 339. The rate of interest is variously stated by Sabry as 6 per cent and by Landes at 7 per cent
6. Colquhoun-Russell, 16.4.66, FO 78/1925
7. *Daira* was the term used for the administrations of the various royal estates. In Ismail's time there were seven such *Dairas*, of which easily the two largest and most important were the *Daira Khassa* and the *Daira Sanieh*. The other *Dairas* were the *Daira Walida*, for the estates of Ismail's mother, the *Daira della Famiglia*, for general property belonging to various members of the royal family, the *Daira Taufiq*, for the estates of Ismail's eldest son, and two other *Dairas* for the administration of the estates of his younger sons
8. Sabry, *op cit*, pp 133–136
9. Stanton-Clarendon, 24.11.66, FO 78/1926
10. Landes, *op cit*, pp 339–44; McCoan, *Egypt Under Ismail*, pp 64–65
11. Stanton-Clarendon, 18.5.66, FO 78/1925
12. *ibid*, 26.7.66, *ibid*
13. Crouchley, *op cit*, p 275
14. Stanton described the new Assembly as 'to some extent a representative one, although its functions are limited to offering advice to the Government on such questions of internal interest as the Viceroy may think proper to submit to them.' Stanton-Clarendon, 24.11.66, FO 78/1926
15. For details of the loan see Sabry, *op cit*, pp 138–147; Landes, *op cit*, pp 339–340; and McCoan, *Egypt Under Ismail*, pp 75–76
16. See Chapter Eight
17. Crouchley, *op cit*, p 275
18. In 1866 1,011,978 cwt of cotton were exported at an average price of 16 pence (old) per lb; in 1867 934,978 cwt at 11 pence per lb; in 1868 1,185,164 cwt at 12 pence per lb; in 1869 1,054,544 cwt at 14 pence per lb; and in 1870 1,078,873 cwt at 11 pence per lb. Landes, *op cit*, p 332
19. Crouchley, *op cit*, p 275. The 1875 figure was certainly exaggerated, or at all events not maintainable. The details of taxation are taken from pp 109–131 of *Egypt Under Ismail Pasha* by B. Jerrold, who uses information provided in *Mémoire du Comité des Européans du Caire sur la Situation Financière de l'Egypte* compiled in 1878
20. For details of this transaction see Marlowe, *op cit*, pp 248–54
21. Granville-Stanton, 31.3.71, FO 78/2186. Granville had replaced Clarendon as FS on Clarendon's death in 1870
22. Stanton-Granville, 5.10.70 and 6.10.70, FO 78/2140
23. *ibid*, 16.2.71, FO 78/2186
24. *ibid*, 3.5.71, *ibid*
25. *ibid*
26. See memo on land tenure by Moore, Acting British C-G, in FO 78/2186

27. Sabry, *op cit*, pp 155–56
28. Sabry, *op cit*, pp 165–57; McCoan, *op cit*, pp 152–55; Landes, *op cit*, pp 349–50
29. Stanton-Granville, 9.5.73, FO 78/2283
30. Most of this had been acquired by Ismail during the course of his reign
31. The above figures are from Stanton-Derby, 4.12.75, FO 78/2404
32. For a detailed account of this transaction see Marlowe, *op cit*, pp 291–304. The total shareholding, which was believed to be 177,642 shares, was actually 176,602 and the price was reduced accordingly. Nobody seems to know what happened to the odd 1,050 shares
33. Stanton-Derby, 6.11.75, FO 78/2404
34. *ibid*, 27.11.75, *ibid*
35. Derby-Stanton, 6.12.75, FO 78/2403
36. Clarendon-Stanton, 10.9.69, FO 78/2091
37. This refers to the bonds issued by Said in 1862 when he took over the Medjidieh Steamship Company. Said had issued ten-year bonds to the value of £E348,718 at 10 per cent interest; of these £E141,109 were still unredeemed at the time of Stanton's despatch
38. This includes the *Daira* revenues
39. Stanton-Clarendon, 9.10.69 and 78/2093
40. *ibid*, 31.3.70, FO 78/2139
41. Clarendon-Stanton, 13.4.70, FO 78/2138
42. Moore-Granville, 5.9.71, FO 78/2186
43. Granville-Stanton, 28.2.71, FO 78/2186
44. In fact, as Cave discovered later, the Halim Pasha and the Mustafa Pasha loans, plus £3 million of the *Daira* floating debt, had been taken on the charge of the State
45. Actually £0.75 million
46. Vivian-Granville, 2.8.73, FO 78/2284
47. *ibid*, 16.8.73, *ibid*
48. *ibid*, 4.10.73, *ibid*
49. *ibid*, 10.10.73, *ibid*
50. Derby-Stanton, 6.12.75, FO 78/2403

10

The Mixed Courts[1]

THE abuses and inconveniences arising from the anomalous position of foreigners in Egypt became more and more serious as the numbers of foreigners increased. The system, or lack of system, as it existed in 1867, when Nubar began his negotiations with the Powers for the setting up of the Mixed Courts, may be summarised as follows:

Criminal Jurisdiction. The Capitulations treaties provided a) that domiciliary searches of a European's private residence by the local police should be preceded by police advice to the European's consul so as to give the consul the opportunity of being represented at the search; b) that a European national should have the right of consular representation when on trial on a criminal charge before an Ottoman court. During the previous fifty years, in Egypt, these treaty rights had been expanded by usage to provide; a) that domiciliary searches of private residences or business premises owned or occupied by a European national could not take place except in the presence of the European owner's or occupier's consular representative; b) that Europeans on a non-capital criminal charge could only be tried according to their own laws before their own consular courts. As far as British subjects were concerned, there had, at the instance of the British Government, who had shown some uneasiness at the extent of criminal jurisdiction claimed and exercised by British consuls in the Levant, been a slight and temporary reversion to the letter of the Capitulations treaties, applied in Cairo only. As from 1852, British subjects in Cairo charged with causing the death of an Ottoman subject were tried before an Ottoman court in the presence of the British Consul. In all other criminal cases in which a British subject was defendant, a local officer was deputed to try the case jointly with the Consul. Apart from this exception all criminal cases in which a European national was a defendant were tried before the defendant's consular court in accordance with the defendant's national laws. Even the small exception admitted in Cairo, which was said to have 'worked well and harmoniously',[2] was abandoned in 1858, when the British consular courts in the Ottoman Empire were re-organised, with consular judges, and with a Supreme Court at Constantinople which claimed criminal jurisdiction over all British subjects in the Ottoman Empire.

Civil Jurisdiction. A system had grown up in Egypt, based on the legal maxim *Actor sequitur forum rei*, which had no foundation in the Capitulation treaties, by which civil cases between suitors of different nationalities were tried before the defendant's court – the consular court in the case of a European defendant, the Ottoman court in the case of an Ottoman defendant. During Mohamed Ali's reign, in an attempt to meet European objections to pursuing claims before an Ottoman court, 'mixed commercial tribunals', with equal numbers of Egyptian and European judges and an Egyptian President, had been set up in Cairo and Alexandria to try commercial cases in which an Ottoman subject was defendant. These tribunals seem to have worked fairly well for small commercial cases, but Europeans refused to have recourse to them in the very many cases in which either the Egyptian Government or some influential Egyptian magnate was the defendant. Such cases came to be settled either by arbitration or by direct negotiation between plaintiff and defendant. In such negotiations the plaintiff was usually assisted by his consul. Sometimes, particularly in cases where the Egyptian Government was the defendant, strong diplomatic pressure was applied and the case settled on terms unduly, and sometimes scandalously, favourable to the plaintiff. Cases in which the plaintiff was unable to secure strong diplomatic backing were usually not settled at all. In hardly any important case was anything like justice done. The resultant dissatisfaction was felt both by the Egyptian Government, which was frequently forced to pay unjustified indemnities as a result of unscrupulous diplomatic pressure, and by numerous European claimants who, lacking strings to pull with their consulates, or with the Viceroy, could not get their claims adjudicated, let alone settled.

Taxation. The question of taxes payable by foreigners on real property owned by them in Egypt had been a vexed one since foreigners started owning such property during the reign of Mohamed Ali. In theory it was admitted that European foreigners were subject to the same taxes and other services as Ottoman nationals in respect of such property. This theory was subscribed to, as far as British subjects were concerned, by a Protocol signed between Great Britain and Turkey in 1868, accepting the provisions of an Ottoman law of 1856, re-enacted in 1867, which officially permitted foreigners to own real property in the Ottoman dominions and provided that they should be subject to the same taxes and so on as Ottoman subjects in respect of such property. But in practice foreigners' liability to such taxes and so on could only be adjudicated in Egypt by the foreigners' consular court since, in most cases in dispute, the foreigner would be the defendant and the Government the plaintiff. The government were reluctant to take such cases to the consular courts and the consuls were reluctant to try to force their nationals to pay their taxes except as the result of a judgement by their own consular court. In 1874 Stanton told HMG that he had 'instructed HM's Consuls that British subjects should pay the house and other property taxes imposed by the Egyptian Government . . . and that, with regard to other taxes, foreigners have no claim under the Capitulations or other commercial treaties existing between the Porte and the several Powers to exemption from such internal imposts'.[3] But it was one thing for the Consul-General to issue instructions; it was another to get them obeyed. When Nubar represented to Stanton that it was the Consuls' duty to assist the Egyptian Government in forcing their nationals to pay their taxes, Stanton 'declined to assist and explained that, although HMG might acknowledge the right of the Egyptian Government to impose taxes on foreigners, it was for them to take proper measures for their collection . . . In reply to his question as to what steps should be taken in the event of British subjects refusing, I stated that the Consular Court was open to him.'[4]

A number of attempts were made to remedy the chaotic state of affairs which had grown up. First, with regard to criminal jurisdiction. By about 1858 the opportunities for profitable employment, and the virtual immunity from any of the restraints of law, characteristic of life for foreigners in Egypt, had attracted to that country, and particularly to Alexandria, a large number of very undesirable foreigners, many of whom had criminal records in their own countries, who used the immunities they enjoyed in Egypt to run drinking-dens, brothels, smuggling rackets and the like. The Egyptian Government, moved by some of the consuls, who complained about the bad state of public security caused by the activities of this European riff-raff, promulgated police regulations restricting entry of foreigners into Egypt by a passport system, and extending rights of domiciliary search without warning to foreign business establishments. Although these regulations were supported by twelve out of the seventeen consuls-general, they were objected to by most of the foreign merchants. HMG, advised by their law officers, objected that the regulations were not in accordance with the Capitulations treaties.[5] Other foreign governments also objected and, in the event, the police regulations became a dead letter.

In the 1840s HMG had tried to compel consuls-general to abandon the exercise of criminal jurisdiction and revert to the letter of the Capitulations treaties. Later they made an about-turn, caused the abolition of the very limited concessions made in this direction in 1852 and opposed any application of Egyptian police regulations to British subjects. They even objected to the Egyptian Government exercising any control over the entry of British subjects into Egypt, and relied instead on the exercise of the powers of British consuls to deport British subjects. British consuls-general generally took the view that it was their duty to ensure the observance by British subjects of duly promulgated criminal laws, even when these laws were not in accordance with English law. In 1864 Colquhoun had a sharp brush with the British Legal Vice-consul who refused to proceed against a British subject who was defying a press law promulgated by the Egyptian Government by publishing a newspaper containing scurrilous criticisms of the Viceroy. Colquhoun overrode his Vice-Consul and arranged direct with the Egyptian police for this person's press to be closed. Colquhoun's view was that if a British subject could not be punished for breaking an Egyptian law unless his offence was also an offence under English law, he must at least be prevented from breaking the Egyptian law, if necessary by removing him from the country.[6] This was not a view unanimously held by the consuls-general.

In civil matters HMG's view was succinctly expressed in the course of a rebuke sent in 1864 to Reade, the acting Consul-General, who had employed more zeal than discretion in

supporting an alleged British subject who was trying to evade
Egyptian Government regulations over the erection and location
of a steam pump. 'By all international law foreigners are bound
to obey the laws and regulations of the country in which they
reside and they are only entitled to exemptions from the
operation of such regulations when by treaty special privileges
have been accorded to them . . . According to local custom in
Egypt foreigners have been in the habit of obtaining privileges
and exemption which are not accorded in Constantinople or in
other parts of the Turkish dominions, and it may be perfectly
right for a British Agent to maintain for a British subject the
enjoyment of privileges and exemptions granted to other
foreigners, but even this would only give him the right to make
such a claim as a matter of favour.'[7]

What was needed was a judicial system which would command
sufficient confidence to put an end to the practice of consular
intervention in civil disputes. In 1856 the British Consul-
General had proposed that the commercial tribunals should be
strengthened by super-imposing a Court of Appeal 'with power
to hear all civil cases from inferior Courts in which foreigners
are interested'. He went on to suggest that 'the European
judges attached to it should form part of the Consular establishments . . . and the sanction of the European Consul representing
the nationality of the foreigner whose interests are involved
ought to be necessary for the validity of the sentence'.[8] This
suggestion did not appeal to the Egyptian Government and
nothing came of it.

In 1860 Sherif Pasha, Egyptian Foreign Minister, proposed
to the Consuls-General of the five Great Powers the setting-up
of civil tribunals which 'shall take cognisance of all claims
exceeding £E10,000'. The Consuls-General 'agreed to meet
the Government in a spirit of fairness and equity; to most of us,
these claims are a source of great vexation and we shall be too
happy if the burden of them were removed'.[8] Sherif then
submitted to the five Consuls-General a draft proposal which
was distributed by them to their twelve other colleagues. The
proposal provided for a tribunal consisting of a president, two
judges and two assessors nominated by the Viceroy, and one
assessor nominated by the Consul-General of each of the five
Powers signatory to the 1841 Convention. Judgement was to
be by majority of votes with right of appeal to Constantinople.

The proposal met with great opposition from some of the Consuls-General. De Leon, the US Consul-General, 'declined in any way to recognise the project'.[9] Colquhoun, the British Consul-General, was in favour, and recommended the proposal to HMG.[10] There followed some detailed negotiation, during which Sherif Pasha was replaced as Foreign Minister by Zulfiqar Pasha. Nearly a year later, Colquhoun reminded HMG of 'the shameful system adopted by my colleagues of supporting claims against the Government which would not bear being submitted before a proper tribunal' and pointed out that the 'sums paid in satisfaction of such claims would have paid off about a quarter of the Government's indebtedness.' He went on to describe the sort of tribunal which had evolved, on paper, from Sherif's original draft. 'A tribunal for mixed cases in which a European is the plaintiff. Our delegate must be present at every suit, would take care that there was no error in procedure, would have the right to be present at the delibera- tions of the judges and at the drawing up of the sentence, and would remonstrate if law or justice were violated.' He told HMG that he recommended the setting-up of such a tribunal but that 'among my colleagues not more than two would support me. I had hoped that my French colleague would be of my way of thinking . . . but this evening M. Beauval called and said he had consulted his *nationnaux* and that they declared they would not submit to an Egyptian tribunal . . . I believe that the Russian and Dutch Consuls-General concur entirely with me.'[11] In the event, the only result of Sherif's initiative was that the existing commercial tribunals were re-organised and a fixed procedure adopted in accordance with the Ottoman Commercial Code (based on the French Commercial Code) which had been promulgated in Constantinople in 1860. The re-organised tribunals still only tried cases in which an Ottoman subject was the defendant. Other cases continued to be tried in the defendant's consular court.

The first really determined attempt to deal with the chaos of foreign jurisdiction was inaugurated by Nubar Pasha, then Foreign Minister, in 1867. While in Constantinople, in the intervals of negotiating with the Porte for another instalment of Egyptian independence, Nubar produced a project for judicial reform which has been described as 'a diplomatic masterpiece, sound in reasoning, eloquent in expression,

A post-chaise on the road between Cairo and Suez

Boulac, the port for Cairo

Both in the 1840s

A view of Suez

Cairo

Both in the 1840s

scathing in its denunciation of existing evils, unanswerable in its appeal to fundamental principles, prophetic in its foresight of the dangers to be avoided, and adroit to the highest degree in its appeal to the self-interest of those upon whose consent the success of the new program would entirely depend.'[12]

This project, in the form of a proposal made to Ismail and communicated to the principal European governments, started by explaining that it was not based on the Capitulations, which were, in reality, no longer in existence. They had been replaced by 'an arbitrary legislation based on custom and conditioned by the prejudices of the various foreign Agents, a legislation based on more or less abusive precedents which the force of circumstances – diplomatic pressure on the one hand and a desire to facilitate the establishment of foreigners in Egypt on the other – have introduced into Egypt and rendered the government impotent and the population deprived of justice in its relations with foreigners. This state of affairs is of no advantage either to the general interests of the foreign communities or to honest individuals, be they Egyptian or foreign. Both government and consuls are agreed on the principles of reform and disagreement only arises over details . . . The government is harassed by claims which the consuls themselves often describe as scandalous, the people have come to distrust foreigners, and the government, although realising that the presence of foreigners is an essential condition of progress, are obliged to keep them at arms' length. During the last four years, the government has paid Fcs. 72 million in indemnities as a result of consular pressure . . . Almost all the public works contracts given to foreigners have led to claims for indemnities. For more than forty years Europeans have been permitted to own property in Egypt; in theory they hold this property subject to the laws and regulations of the country, and in theory the consuls accept that this is so, but in practice foreigners invoke the Capitulations in order to avoid paying any taxes in respect of this property and, being supported by their consuls, almost invariably succeed in such avoidance.'

Nubar went on to explain the principle behind his project, which was 'the complete separation of justice and administration. In the same way as she has done in her army, in her railways etc., Egypt must introduce foreigners into her Courts in order to train the Egyptian element. Constantinople has

G

introduced Mixed Tribunals of Commerce where all commercial cases between Ottoman subjects and foreigners are tried irrespective of who is the plaintiff and who the defendant. The object should be to extend this system to apply both to civil and criminal suits. The existing commercial tribunals should be taken as a basis on which to build.' He explained that these tribunals only tried suits in which an Ottoman subject was the defendant since the consuls insisted on their own jurisdiction when the defendant was a European national.

After these preliminary remarks, Nubar went on to make his specific proposals:

(i) The conservation of the existing mixed commercial courts in Cairo and Alexandria but, instead of their existing constitution of three Egyptian members and three members chosen by the consuls, he proposed a court of two Egyptian and two foreign judges, with an Egyptian president, all nominated by the Viceroy.

(ii) Civil courts of First Instance in Cairo and Alexandria with two Egyptian and two European judges, all nominated by the Viceroy.

(iii) A Court of Appeal sitting at Alexandria composed of three Egyptian and three foreign judges and an Egyptian president, all nominated by the Viceroy, to which decisions of the courts proposed under (i) and (ii) could be referred.

(iv) After pointing out that the Capitulations did not confer extra-territorial rights in criminal matters, but merely the right of a foreign national to have his consul present when he was being tried before an Ottoman court, and that every government had an indisputable right to apply its criminal laws applied to all the inhabitants of the country, Nubar proposed, in general terms, the setting up of mixed criminal courts in Cairo and Alexandria, with a Court of Appeal sitting in Alexandria. In a later note he added: 'Simple police matters could be tried by a European magistrate appointed by the Civil Tribunal. More serious cases would be tried by a tribunal consisting of three magistrates, of which two would be European, sitting with a jury if the accused opted for one.'[13]

(v) Judges to be appointed for a period of five years and to be irremovable during that period.

(vi) In commercial cases the code of law should be the French Commercial Code as in the commercial tribunals at Constantinople, and in other civil cases, the Code Napoleon.

Nubar's idea was to bring all the European communities in Egypt under Egyptian jurisdiction by offering them guarantees in the form of a European system of law and of a judiciary which, although nominated by the head of State, would be independent of the executive and contain a considerable European element. It aimed at the end of the Capitulations (except in so far as it retained consular jurisdiction in matters of personal status) and justified this by providing Egyptian courts with standards of law and procedure which could reasonably be accepted by Europeans. Implicit in the project was the assumption that the Egyptian ruler and Government would be subject to the law as dispensed by the proposed courts. This was a necessary *quid pro quo* for the substitution of judicial procedure for diplomatic pressure in cases to which the ruler or Government were parties. It has been surmised that one of the attractions of the project from Nubar's point of view was that it would serve to contain Khedivial despotism. One of the things which made European governments and consuls and, still more, Euroean residents, sceptical was that they did not believe that the judiciary would, in practice, be independent of the executive.

It is unlikely that Nubar believed that his project had any chance of being accepted *in toto*. In particular, he seems to have regarded the criminal proposals as expendable. He was to devote the next seven years to negotiations on the basis of his project in Constantinople and in most of the capitals of Europe. Such success as he achieved is, in the words of one writer, 'entitled to be ranked among the foremost diplomatic achievements of modern history'.[14]

HMG's first reaction to the project was moderately favourable. Lord Stanley, the Foreign Minister, wrote: 'The system now in Egypt regarding suits in which foreigners are concerned is as injurious to the interests of all parties as it is certainly without the warrant of any treaty engagements. HMG . . . is perfectly willing . . . to help the Egyptian Government to establish a better system.' As Nubar had remarked, everyone was agreed on the principle of reform; they only disagreed about the details. Stanley went on to suggest that it might be better not to attempt to devise a new code of law but to apply a new form of procedure to the law as it stood. After remarking that HMG had no intention of insisting on the embodiment of the maxims of English law into any system applicable to foreigners as a whole, Stanley continued: 'The basis on which proceedings might be initiated might be the adaptation to altered circumstances of the principles laid down in the Capitulations, the departure from which has led in a great measure to the evils so justly felt . . . The Capitulations did not pretend to deprive the local government of jurisdiction over foreigners in matters, whether criminal or civil, in which they were brought into collision with the laws of the territorial Sovereign. They reserved however a certain right of super-vision which would act as a check on abuses. In process of time however these checks, especially in Egypt, have become the great abuse and by degrees the authority of the local tribunals has been abused and set aside by the encroachment of an extra-territorial jurisdiction. This is the state of affairs which the Egyptian Government desires to remedy, and they cannot be more disposed to make the attempt than HMG are to second them in it.' He concluded by stating that 'although HMG were not inclined to hold out for a jurisdiction to which they had no treaty rights, foreign Powers had a right to expect that any new system should afford ample security to the foreigner that in pleading before an Egyptian tribunal, he will have nothing to apprehend from the venality, the ignorance, or the fanaticism of his judges, that the law is clear, and the procedure well-defined'. He intimated that HMG would be willing to take part in any enquiry with a view to arriving at 'something really practicable rather than desirable in the abstract'.[15] Behind all this benevolent verbiage, it was clear that HMG had no intention of waiving such rights as were conferred by the Capitulations treaties and that they saw reform, not as a replacement of the Capitulations, as Nubar saw it, but as a removal of the abuses which had grown up around the Capitulations.

Stanton, who had at first thought Nubar's project 'too drastic',[16] saw Nubar in Paris in November 1867 and seems to have taken a more favourable view. He agreed that such courts as might be set up should be quite independent of the con-sulates, that they should have the power of executing their own judgements by their own officers without reference to the consulates, and that the Viceroy should nominate the judges. He told Stanley that Nubar agreed that European judges should be in a majority in each court.[17] Stanley minuted his agreement with all this, but prudently added that 'it would be premature to come to any definite conclusion until we hear what the other Powers have to say'. A few weeks later, on the advice of the Law Officers, he told Stanton that HMG would not be willing to consider changing the existing consular jurisdiction in criminal cases.[18]

Any proposed change in the existing system of jurisdiction over foreigners was bound to excite the suspicions of the European communities in Egypt. These were by this time very numerous. The largest was that of the Greeks, which numbered about 35,000.[19] It was generally considered that the Greek Consulates abused the privileges accorded to foreign nationals more scandalously than those of any other foreign Power.[20] But the views of the Greek Government were unlikely to weigh very heavily in the councils of the Powers. The next biggest community was the French, numbering about 18,000. Some of these had influential connections in France and many of them had important interests in Egypt. Most of the public utility concessions were held by French interests; much money was owed by the Khedive and by the Egyptian Government to them, and many of them were employed by the Egyptian Government. They naturally attached great importance to the safeguards and privileges which the *status quo* gave them, and both the French Government and the French Consuls were extremely sensitive to pressure from French interests in Egypt.

The other considerable foreign communities in Egypt were the Italian, numbering about 14,000, and the British and Austrian, numbering about 6,000 each. Most of the foreign trade of Egypt was in British hands and the British merchant community in Alexandria was prosperous and influential. But its members were a good deal less in contractual relationship with the Khedive or the Egyptian Government than were the members of the French community. Nevertheless the British were equally vociferous with the other foreign communities in objecting to the changes proposed by Nubar, although their protests received less attention from HMG.

It was predictable that the French Government would be foremost in opposition to Nubar's project, the more so since M. de Moustier, the French Foreign Minister, had fallen foul of Nubar over the Suez Canal negotiations two years previously, when he had been French Ambassador in Constantinople. Moustier's reaction was to appoint a Commission to study the project. One of the members of the Commission was Outrey, previously French Consul-General in Egypt, who had just been declared *persona non grata* by the Khedive. Nubar was invited to explain his project to the Commission, which started sitting in November 1867. In a memorandum Nubar stated his willingness to concede a majority of European judges in the courts to be set up. He also agreed to merge the proposed commercial and civil Courts of First Instance. He was insistent on the necessity for separating the courts entirely from the consulates, whether in the nomination of judges, or in the execution of judgements, or in the consular representation of parties to the suit. The Commission, which showed itself greatly affronted by Nubar's strictures on existing foreign jurisdiction, recommended that the proposed courts should only be competent to try civil and commercial mixed suits in which an Ottoman subject was the defendant (except for small cases involving hire and rent and cases in which both parties agreed to the jurisdiction of the mixed courts), and that the procedure in all other suits should remain *in statu quo*. Moustier accepted the Commission's recommendations, which were presented to him in December 1867 and, in the course of a number of stormy interviews with Nubar over the next few weeks, made it clear that he would not agree to anything beyond what the Commission recommended. He also refused to agree to participate in an International Commission, which Nubar proposed should be held in Alexandria, except on the basis of the French Commission's recommendations.

Having come up against a brick wall in Paris, Nubar, in May 1868, went to London. He had been encouraged by Stanley's initial reception of his project to hope that HMG would assist him against the French opposition. In this he was disappointed. Stanley, under the influence of the Law Officers, of the permanent officials of the Foreign Office, and of the British community of Alexandria, which had sent him a memorandum protesting against the Nubar project, had been retreating uncertainly towards Moustier's entrenched position. The basis of this position was that the usages which had grown up in Egypt were just as inviolable as the Capitulations treaties themselves and that any new arrangements must conform with both. So, in spite of the views he had initially expressed, Stanley now changed his mind. First he insisted on the maintenance of consular criminal jurisdiction over all British subjects in Egypt. Then, in a despatch written to Lord Lyons, the British Ambassador in Paris, for communication to the French Government, he wrote that there existed in Egypt, in matters of foreign privileges, 'usages so ancient and well-established that they constituted *"droits acquis"* which were to be regarded as sacrosanct as the Capitulations treaties themselves'.[21] He added that not all such usages were to be so regarded and that it would be the business of an International Commission to decide which usages were sacrosanct and which were not. While HMG did not accept all the recommendations of the French Commission, they would agree that they should form the basis for the deliberations of an International Commission.[22]

After Nubar had communicated the result of his negotiations to Ismail, it was decided that he should get the consent of as many of the Capitulatory Powers as possible[23] to nominate representatives to an International Commission at Alexandria, whether the French agreed to attend or not. It was accepted that the recommendations of the French Commission would form the basis of discussion, but it was hoped that these would be regarded as a minimum from which it would be possible to advance. Nubar then visited the Prussian Government in Berlin and the Italian Government in Florence and obtained the agreement of both to send representatives. Ismail, on a visit to Constantinople, through the Russian Ambassador there, obtained a similar agreement from the Russian Government. In December 1868 Moustier was replaced as French Foreign Minister by the Marquis de la Valette. This seemed to remove one of the obstacles in the way and negotiations were resumed in Paris in February 1869. Nubar got on better with Valette than he had with Moustier and, with some assistance from Lesseps (who had agreed to support him over foreign jurisdiction in return for the favours being shown to the Canal Company by the Egyptian Government), got him to agree to send representatives to the Commission on the understanding that the Commission would have no power to decide anything, but only to make recommendations.

At this point the Porte, which had been kept informed of the negotiations from the beginning, started objecting to the whole business on the ground that it was in contravention of the 1841 settlement. But the British and French Governments, which had never raised this objection in their discussions with Nubar, overruled Ottoman objections, the British pointing out that nothing which was contemplated could reasonably be regarded as encroaching on the Sultan's rights. The Porte professed themselves satisfied and the International Commission opened in Cairo in October 1869, when the opening of the Suez Canal was being so extravagantly celebrated.

The members of the Commission consisted of representatives from the five Powers associated with the 1841 settlement – Great Britain, France, Austria (by this time Austria-Hungary), Russia, Prussia (which had now absorbed the North German Confederation), plus Italy (which had achieved national independence since 1841 and absorbed the old States of Tuscany, Sardinia and Naples). The British Government was represented by Colonel Stanton, the Consul-General in Egypt, and Sir Philip Francis, Consular Judge in Constantinople, who had previously been Legal Vice-Consul in Egypt. Their instructions from HMG had been widely drawn. They were not committed to support of the French Commission's, or any other, recommendations and were enjoined not to agree to any proposal which would derogate from the authority of the Porte, and to ensure that British rights under the Capitulations were not infringed, on the basis that these rights consisted not only of the provisions of the treaties themselves but also of such usages which could be regarded as having developed out of the treaties.

Given the attitude of the French delegates, whose instructions were to keep within the recommendations of the French Commission, the findings of the International Commission, which were produced in January 1870, were more favourable to reform than might has been expected. Subject (a) to a majority of European judges in each court, to be nominated by the Viceroy from lists submitted to him by the Governments of the Powers, (b) to three tiers of jurisdiction – First Instance, Appeal and Cassation, (c) to the nomination of two European assessors in commercial cases, and (d) to the appointment of Europeans as principal officers of the courts, it recommended that the proposed courts should be competent (a) to try all civil and commercial suits between Ottoman and European subjects, except suits concerning immovable property, which were to be tried by Ottoman Courts and (b) to appoint magistrates to try contraventions (minor criminal cases) in which Europeans were accused. Civil and commercial cases between Europeans of different nationality were to be reserved for the jurisdiction of the defendant's consular court as before. (Nubar had indicated that he would be willing to transfer the right of the Ottoman courts to try 'mixed' cases concerning immovable property to the proposed courts if the Powers would concede the jurisdiction of the proposed courts in other civil cases between foreigners of different nationality.) Serious criminal cases and matters of personal status were to be reserved to the jurisdiction of the consular courts. The setting up of the proposed courts was to be dependent on the approval by the Powers of a suitable Civil Code. The delegates of four of the Powers – Great Britain, Austria-Hungary, Prussia and Italy – indicated that they would be willing to concede all criminal jurisdiction affecting Europeans to the proposed courts on condition of a suitable criminal code being approved by the Powers. But the French and Russian delegates were opposed to this.

After the Commission had reported, Nubar hurried off to Constantinople and got the Porte to agree to 'a project of organisation for Mixed Courts in Egypt' based on the Commission's recommendations. This project was sent by Ali Pasha, the Grand Vizier, to the governments of the six Powers. The end seemed in sight. But the French Government, moved by furious protests from their nationals in Egypt, appointed yet another commission to examine the new project. This commission, which seems to have been influenced by the advocacy of the Canal Company in favour of the proposed reforms, produced a counter-project, which was closely in accordance with Nubar's new project, except that it recommended the abolition of the proposed Court of Cassation and stipulated that the new system should be regarded as being on trial for the first five years of its operation.

Apart from a proposal by Austria-Hungary that the new courts should have jurisdiction over all civil cases concerning foreigners of different nationality,[24] the other Powers approved the French counter-project in principle. Lord Granville, British Foreign Secretary, told the French Government in July 1970 that the Law Officers, without necessarily agreeing with every

detail, 'consider that it appears to have been drawn up with
very great care and to rest on principles sufficiently in accordance
with European principles of jurisprudence as to authorise HMG
to adopt it as a basis for judicial reforms in Egypt.[25]

At this point, a dispute arose as to the way in which the
Porte should be associated with the proposed reforms. Nubar,
supported by the Austro-Hungarian Government, considered
that the Sultan should give his permission for the setting up of
the Mixed Courts on the basis of the French counter-project
and that the Powers should negotiate the details direct with the
Egyptian Government. The Porte, supported by the British
and French Governments, considered that the details should be
worked out between the Powers and the Porte and that the
Sultan should then authorise the Khedive to put the agreed
scheme into execution. The real point at issue was the extent
of independence which had been conferred on Egypt by the
1867 Firman, and Ismail preferred to delay the implementation
of the reforms rather than defer to the Turkish-British-French
viewpoint. Therefore, in August 1870, on the pretext of minor
objections to the French counter-project expressed by the
Porte, Austria-Hungary and Italy, he told the French Consul-
General that he was abandoning the whole question of judicial
reform for the time being. By this time, war had broken out
between France and Prussia and the French Government had
more pressing matters to pursue.

Negotiations were resumed two years later, in the autumn
of 1872, after France had been defeated by Prussia, after the
death of Ali Pasha, and after Ismail had bribed himself into the
good graces of Sultan Abdul Aziz. Another international commission was convened in Constantinople and, on the basis of
the recommendations made by it, Nubar, in February 1873,
distributed to the six Powers a detailed project for setting up
Mixed Courts in Egypt, on the general basis agreed on in
1870, together with codes of law, based on the Code Napoleon,
which had been drawn up by M. Manoury, a French lawyer
resident in Egypt. This project was accepted by all the six
Powers except France. French approval was given in November
1874, subject to various amendments, and subject to ratification
by the French Chamber.

By this time Nubar, the architect of the reforms, had left the
Egyptian Government, and the conclusion of the matter was

left to Sherif Pasha, the new Foreign Minister. The French Chamber, fighting a rearguard action against the reforms, appointed yet another commission to examine the project. This commission recommended against its adoption but, in the meantime, the Egyptian Government, having been assured of the support of the other Powers (who were a good deal less deferential towards France than they had been before the Franco-Prussian war) went ahead and, on 28 July 1875, formally inaugurated the new Courts. The French Chamber, faced with the *fait accompli*, ratified in December 1875. This ratification was, however, qualified by a declaration from the French Government dated 25 October 1876 which made the following points:

(i) That they did not recognise the right of the Mixed Courts to legalise by their decisions any new taxes applicable to foreigners.

(ii) That they reserved the right of diplomatic intervention to procure the cessation of and/or reparation for acts contrary to treaties or to human rights perpetrated against French nationals by the Egyptian Government or its agents;

(iii) That French Consuls in Egypt would continue to exercise the same jurisdiction as before except in cases specifically transferred to the Mixed Courts by international agreement;

(iv) That the Capitulations treaties, and the usages deriving from them, remained in force in respect of all relations between the Egyptian Government and French nationals except in so far as they had been replaced *à titre d'essai* by the powers of the Mixed Courts.

The first of these qualifications, although unilaterally put forward and without any treaty sanction, was tacitly accepted by the other Capitulatory Powers and meant in effect that, before any new project of law involving taxation could be promulgated in Egypt, it had to be approved by the governments of the fourteen Capitulatory Powers. The second qualification meant that the Mixed Courts were to be regarded, not as a substitute for but as a possible alternative to, diplomatic pressure as a means of settling disputes between the Egyptian Government and foreigners. In short, the French qualifications meant that the Mixed Courts, so far from releasing the Egyptian Government from its previous legislative disabilities vis-a-vis foreigners, actually increased their extent.

But in practice the Mixed Courts, which started operating in February 1876, were an improvement on the previous system. Exaggerated and unjustified claims were cut down to size and justified claims settled more expeditiously. The fears expressed lest the Courts should become subordinate to the will of the Viceroy proved unfounded. Nubar's opposite fears lest the Courts should, through lack of the safeguards with which he had been compelled to dispense, fall under the influence of the consuls, also, on the whole, proved unfounded.

Nevertheless, the Mixed Courts, as inaugurated in 1876, fell far short of the comprehensive system of reform which Nubar had adumbrated in 1867. The Egyptian Government still had virtually no jurisdiction over foreigners in criminal matters, and the previous abuses arising from this immunity continued unchecked, as did the chaotic conditions created by the existence of a multiplicity of jurisdictions in disputes between foreigners of different nationalities. Nubar's ultimate ambition of making the Mixed Courts into a comprehensive system of civil and criminal jurisdiction applicable to all the inhabitants of Egypt remained frustrated.[26]

One important, and extremely undesirable, result of the establishment of the Mixed Courts was the legalisation of the pledging of land as security for loans and its forfeiture against non-payment. Moslem law forbade foreclosure (although this was often got round in various ways), but the establishment of the Mixed Courts resulted in a great deal of agricultural land passing to foreigners as a result of foreclosed mortgages.

The extent of the Mixed Courts' jurisdiction over the acts of the Egyptian Government, as defined in Article II of the *Règlement*, providing that the Courts had jurisdiction over 'acts of administration prejudicing rights acquired by foreigners', was to cause much trouble and confusion. The great question which arose was 'as to how far the Egyptian Government has the power of legislation and whether every law . . . which may affect a foreigner must be accepted by the Governments of the States represented in the Mixed Courts before it can be made applicable to their subjects, or is in fact valid.'[27] Legal opinion was divided, some lawyers holding that the *Règlement* only gave jurisdiction over legislative acts specifically directed towards foreigners and could not cover legislation applicable to all residents of Egypt and only incidentally affecting foreigners.

The official French view was that all financial legislation affecting foreigners, even incidentally, required the consent of all the Capitulatory Powers in order to become valid in its application to foreigners. The German Government, as will be seen, precipitated Ismail's deposition in 1879 by a similar interpretation of a financial decree. The Mixed Court of Appeal upheld the wider interpretation of Article II in one early judgement and later reversed itself. In England the Lord Chancellor of the day accepted the wider interpretation and the Law Officers disagreed with him. Generally, the Powers adopted the interpretation which suited them best at the time.

Notes

1. For official British correspondence covering the negotiations leading up to the inauguration of the Mixed Courts see FO 78/2742–2749
2. Reade-Stanton, 2.11.67, FO 78/1877
3. Stanton-Derby, 15.3.74, FO 78/2342
4. *ibid*, 8.5.74, *ibid*
5. Malmesbury-Green, 30.6.58, FO 78/1401
6. See correspondence in FO 78/1818
7. Russell-Reade, 31.8.64, FO 78/1817
8. Colquhoun-Russell, 25.6.60, FO 78/1522
9. *ibid*, 27.7.60, *ibid*
10. *ibid*, 3.10.60, *ibid*
11. *ibid*, 12.8.61, FO 78/1591
12. Brinton, *The Mixed Courts of Egypt*, pp 13–14
13. Stanton-Stanley, 1.1.68, FO 78/2038
14. Brinton, *op cit*, p 19
15. Stanley-Stanton, 18.10.67, FO 78/1975
16. Stanton-Lyons, 27.3.67, FO 78/1926
17. Stanton-Stanley, 4.11.67, FO 78/1977
18. Stanley-Stanton, 15.1.68, FO 78/2037
19. These and the other figures for foreign communities given below, are taken from Brinton, *op cit*, p 28
20. See *inter alia* Douin, *op cit*, Vol II, p 168
21. This in spite of the fact that none of the usages were more than forty years old
22. Douin, *op cit*, Vol II, pp 224–5
23. The original seventeen Capitulatory Powers had by this time been reduced to fourteen. Naples, Sardinia and Sicily had been merged into Italy, and Prussia had absorbed the North German Federation
24. This was due to domestic political reasons deriving from Hungarian insistence that both Austrian and Hungarian codes be applied in the Austro-Hungarian Consular Courts
25. Douin, *op cit*, Vol II, p 537
26. Such a comprehensive scheme was outlined by Nubar at the International Commission in Cairo, but it was rejected almost without discussion
27. Malet-Granville, 19.12.81, FO 141/144

11

The Reckoning

IN his letter of appointment to Mr Cave Lord Derby told him:
'Although the primary object of your mission will be to confer
with the Khedive upon the subject of the advice and assistance
for which HH has applied, you cannot fail to obtain incidentally
much information of the greatest value both to Egypt and to
this country . . . HMG do not consider it necessary to give you
detailed instructions as they prefer to leave the conduct of the
mission to your discretion, relying on you to be careful not to
pledge them to any course of proceeding, by advice or otherwise, which might be taken to imply a desire to interfere unduly
with the internal affairs of Egypt.'[1]

Ismail's object in asking for the mission was quite clear. He
wanted to excite French jealousy of Great Britain, and *vice
versa*, in order to obtain, either from French or British sources,
or from both, the financial assistance which he urgently needed
without submitting to any diminution of his independence or to
any real control over his finances. His financial needs were
becoming desperate. Immediately, he required a few millions
of short-term money in order to meet maturing Treasury
bonds; ultimately he needed to consolidate his floating and to
convert his funded debt so as to release some of the revenues
which had been allocated to the existing debt service and, by
this means, to clear the way for another long-term loan.

Cave and his party arrived in Egypt on 17 December. The
Khedive lost no time in making it clear to him 'that it was
utterly out of his power to permit any official enquiry into the
finances of Egypt', as such an enquiry 'would be virtually
allowing foreign intervention in the affairs of the country. He
could not suppose that HMG had any such intention, but if the
enquiry contemplated by Mr Cave were carried out, it would
be out of his power to refuse similar facilities for an enquiry
from any other Power, and thus an international commission on

his finances would be instituted. The Porte would also probably follow their example and his administrative autonomy would be at an end.' Ismail went on to explain that, when the two financial experts for whom he had asked should arrive, 'every detail of the State's receipts and expenditure would be at their disposal, as he had no desire to hide anything, but these gentlemen would be employees of his Government and not in the service of any foreign State'.[2] Cave eventually satisfied the Khedive that he had come, not for the purpose of any official enquiry but to obtain a general picture of the financial situation, and the Khedive agreed to provide such general information as he might require.[3]

Having settled this point to his satisfaction, Ismail, determined to try to use Cave as a means of getting financial support from the British Government, proceeded to let him know about various schemes he had in train for obtaining money from other sources. He told him that Lesseps had offered to find him a loan of £2 million at 9 per cent on the security of his Suez Canal Company Preference shares (entitling the Egyptian Government to 15 per cent of the net profits of the Company). There was another scheme for mortgaging these Preference shares against a £2 million loan at 8 per cent, a scheme for leasing the railways for thirty years for £1,250,000 a year, the telegraphs for a similar period for £50,000 a year, and the tobacco Customs for £300,000 a year.[4] A third scheme concerning the Preference shares was said to have been put forward by Baron Hirsch who had offered to lend him £2 million on their security at 5 per cent. Sir George Elliot, MP for Durham and contractor for the Alexandria harbour works then in progress, was interested in leasing the railway and harbour. Outrey, previously French Consul-General in Egypt, was on the point of arriving on behalf of a Paris syndicate to bid for a lease of the railways and to arrange for a loan.

Cave duly reported all this to HMG and, as Ismail had no doubt intended, suggested that they might assist in raising a loan to pay off the floating debt. 'The present financial position of Egypt allows of effective financial assistance being given, but, if its resources are too heavily mortgaged, relief will come too late. Here is an opportunity of real support which may not occur again. The Viceroy may arrange his affairs soon without England's assistance and may thus tide over his difficulties. But

he would then carry on his former expenditure without our
being able to check it. If HMG obtain for him easier terms now,
they will acquire a right to proper control which will ensure
the stability of the revenue.'[6]

Cave's original idea had been that a British-sponsored loan
might be secured on the railway revenues, but he soon discovered that these were already pledged to the service of the
1873 loan. Ten days later, he suggested that HMG might
support 'a more comprehensive operation'. After pointing out
that 'the immediate financial pressure arises from HH's inability
to take up the bonds of the unfunded floating debt now falling
due at short intervals and estimated by HH at £12 million',
and that 'without the means of meeting the floating debt a very
serious crisis must take place which would be fatal to the
interests of the bondholders', he proposed a scheme which
involved devoting the proceeds of the *Muqabala* to the service
of the 1864 loan and the 1866 and 1867 *Daira* loans, and
reducing the principal of the other funded loans by 20 per cent
from £44 to £35 million, adding £12 million floating debt,
and converting it into £48 million new stock at 6 per cent
repayable over fourteen years at an estimated annual charge of
£5,116,128.[7] A week later, he informed HMG of a similar
refunding scheme which had been suggested to Ismail by Sir
George Elliot and which involved the compulsory conversion
of the funded debt at existing market prices. Cave told HMG
that he thought well of this suggestion, which Ismail had
expressed his readiness to accept, and asked them to approve
either his or Elliot's scheme as 'the pressure on the Khedive
required an early solution which would prevent him entertaining
offers affording immediate relief but involving far more serious
embarrassments later'.[8]

HMG would have nothing to do with either of these schemes.
Lord Tenterden, the Permanent Under-Secretary at the Foreign
Office, minuted that both schemes amounted to a partial
repudiation and that he could 'foresee pretty plain the sort of
tumult that would storm the Foreign Office if HMG advise the
Khedive to accept even partial repudiation. I do not mean to
say that either scheme may not be a very good one, or question
the right of Mr Cave to advise HH to adopt one of them, but
for HMG to advise him to do so is another matter.'[9] Derby
agreed with Tenterden and Cave was told that 'HMG cannot

express any opinion on the Khedive's proposed plans or incur any responsibility in connection with them.'[10] Derby was also getting alarmed at the extent to which Cave appeared to be exceeding his instructions and, on 26 January, had cabled him to return home as soon as possible.[11] In reply Cave, protesting that his recall would have an adverse effect on Egyptian credit, stressed that he had not committed HMG in any way. Derby did not insist and Cave stayed on in Egypt for another three weeks.

Meanwhile, events had been moving in other directions. On 5 January Nubar had again resigned his post as Foreign Minister and had been replaced by Sherif. After a few weeks he was again to leave Egypt. Ever since his return and re-assumption of the Foreign Ministry only a few weeks before, he had been on bad terms with Ismail. In a meeting with the Cave mission soon after their arrival he had openly criticised the Khedive's financial policies, his abuse of the *corvée*, and the administration of his estates.[12] To other people, he had criticised the Khedive's action in accepting the Cave mission and, through his friend Jules Pastré of the Anglo-Egyptian Bank, was instrumental in arranging with the French Government to send M. Outrey to Egypt on a financial mission to off-set the Cave mission. Ismail took umbrage at this, since he had declared Outrey *persona non grata* a few years previously, when he had been Consul-General in Egypt. He told Cave that he had dismissed Nubar from the Ministry of Commerce (a post usually combined with that of Foreign Minister) because of it, and that Nubar had resigned the Foreign Ministry as well, realising that he had lost the confidence of his master.[13] (The probable real reason for Nubar's disgrace was that Ismail was coming to realise the implications of the Mixed Courts regime, designed by Nubar, which provided that the Egyptian Government and his own *Dairas* were subject to the jurisdiction of, and could be sued in, these courts, thus cutting at the roots of his absolute authority.)

Ismail's first reaction on hearing of Outrey's mission was that he would not have the man in the country. But he could not afford to be particular. He had to have money and by the end of January it was apparent, not only that he was unlikely to get it as a result of the Cave mission, but that the existence of the mission had lessened his chances of obtaining it from elsewhere.[14]

The French Government had viewed the Cave mission with

the gravest suspicion. The French Ambassador in London had told Derby that his Government were seriously concerned at what appeared to be 'a financial intervention by the British Government in the domestic administration of Egypt which amounted to an infringement of Egyptian independence'.[15] He was unimpressed by Derby's denials. Moreover, the French Government was worried about the large Crédit Foncier holding of Egyptian Treasury bonds. The British purchase of the Canal shares had defeated Crédit Foncier's plans for funding these bonds on the security of the Canal shares and it was more urgent than ever to try to make some other arrangement. Plans were already afoot in connection with the Preference shares, which were later pledged to the Crédit Foncier as part security for a £5 million loan.

In view of these considerations the French Government welcomed Nubar's suggestion, made at the end of December, that a French mission should be sent to Egypt to discuss both an immediate short-term loan to provide for the Treasury bonds then maturing, and a long-term arrangement providing for a consolidation of the funded and floating debt. And when Ismail realised that there was nothing to be hoped for from the British Government, he reconciled himself to dealing with Outrey and with Pastré, who had been authorised by Crédit Foncier to make some arrangements for the greater security of the floating debt.

At the beginning of February, Ismail, in a last attempt to use the Cave mission to prop up his collapsing credit, proposed to Stanton that HMG should make a public announcement in which Cave would be quoted as expressing confidence in the state of Egyptian finances.[16] This proposal was made to Stanton without Cave's knowledge or approval and HMG turned it down indignantly. Tenterden minuted that it was 'an outrageous proposition by which the Khedive deliberately puts words into Cave's mouth and then asks us to publish them in order to assist him in raising money'. Derby agreed and Stanton was told that 'HMG could not undertake to comply with the Khedive's request and trusts that HH will not again advert to the matter.'[17]

By this time Ismail was already in negotiation with Pastré and with Outrey, who had arrived in Egypt in the middle of January. On 28 January Cave reported that the Khedive was trying to arrange a loan of £14 million at 9 per cent 'furnished by French contractors'.[18] This proved a false alarm but, on 1 February, Cave cabled that the Khedive would now only require one, and not two, financial experts from England.[19] In a letter he explained what had happened. On his pressing the Khedive for more information about the functions of the British experts asked for, Ismail explained that 'negotiations were on foot on the one hand with Sir George Elliot and on the other hand with the French for an immediate advance of £2½ million. It depended on which of the two would come forward. If Elliot found the money, the unification scheme [the scheme proposed by Elliot for the conversion of the funded debt] would go on and the new Department would be created, but that it was now contemplated under that arrangement to appoint a French member of the Control Department, so that HH proposed . . . to ask HMG to nominate only one official.' When Cave pressed him about the duties of this official, the Khedive told him that 'the whole business had aroused so much foreign comment that he simply wanted an official to act as financial adviser without executive duties'.[20]

After receiving Cave's cable of 1 February, and before receiving this rather confusing explanation, HMG, who had clearly lost much of their confidence in Cave's judgement, advised Stanton that they recommended 'Mr C. Rivers Wilson as a gentleman to assist in the re-organisation of the Egyptian Department of Finance.' They explained that 'Mr Wilson now holds the office of Controller of the Public Debt,' and pointed out that, if he were to take office under the Khedive, he would have to give up 'that important and lucrative appointment' and suggested that it would be best for Wilson to go out to Egypt and 'make his own enquiries as to the position which he is to hold'.[21]

It seems likely that HMG, despairing of getting any coherent information from Cave, and anxious about the rumours reaching them (*inter alia* from Rothschilds) of Outrey's activities, arranged for Rivers Wilson to go to Egypt, not with any serious intention of taking office under the Khedive, but in order to 'spy out the land' and see what Outrey and his associates were up to. Throughout his visit to Egypt Wilson was in correspondence with Stafford Northcote, the Chancellor of the Exchequer and his official chief, and with Rothschilds, with whom he was in close touch as a result of his duties as Controller of the National Debt. Rothschilds, with HMG's knowledge, were considering making an offer to Ismail in competition with the offers then being made by Outrey and his associates, and one of Wilson's functions was to act as intermediary.

During March, while Rivers Wilson was on his way to Egypt, HMG were urging the Khedive not to commit himself to French interests before Wilson arrived, since they had 'reason to know that proposals are under consideration by English financiers which may lead to a satisfactory settlement of his affairs'.[22] Stanton was also told to inform the Khedive unofficially that an invitation to a French official to assist in the reorganisation of Egyptian finances would 'lead to Wilson's recall and prove an impediment to an arrangement which might otherwise be possible'.[23]

The French negotiations, which had brought about the attempted combination between HMG and Rothschilds, had been going on in Cairo since the middle of January. The first French proposal was for the establishment of a National Bank which would collect the revenue and manage the service of the debt; and would fund the floating debt at 6 per cent interest, repayable over thirty years, and secured on such revenues as were not already mortgaged – the *octrois*, the Upper Egypt railway and the Alexandria port dues – and on the Suez Canal Preference shares. A condition of this arrangement was that a French financial adviser should be appointed to counter-balance the English one, and it was provided that the Bank should be placed under the management of three Commissioners appointed by the British, French and Italian Governments respectively. This arrangement was commended by the French Government to HMG.[24] But HMG, after receiving details from Stanton, rejected it. 'HMG cannot send a Commissioner to take part in the management of a Bank. If a workable plan to receive revenue and apply it to the payment of debt were proposed we would give it our consideration.'[25] We have already seen their reaction to the appointment of a French financial adviser. This adviser, M. Villet, arrived in Egypt in the middle of March and brought with him a proposal, backed by the French Government, substituting the proposed National Bank by a *'caisse d'amortisation'* administered by four international Commissioners who would act as receivers and distributors of the 'affected'[26] portions of the revenue after the consolidation and re-funding of the debt on the lines then under negotiation.

This negotiation was carried on without any information being given to HMG, either by the French or by the Egyptian Governments. They heard what was going on indirectly, through reports from Stanton, through the newspapers and, probably, through Rothschilds. (Wilson had not yet arrived in Cairo and Cave had left.) They rather querulously asked Stanton to find out what the proposed '*Commission de la Dette*' was all about, whether French and Italian Commissioners had been appointed, and what arrangements, if any, had been made for the unification and conversion of the debt.[27]

Meanwhile, Cave had returned to England and written his report, which was dated 22 March but not published until 3 April. The delay in publication was due to a misunderstanding with the Khedive which was to have unfortunate repercussions on Egyptian credit. On 20 March Derby cabled Stanton that Cave's report was finished, that its contents were, in substance, already known to the Khedive, and that 'we think it desirable to lay it before Parliament at once and believe that it will have a good effect'.[28] Ismail immediately objected on the ground that the report was based on information supplied to Cave confidentially.[29] On 23 March Disraeli, the Prime Minister, told the House of Commons that the report would not be published because of the Khedive's objections.[30] This announcement tended to confirm the fears being expressed about the state of Egyptian finances and the price of Egyptian 1873 loan stock fell from 63 to 51.[31] On 25 March Derby cabled Stanton that 'the refusal of the Khedive to consent to the publication of the Cave report is injuring his credit in this country. It would be much wiser for him to withdraw his opposition.'[32] The Khedive did so and the report was published on 3 April. Its contents were, on the whole, fairly reassuring. But they did not repair the damage done by Ismail's original objection to its publication and by Disraeli's announcement of this objection in Parliament.[33] On 6 April, three days after the publication of the report, the Egyptian Government issued a decree announcing that, pending financial arrangements for a settlement of the debt, the payment of obligations falling due in April and May would be postponed for three months, subject to payment of 7 per cent interest for the period of delay.[34]

The Cave report[35] opened by stating: 'The Viceroy has attempted to carry out with a limited revenue, in the course of a few years, works which ought to have been spread over a far longer period and which would tax the resources of far richer Exchequers.' It made some reference to waste and extravagance, but commented that 'probably nothing in Egypt has even approached the profligate expenditure which characterised the commencement of the railway system in England'. He described the Egyptian system of agriculture, irrigation and land tenure, characterised Ismail's expenditure as unproductive, and criticised the improvidence of the *Muqabala*. He estimated the current annual revenue at £10,698,070,[36] but pointed out that of this £1,531,118 consisted of *Muqabala* receipts, which were only temporary and would eventually, according to the Law of the *Muqabala*, involve a substantial reduction in the proceeds of the *miri*. He gave State expenditure as £9,080,681 a year, of which £5,036,675 was devoted to debt service. He made it clear, which had not been done before, that the *Daira* loans of 1866 and 1867, as well as £3 million of the *Daira* floating debt, 'had been taken over by the State for value received'. He described the considerable material progress made during Ismail's reign and stated that its results would probably lead to a small but steady increase in the future revenue. He gave details of the various foreign loans and the arrangements made for servicing them. 'None of these loans costs less than 12 per cent p.a., while some cost $13\frac{1}{4}$ per cent and the railway loan 26.9 per cent including sinking fund.' Dealing with the *Muqabala*, Cave stated that, in return for proceeds which the Government estimated at £26,365,878 by the time the twelve-year annuities had been paid by 1885, the Government had surrendered in perpetuity $£2\frac{1}{2}$ million a year in revenue. Commenting on the figures furnished by the Egyptian Government covering receipts and expenditure during Ismail's reign (see pp. 112–13), Cave commented: 'The sum raised in revenue is little less than that spent in administration, tribute and works of unquestionable utility. For the present large amount of indebtedness there is absolutely nothing to show but the Suez Canal, the whole product of the loans and floating debt having been absorbed in the payment of interest and sinking fund with the exception of the sums debited to the Suez Canal.'

With regard to the immediate future, Cave had this to say; 'The immediate pressure arises from the Khedive's inability to take up the bonds of his unfunded floating debt now falling due at short intervals and estimated by HH at £18,243,076 at least.[37] This unfortunate position is due in great measure to the onerous conditions of the 1873 loan.' After illustrating this statement, Cave went on to suggest a plan of consolidation and re-funding. This proposed that the 1862, 1868, 1870 and 1873 loans, plus State floating debt of £18 million, plus *Daira* debt of £3 million, should be funded in a new consolidated loan of £72 million at 7 per cent interest and repayable over fifty years. He estimated that the cost of conversion would be £4,473,000. He proposed that the shorter-dated loans should be serviced out of the proceeds of the *Muqabala* and that £4 million a year should be set aside for administration, including a Civil List for the Khedive. On the estimated revenue of £10,689,000 a year Cave concluded that the servicing of such a plan would be practicable, but that 'an essential condition . . . is that the Khedive should place a person who would command general confidence, such as the financial agent sent out by HMG to take employment under HH at the head of a Control Department which would receive from the tax-collector certain branches of revenue to be defined, but including land tax and *Muqabala*, and should have a general supervision of the incidence and levying of taxes'. The report concluded: 'Egypt is well able to bear the charge of the whole of her indebtedness at a reasonable rate of interest, but she cannot go on renewing floating debts at 25 per cent and raising fresh loans at 12 per cent and 13 per cent to meet these additions to her debt and which do not bring in a single piastre to her Exchequer.'

As we have seen, the publication of the Cave report was followed almost immediately by the announcement of a three months' moratorium. For some two months previously, maturing Treasury bonds had only been met with the assistance of Outrey and his associates, who had advanced Ismail about £5 million at 14 per cent interest on the understanding that this amount would be included, on favourable terms, in the re-funding arrangement they were negotiating with him. The moratorium was declared on the advice of Rivers Wilson, who regarded it as less ruinous than continuing to borrow money on such terms.

Ismail still seems to have been anxious to extricate himself from the French by making an arrangement with Rothschilds and, on 15 April, handed to Stanton two draft decrees, one of which provided for a settlement of the debt on the lines proposed in the Cave report, and the other for the setting-up of a *Caisse de la Dette* with European Commissioners for the receipt and distribution of the revenues 'affected' to the debt.[38] The intention was that Rothschilds should finance and manage the re-funding. HMG expressed a guarded approval of the plan and told the Khedive that 'in the event of his being able to obtain the means necessary for carrying it through', they would 'have much pleasure in assisting him by recommending a Commissioner'. They asked for more details and for an assurance that the Canal share annuities would be included in the consolidation.[39] Further than this HMG would not go, and Rothschilds would not touch the re-funding as Ismail would not agree to the amount of control on which they insisted.

Since he could get no help from HMG or from Rothschilds, Ismail was compelled to make the best terms he could with Outrey and his associates. He gave details of these terms to Stanton on 25 April and had them published in two decrees dated 2 and 7 May. The first of these provided for the setting-up of a *Caisse de la Dette* to be administered by French, British, Austrian and Italian Commissioners on the lines communicated to Stanton ten days before. The second decree provided for the conversion of the whole funded and floating debt,[40] calculated at a total of £91 million, into a Consolidated Debt bearing interest at 7 per cent and repayable over sixty-five years. The principal features of this scheme of consolidation were: (i) The 1862, 1868, 1870 and 1873 loans were converted at par; (ii) The 1864, 1866 and 1867 loans were converted at 95; (iii) The floating debt was converted at 80, the holders thus receiving a bonus of 25 per cent; (iv) The *Muqabala* was cancelled. Of the £11,758,140 said to have been paid, £5,469,188 was to be deducted for alleged arrears of tax, £1 million was to be included in the Consolidated Debt, and the balance repaid over sixty-five years at 7 per cent interest; (v) The service of the debt was fixed at £6,443,600 a year, of which £5,790,845 was to come out of State revenues and £684,411 out of the *Daira* revenues. A group of French capitalists was to manage the conversion. Certain specific revenues, estimated to produce enough to service the debt, were 'affected' for the purpose and were to be paid direct to the *Caisse*.[41]

HMG were not impressed. They enquired how the total debt, which had been estimated by Cave at some £76½ million a few weeks before, had increased to £91 million. It was explained that the difference was due to £3 million which had been borrowed since; to a loan of £5 million advanced by the loan contractors on which a bonus of £2,740,000 had been provided; and to a bonus of £6,440,000 to the holders of the floating debt in consideration of their obligations being converted from short to long term. HMG expressed regret that 'HH has not been able to induce the leading houses of Europe to act for him,' and that 'he had not thought fit to adopt Mr Cave's recommendations for dealing with the debt'. They were disturbed at the apparent increase in the debt and were not reassured by the explanations given. 'A large part of the admitted increase is due to a bonus to the holders of the floating debt – a concession to equity which is, to say the least, doubtful. On the other hand, the holders of the short loans are treated unjustly. Furthermore, it appears that a new loan is in contemplation, the charge for which is beyond all reason onerous.'[42] It was pointed out that the abrogation of the *Muqabala* would involve compensation charges equivalent to an increase of nearly £12 million in the debt, the alternative being a breach of faith. In conclusion, HMG stated; 'They sincerely hope that the scheme which HH has adopted may lead to an improvement in the administration of his finances but it will not be within their power to accept the responsibility in which the nomination of a Commissioner would involve them.'[43]

Rivers Wilson expressed his disapproval of the scheme. He thought that it placed a heavy burden on the Egyptian taxpayer and that it was unduly generous to the floating debtholders. He told Northcote, the Chancellor of the Exchequer, that he would act as a Commissioner for a limited period if HMG nominated him, and if he were appointed President, but that otherwise he would prefer to return to England as 'considering that French influence is paramount, it is high improbable that any acceptable offer would be made to me'.[44] In the event, although Ismail offered him the Presidency of the *Caisse*, Northcote told him that his remaining in Egypt would cause misunderstanding unless he resigned from British Government service, and he returned to his Controllership of the Public Debt.[45] But, as we shall see, he was not yet finished with Egypt.

French, Austrian and Italian Commissioners were nominated by their respective governments and appointed by the Khedive, and the *Caisse de la Dette* was officially inaugurated on 10 June 1876. A Supreme Council of the Treasury consisting of an Italian President and five Egyptian and five European members was set up with undefined duties of supervising the finances. But the new arrangement was doomed before it got off the ground. There was no real control over revenue and expenditure since the powers of the *Caisse* were confined to the distribution of such sums as the Egyptian Treasury chose to put at its disposal. The annual debt service, based on an exaggerated estimate of the revenue, was impossibly onerous. There was nothing to stop creditors who had not been included in the settlement from suing the government or the *Dairas* in the newly set up Mixed Courts. HMG, the British bondholders, and various powerful international banking interests, including Rothschilds, Fruhling & Goschen and the Oppenheims, disapproved.

Ismail told Charles Cookson,[46] the acting British Consul-General, that 'it was not until he had lost all hope of effecting the conversion of the debt by the agency of a great European financial house that pressing necessity had led him to accept the proposals of the French group'.[47] He continued to keep his lines open with HMG. He appointed Acton, a British official at the Ministry of Commerce, to the 'Supreme Council of the Treasury'.[48] He obviously expected that before long HMG would step in to redress the imbalance created by French dominance, and he hoped by this means to reduce the burden of the debt without having to accept any too onerous system of control. To some extent, his hopes and expectations were justified.

The cancellation of the *Muqabala* proved so unpopular with Egyptian landowners that the Egyptian Government decided that it would have to be restored. This, in itself, would have involved a radical revision of the French settlement. Then, the Egyptian Government were confronted with a judgement by the Court of Appeal of the Mixed Courts which, if maintained, would knock the bottom out of the whole settlement. In April judgement had been given in the Court of First Instance against the *Daira* in respect of a bill which had fallen due and remained unpaid, and the bill was ordered to be paid forthwith against threat of execution on the *Daira's* property. Subsequently, the bill formed part of the floating debt which had been consolidated according to the terms of the decree of 7 May. After the promulgation of the decree the Court of Appeal upheld the judgement of the Court of First Instance on the ground that the *Règlement Judicaire* of the Mixed Courts provided that they had jurisdiction over 'acts of administration which prejudice rights acquired by a foreigner'. This meant that a foreigner could challenge in the Mixed Courts any 'administrative act' affecting foreigners promulgated by the Egyptian Government after the inauguration of the Mixed Courts.

Following on the Court of Appeal's judgement, Cookson warned HMG that 'several such actions are being brought against the *Daira*, which cannot fail to cause serious inconvenience and may produce a collision between the Administration and the Courts, which cannot fail to be very prejudicial to the success of the new jurisdiction'.[49] A few weeks later, he reported that 'over fifty sentences involving thousands have been given against the *Daira* and the government. By an understanding with the plaintiffs no steps have been taken to execute the sentences until recently. But now the question has come to a serious crisis.'[50] He went on to describe how an attempt had been made to levy execution on the treasure-chest of the Governor of Alexandria and how this had been successfully resisted by order of the government. A few days later an attempt was made to levy execution on the contents of Ramle Palace in Alexandria in satisfaction of a judgement for £3,000 against the *Daira*. 'The Court of Appeal,' reported Cookson, 'appears to acquiesce in the defiance of its authority.'[51] A public protest by one of the foreign judges in the Court of First Instance was not supported by his colleagues.

Meanwhile, HMG had referred the matter to their Law Officers, who expressed the opinion that the decree of 7 May, although 'a breach of the compact entered into with the Powers who were consenting parties to the establishment of the new Tribunals' had 'taken away the plaintiffs' right of action and the judgements against the Khedive were wrong.'[52] The Lord Chancellor disagreed with the Law Officers and held that the Court of Appeal was right. HMG addressed a circular to all the Capitulatory Powers suggesting that 'it is most desirable that the Powers who joined in setting up the Courts should unite in addressing a joint protest at the action of the Khedive and his Government, which is weakening the position of his judges and destroying the efficiency of the Courts'.[53] There followed a long correspondence with these Powers and the receipt of a reasoned memorandum from the Egyptian Government. In October, the Hon. H. C. Vivian, who had taken over as British Agent and Consul-General in Egypt, told HMG that the Mixed Courts had postponed all suits against the Egyptian Government and *Daira* until 7 November 'to give the Viceroy time to negotiate an amicable arrangement with his creditors and to learn the views of the European Governments about the powers of the Courts'. He urged that these views should be communicated to the Consuls-General before 7 November.[54] By this time there were 222 suits pending against the Government and *Daira* involving amounts of nearly half-a-million sterling.

Meanwhile, in August 1876, Mr (later Lord) Goschen, a partner in the banking house of Fruhling and Goschen, and a member of the previous Liberal administration in England, undertook 'to represent the interest of the [British] holders of Egyptian stock with a view to obtaining some modification of the late decree by the Khedive, which has affected the position of the holders of the funded debt'.[55] Vivian was instructed to 'give such unofficial assistance as you can to Mr Goschen' and authorised to inform the Khedive that 'Mr Goschen was a member of the late Cabinet and is a person of high reputation and position in the country'.[56]

Goschen went to Paris at the end of August and conferred with M. Joubert, the representative of the French creditors. They produced a draft plan which secured the backing of the French Government. In September, Baron des Michels, the new French Consul-General in Egypt, recommended Ismail to invite Messrs Goschen and Joubert to Cairo. On Ismail's remarking that the Mixed Court judgement had upset the French arrangement anyway, des Michels pointed out that his Government would insist on the decree of 7 May being put into operation unless it was varied as the result of an agreement with Messrs Goschen and Joubert. Vivian, quoting Ismail's version of des Michels' communication to him, commented: 'It seems impossible to reconcile the contradiction between the purpose of forcing the Egyptian Government to carry out the financial decree unaltered with the intention of HMG to maintain the decision of the Courts, and an invitation to Mr Goschen seems useless if the two Governments are united in compelling HH to carry out his financial decree.'[57]

HMG who then and afterwards dissociated themselves from any official responsibility for the Goschen-Joubert mission, apparently left Goschen, who arrived in Egypt with Joubert in mid-October, to explain the apparent contradiction to Vivian. What was happening was, in fact, obvious and Vivian could not have been unaware of it. With the French Government insisting on the fulfilment of the French-sponsored settlement of 7 May, and the British Government upholding the judgment of the Court of Appeal, Ismail was to be subjected to converging pressures in order to compel him to agree to a revised settlement agreed on between Goschen and Joubert and approved, officially by the French, and unofficially by the British, Governments. HMG's attitude towards the Court of Appeal judgment was dictated, not by any legal consideration, but by a determination to wreck the French settlement of 7 May and compel the French Government to agree to a revision of this settlement which Ismail would then be compelled to accept.

After some negotiation in Cairo, a revised proposal, which was 'leaked' to Reuters and published in Europe, was presented by Messrs Goschen and Joubert to the Khedive on 3 November. It provided: (i) For the separation of the Consolidated Debt from the *Daira* debt, which would be the subject of a separate arrangement; (ii) For the reduction of the bonus on the floating debt from 25 per cent to 10 per cent; (iii) For the extinction of £15 million of Consolidated Debt by the issue of 5 per cent railway debentures for the same amount. A Railway Commission consisting of two Englishmen and one Frenchman was to be set up to manage the railways;[58] (iv) For the re-establishment of the *Muqabala* and the application of its proceeds to the 'short' loans.

This proposal reduced the Consolidated Debt from £91 million to £59 million, which was to be funded at 7 per cent, of which 1 per cent, together with the balance of the *Muqabala* proceeds, would be put into a sinking fund until 1885 to reduce the debt to £40 million, after which the full 7 per cent would be paid to the bondholders. (The point was that, assuming the continuance of the *Muqabala*, the revenue could be expected to fall after 1885 by the amount of the *miri* remissions provided for in the *Muqabala*; it was therefore desirable to reduce the capital of the debt after that date.) An English Commissioner was to be appointed to the *Caisse* and English and French Controllers-General to supervise revenues and expenditure respectively. As in the 7 May settlement, certain specific sources of revenue were 'affected' to the service of the debt and were to be paid direct into the *Caisse*.

The service of the funded debt under this proposal would amount to about £5,480,000 a year, exclusive of the *Daira* debt, which was to be the subject of a separate arrangement. It was slightly less onerous than the original French settlement but, like that settlement, it was based on an exaggerated estimate of Egypt's maintainable revenue. For this, the Egyptian Government were to blame, as they had provided the figures and refused to allow any investigation into them.

The man behind the Khedive in this refusal was Ismail Sadiq, Minister of Finance since 1868, known as the Mufattish, and feared and hated throughout the country as a result of the heavy taxation he had exacted on behalf of his master. (He had also managed to become very rich himself.) Goschen and Joubert, holding the Mufattish responsible for the financial confusion, refused to treat with him and 'informed the Khedive of the false accounts, glaring discrepancies and evident suppression of revenue which, with still more disgraceful scandals, their searching enquiries had disclosed'.[59] Possibly guided by Vivian, they took the view that the real obstacle to a proper control of the finances, and to an honest implementation of an agreed settlement, was not Ismail himself but the Mufattish. In this they were wrong. But Ismail was not unwilling to listen to, and to act upon, complaints about his Finance Minister. He had to have a settlement and regain the confidence of the Powers. Also, in view of the increasing discontent in the country at the heavy incidence of taxation,[60] he may have found it convenient to transfer the resulting unpopularity from himself to the Mufattish. In effect, there seems to have been a tacit bargain between the Khedive on one side and Goschen and Joubert on the other that the Mufattish must be got rid of as an essential condition for a settlement.

On 9 December, after the Goschen-Joubert proposal had been presented to the Khedive, and before he had accepted it, the Mufattish was arrested on a charge of conspiracy against the Khedive. What happened afterwards has always remained a mystery. The official account was that he was tried by a special court, sentenced to exile in Dongola, and shipped there by Nile forthwith. Some weeks later it was announced that he had died in Dongola from the effects of over-drinking. It was generally believed that he had been murdered in Gezira Palace by Ismail's orders soon after his arrest.[61]

The Mufattish was succeeded as Finance Minister by Husain Pasha, the Khedive's second son,[62] who was more or less of a puppet. On 14 November the Goschen-Joubert proposals were officially accepted by the Khedive, subject to a few minor amendments. The operation of the sinking fund was limited to provide a sum of £4,200,000 a year for administration. The issue of railway debentures was increased from £15 million to £17 million in exchange for £2 million worth of Consolidated debt which was to be surrendered to the Khedive to enable him to raise money to pay the contractors for the Alexandria harbour works.[63] It was arranged that execution of judgements against the *Daira* should be postponed to enable an arrangement to be worked out for a settlement of the *Daira* debts. It was stipulated that the British and French Controllers-General should have the power of appointing and dismissing tax-collectors in the provinces, and that no more loans should be raised except with their consent and that of the *Caisse*. The settlement was promulgated in a decree dated 18 November 1876.

The effect of the Goschen-Joubert settlement was to create three stocks: (i) £59 million worth of 7 per cent Unified Stock with half-yearly coupons amounting to about £2 million payable on 15 January and 15 July; (ii) £17 million worth of Privileged Stock with half-yearly coupons amounting to about £450,000 due on 15 April and 15 October; (ii) About £4 million worth of 7 per cent Short-term Stock with half-yearly coupons amounting to about £250,000 plus 2 per cent for sinking fund due on 1 April and 1 October. This involved an allocation of about £5½ million a year for the service of the funded debt, excluding the *Daira* debt. Later, it was arranged as a temporary measure that the third half-yearly Unified

Shepheard's Hotel in about 1850

'Disgorging': a drawing for a cartoon by Tenniel

coupon due in April 1878 should be met in two instalments, the first in anticipation on 1 November 1877 and the second in arrear due on 1 May 1878.

European officials were already arriving in Egypt in anticipation of the settlement. On 4 November Mr Romaine arrived as the English Controller of Revenue designate, accompanied by General Marriott, Chief Commissioner designate of the railways. Later, Captain Evelyn Baring (afterwards Lord Cromer), previously secretary to the Viceroy of India and a member of the banking family, was appointed British Commissioner of the Caisse, arriving in Egypt in March 1877. Another Englishman, Mr Scrivener, was appointed Director-General of Customs. These British officials were nominated, not by HMG but by Goschen on behalf of the English bondholders, and were appointed by the Khedive. HMG, on being advised of the nominations, stated that they 'accepted no responsibility but had no objection'.[64] Goschen had previously suggested that HMG might nominate officials in return for the Suez Canal annuities being included in the funding scheme, but this offer had been declined. The French officials were nominated by the French Government. There was some difficulty about the French Controller-General. The French Government wished to nominate de Blignières, the French Debt Commissioner. But Ismail objected to him personally and Baron de Malaret was appointed instead, de Blignières remaining at the *Caisse*.

Goschen was not very optimistic about the working of the settlement. On his return from Egypt in December he told Derby that 'he thought Ismail would repudiate if he got the chance' and that 'there was reason to believe that he was holding back funds which he had in hand'. He urged that HMG should 'express their satisfaction at the arrangement which has been come to between HH and his creditors and their hope that he would keep to it'. Derby told Vivian that 'it would not be desirable that HMG should be committed to an opinion of a scheme to which the Khedive has given his approval, but it cannot be otherwise than a matter of satisfaction that the efforts of Messrs Goschen and Joubert should have resulted in an arrangement between HH and his creditors acceptable to the parties concerned. They can feel no doubt that HH will be actuated by an honourable desire to fulfil the engagements which he has contracted, and they trust that, in the interests of

H

Egypt, which would be gravely compromised by any failure in this respect, he will persevere in doing so, whatever difficulties in detail he may have.'[65]

Early in 1877 Goschen returned to Egypt to negotiate a settlement of the *Daira* debt. This took some time, but an agreement was eventually arrived at in July 1877. The total debt was agreed at £9 million. The supervision of the *Dairas* was entrusted to two Controllers, one nominated by Goschen, the other by Joubert. £450,000 a year, being the estimated minimum income of the *Dairas*, plus £250,000 a year from the Khedive's Civil List, was allocated for the service of the debt at 5 per cent, of which 1 per cent was allocated to a sinking fund. Any income in excess of £450,000 a year from the *Dairas* was to be paid over to the Khedive.

This settlement only concerned the *Daira Khassa* and the *Daira Sanieh*, which administered about 485,000 *feddans* out of the total royal estates of between 900,000 and 1,000,000 *feddans*. The other royal *Dairas* were left under the Khedive's control. The settlement also assumed the correctness of the Khedive's official Civil List of £390,000 a year. In fact, the total sum estimated to be drawn by the Khedive and his family from public funds was about £700,000 a year.[66]

Another category of debt, not included in the funding arrangements, was the amount owing on current account by the Treasury and *Dairas* for commercial supplies and services. These were found by a Commission appointed for the purpose to amount to some £3½ million, of which about 1¾ million was owing to Europeans. After a good deal of delay, and some pressure from the Consuls-General on behalf of the European creditors, the Egyptian Government produced a scheme for paying the European creditors over the next three-and-a-half years in negotiable bonds bearing 5 per cent interest, provided that the *Caisse* and the Controllers agreed that such an arrangement was in accordance with the Goschen-Joubert settlement, which stipulated that no further loan should be raised without the consent of the *Caisse* and Controllers. Vivian, after remarking that the arrangement provided for paying all European creditors first, pointed out that 'the whole value of the proposal depends on the real existence of the resources pledged, which are said to come from "unpaid arrears of taxes".' He expressed doubts as to whether these really existed.[67] In the event nothing came of the proposal, and in August 1877 Vivian warned Sherif, the Foreign Minister, that the waiting creditors 'would certainly fall back on their indisputable right to attack the Government before the Tribunals'.[68] By the end of August, all foreign commercial houses were refusing supplies to the Government except against cash on delivery, and some of the claims against the Government were 'being hawked about for sale at 50 per cent discount'.[69]

By this time it was becoming apparent that the Goschen-Joubert settlement was unworkable. The normal financial embarrassments of the Egyptian Government had been increased by the outbreak of war between Turkey and Russia in April 1877. In January, when the prospect of war was imminent, and when it appeared probable that the Sultan[70] would call upon the Khedive for assistance, Vivian had suggested that 'the financial position of Egypt, the limited allowance apportioned for the administration of the country, and the solemn engagement contracted by the Viceroy not to exceed it, forbids him from incurring any further expenditure in reinforcing the contingent that Egypt has already sent'.[71] After war had broken out the French and Russian Consuls-General advised the Khedive to ignore any request from the Porte for military assistance and warned him of the possibility of a Russian blockade if he tried to send such assistance. Vivian was told 'carefully to avoid joining any pressure which may be attempted to be put on the Khedive with reference to the amount of assistance he shall send to the Porte'.[72]

Ismail, realising that he would get no support from HMG in a refusal to send assistance to the Sultan, and realising that, in the light of the British attitude, the Russian blockade threat was nugatory, told Constantinople that 'within the limits of possibility and with due regard to financial engagements Egypt will furnish all the assistance she can afford'.[73] In fact, Ismail supplied Turkey with 25,000 troops and was continually being asked for more. Vivian warned HMG of the effect of this assistance on Egypt's finances. 'The drain of so large a body of reinforcements must seriously cripple the country, but in view of Your Lordship's instructions I have not thought it right to make any remonstrance.'[74] A few days later he told Derby that the additional reinforcements being sent 'would not improbably be incompatible with the maintenance of the

Khedive's financial engagements', and that 'the financial position of the Egyptian Government was sufficiently serious before the war broke out, but the increasing military expenditure . . . is rapidly adding to the difficulties and eating up the country's resources'.

While HMG were, in effect, encouraging Ismail to send assistance to Turkey, the European Controllers were objecting to the war taxes imposed, and Vivian was objecting to a 10 per cent 'war surcharge' on port dues at Alexandria.

Apart from the war expenses, the European controls instituted by Goschen and Joubert were not working well. Vivian complained that the salaries of the European officials, which were between £2,000 and £3,000 a year, added to the cost without increasing the efficiency of administration. He had told Ismail in October 1876 that he 'doubted whether the appointment of Englishmen at high salaries in subordinate positions where they had no real power of re-organisation or reform' was the best guarantee for financial amelioration.[75] He was not enthusiastic about some of the British officials appointed. He particularly complained of the incapacity of Romaine, the British Controller of Revenue, who, he told Derby, was put in the shade by his French colleague, Baron de Malaret, who 'with the tact of an old diplomat knows how to profit by daily access to the Khedive and has become his financial adviser in all matters'.[76] He told Derby that the salaries of the European officials amounted to £33,500 a year, of which £15,000 a year was drawn by British officials, but that in spite of this expensive form of 'control', receipts from the 'affected' portions of the revenue had decreased and that it was only as a result of taxes being collected in advance that the coupons on the funded debt were being paid on due dates. HMG's only comment on all this was that they were 'in no way responsible for the salaries of the gentlemen recently appointed to positions in the civil administration'.[77]

The shortfall in the 'affected' revenue was partly because of systematic 'milking' between the taxpayer and the *Caisse*. But it was mainly because the service of the debt had been fixed at a figure which was beyond Egypt's reasonable capacity to pay. Vivian, who had been in favour of the settlement, soon came to see this. In July, he told Derby that the Controllers had not succeeded 'in checking to any great extent the abuses and extortion that prevail in the provinces' and doubted if they could tell 'whether the legal taxes and only these are honestly collected and paid over', or whether 'the country is taxed beyond its means'. He thought 'it is just as important that they [the Controllers] should protect the peasantry as the bond-holders and prevent the killing of the goose that lays the golden eggs'.[78] He warned HMG that 'great mischief may be done both to the country and to our own reputation as taking a leading part among the European advisers, by the perpetuation of abuses and oppression under the shelter of their authority, and unfriendly critics are not wanting to call attention to their shortcomings'. A few days later, when telling Derby that the money for meeting the July coupon on the Unified debt had been paid into the *Caisse*, he wrote that 'this result may have been achieved at the expense of ruinous sacrifices by the peasantry, through forced sales of growing crops and collecting taxes in advance, while the native employees' pay is heavily in arrears'.[79] He expressed the fear lest 'the European advisers may be unconsciously sanctioning the utter ruin of the peasantry, the creators of the wealth of the country, for which, as the English element is predominant, we are incurring a serious responsibility'.

At the end of July Vivian told HMG that an analysis of the revenue receipts had led him to the conclusion that the Goschen-Joubert settlement was unworkable.[80] He attributed a falling-off of customs revenue partly to 'the smuggling which is being carried out on a large scale by Europeans, who are protected by the Capitulations, or rather by the abuses of the Capitulations which have crept in here . . . It seems to me most unjust that, while we have our grip on the throat of Egypt and are exacting from her the uttermost farthing of her debts, we should allow her to be cheated of a great proportion of the revenue honestly hers, which might have been used to pay them.'

In September 1877 Ismail, who, in the days when he had been looking for loans, had persistently exaggerated the amount and buoyancy of Egypt's revenues and who now showed an equally persistent pessimism, told Vivian that the Goschen-Joubert settlement must be revised but that it was for the Controllers to take the intiative in proposing this. Vivian reported that Ismail was not exaggerating the position and that the expenses of the war and a low Nile had brought on a crisis somewhat

H*

earlier than expected. The Commissioners of the *Caisse* thought that 'a thorough and searching enquiry must now be held into the real state of affairs with a view probably to some modification of the 18 November Decree. Captain Baring thinks that it should be conducted by a Commission composed of the two Controllers and the French and English Commissioners of the *Caisse*. The Khedive thinks that the Controllers alone should do it. The investigation, if held, should go into the question of reducing expenditure as well as increasing revenue; it should suggest means of acquiring a stronger control in the provinces over the collection and payment of taxes and protecting the *fellah* from arbitrary and illegal taxation, the expediency of changing the dates of the coupons to coincide with the harvests, and should further devise a practical mode of dealing with the large mass of floating debt.'

This 'large mass of floating debt' consisted of those Government and *Daira* debts which had not been funded under the Goschen-Joubert settlement. These were estimated at about £11.5 million, of which some £7.2 million was secured by various assets, and £4.3 million unsecured. A number of judgments for the recovery of these debts had been obtained from the Mixed Courts, but had not been executed. This non-execution was causing great dissatisfaction to the creditors affected, and introduced a note of urgency into the situation as far as the British and French Governments were concerned. The funded debt, and the secured part of the floating debt, were held mainly by British and French nationals.[81] The unsecured part of the floating debt was owed mainly to Italian, Austrian and German nationals whose governments were beginning to get restive at the non-execution of the Mixed Courts judgments and at the concentration of payments on the funded debt coupons. Unless this situation were relieved it seemed likely that these governments would no longer be content to leave the management of Egyptian affairs to Great Britain and France. It was therefore an Anglo-French interest to devise some means of satisfying the floating debtholders, if possible without prejudice to the secured bondholders.[82]

Towards the end of 1877 Baring, the English Commissioner of the *Caisse*, produced a plan for raising a loan of £11.5 million at 5 per cent, to be guaranteed by the British and French Governments, for paying off the whole of the secured and unsecured floating debt (in which he included £½ million arrears of pay to Government officials and the army). He calculated that, with proper control, and by a drastic reduction in the estimated £700,000 a year which the Khedive took from the revenue for his private purposes, it would be possible to keep administrative expenses down to an annual £3.5 million and provide for the service of the whole debt, including the new loan.

HMG refused to consider guaranteeing a loan. But, in view of the pressure of the floating debt, and the increasing difficulty and hardship involved in providing for the service of the funded debt, it was becoming urgently necessary to do something. And there was a growing consensus of opinion among Egypt's creditors that that 'something' must involve a far stricter control over the Khedive than anything which had yet been contemplated. (This consensus was probably assisted by the exiled Nubar who was busy telling tales in London and Paris about Ismail and his methods.) Over the next eighteen months an intricate battle of wits and wills was waged between Ismail and his creditors, in which the latter tried to establish and the former to evade the imposition of some effective form of financial investigation and control. Ismail was beaten in the end. But he put up a good fight, using every desperate expedient to which he could put his hand. Appreciating that HMG were less interested in Egypt's creditors than in Egypt's strategic position as a staging-post on the route to India, he tried to placate them by the appointment of British officials, by co-operation over anti-slavery measures, and by subservience to British interests in the Red Sea and Central Africa. He exploited local rivalries between British and French officials. He played upon the divergent interests of the funded bondholders and the floating debtholders. He used the pretensions of the Mixed Courts judges against those of the Consuls-General and vice versa. He sowed the seeds of dissension between the Controllers and the Commissioners of the Caisse. He invoked the help of distinguished Europeans such as Gordon and Lesseps who, for different reasons, were sympathetic to him. He sought the aid of the Porte against European interference; he invoked the indignation of the rich against European proposals to increase their taxes; he encouraged the discontent of army officers against the European-imposed reduction of army establishments; he played with nascent Egyptian nationalism and traditional Moslem fanaticism in order to arouse indignation against European methods. He tried to transfer from himself to the European officials the odium for all the misfortunes from which the country was suffering. It was a virtuoso performance, a classic example of the ingenuity of a bankrupt in keeping his creditors at bay.

The first stage of the struggle was fought over the terms of reference and membership of the Commission of Enquiry which most of those concerned now agreed to be necessary.[83] The Commissioners of the *Caisse*, supported by the British and French Consuls-General, insisted that the enquiry must investigate expenditure as well as revenue and that the Commissioners must take part. The Khedive insisted that the enquiry should confine itself to establishing the maintainable revenue and that the Commissioners of the *Caisse* should be excluded from it. The British and French Governments were both reluctant to put pressure on Ismail. HMG still wanted to keep more or less aloof. The French Government, appreciating that any enquiry would probably result in a scaling-down of the amounts due to creditors, and suspecting that Ismail still had some undisclosed assets up his sleeve, were not keen on having an enquiry at all. Eventually, HMG's reluctance was overcome by Vivian's warning that, if matters were allowed to go on as they were, other Powers might intervene on behalf of the judgment creditors.[84]

As in the case of the Goschen-Joubert settlement, Ismail was eventually brought to heel as a result of converging pressures applied to him by the British and French Governments acting more or less in concert. Vivian was instructed, on the one hand, to join with the other Consuls-General in a protest against the non-execution of Mixed Courts judgements against the Government and *Daira*. On the other hand, he was told 'to act in concert with your French colleague to support the claims of the bondholders that they should be adequately represented on the Commission of Enquiry and to say that HMG think that the enquiry should be full and comprehensive, that Captain Baring should be a Commissioner and that, if a second British Commissioner were required, they would be prepared to nominate Mr Rivers Wilson'.[85]

As usual, when Britain and France were united, Ismail gave

way. After a little further haggling, a decree promulgating the Commission of Enquiry was issued on 27 March 1878. Lesseps was named as President, Rivers Wilson as first Vice-President, and Riaz Pasha, a respected Turco-Egyptian statesman, as second Vice-President. The other four members were the four Commissioners of the *Caisse*. It was understood that Lesseps would take no part in the detailed work of the Commission and that the *de facto* President would be Rivers Wilson. This seems to have been regarded hopefully by Ismail who, from his dealings with Rivers Wilson in 1876, was inclined to regard him as an ally. He was soon undeceived.

During the course of Nubar's tale-bearing in London and Paris, he had seen much of Rivers Wilson, who was advising HMG on Egyptian financial affairs. He impressed him with various undesirable aspects of Ismail's behaviour and convinced him that Ismail's absolute power was the major obstacle against any reform and that the solution lay in compelling him to resign his authority into the hands of a constitutional Ministry composed partly of Europeans.[86] In particular Nubar gave Wilson details of the oppressive methods by which Ismail's estates had been acquired and were being cultivated, and reminded him that the *Daira Khassa* and *Daira Sanieh* estates, the incomes from which were pledged under the Goschen-Joubert settlement, only represented about half the total Khedivial landholding. He also reminded him that the other half represented about the only remaining free asset which might be pledged as security for any additional loan to pay off the floating debtholders.

The terms of reference of the Commission, as laid down in the decree of 27 March, provided that their investigations '*porteront sur tous les éléments de la situation financière en tenant compte des droits legitimes du gouvernment . . . Les Ministres et fonctionnaires devront fournir directement à la Commission sur sa demande et dans le plus bref delai tous les renseignments que leur seront demandés.*'

Vivian reported that des Michels and de Blignières were 'so fully imbued with the idea that the Khedive is defrauding his creditors, and so anxious to show that the country can pay all that it is engaged to pay, that it is difficult to make them look at the question from any other point of view'. He believed that they were 'so bitterly prejudiced against the Khedive that they were incapable of doing him justice'. He described his own view, and Baring's, as being that, 'although they do not want to see the bondholders defrauded, neither do they want to see the *fellahs* oppressed and that, in any new arrangement, the welfare of Egypt, as well as that of its foreign creditors, is to be considered'.[87]

Point was given to Vivian's estimate of these contrasting viewpoints when the payment of the 'intercalary' coupon of the Unified Debt, amounting to about £1 million, came up. By agreement with the *Caisse*, the half-yearly Unified April coupon had been split into two, the first half, which had already been paid, falling due by anticipation the previous November, and the second half, in arrear, on 1 May. On 13 April Vivian reported that 'there is a great divergence of opinion among my colleagues as to the treatment of the various classes of debt. My French colleague holds that the next (Unified) coupon should be paid before anything else . . . and his Government endorses this opinion. My German, Austrian and Italian colleagues will not admit that the necessity for paying the next coupon can be pleaded as an excuse for not settling with the judgment creditors, while the Khedive will avoid as long as he can paying either. The instructions sent to the Austrian and Italian Consuls-General authorise them to threaten to hold the Khedive personally responsible for the execution of the sentences of the Tribunals.' Vivian also referred to the arrears of pay due to Government employees, 'many of whom are literally starving'. 'The situation is full of difficulties . . . On the one hand the non-payment of the coupon would be a breach of contract and would involve bankruptcy; on the other hand the strong official support which is being given to the judgment creditors and the urgent necessities of the Government employees may compel the Khedive to prefer their claims to those of the bondholders'. He told HMG that the French Consul-General had asked him for his support in insisting that the 1 May coupon be paid, and asked for instructions.[88] Two days later Vivian cabled that payment of the May coupon 'would absorb every available resource of the Government and leave nothing to pay the tribute which we are instructed officially to demand[89] or arrears of pay to Government clerks who are in great distress. I contemplate that the payment of the coupon will certainly produce disastrous effects, but I doubt if I can do more than warn the Viceroy of its very serious consequences, leaving to him the entire responsibility of deciding how to act.'[90] HMG's reply was sent by Lord Salisbury, who had just taken over the Foreign Office from Lord Derby. After stating that the French Government had told him that 'there is every reason to believe the Khedive can pay the coupon of the Unified Debt which falls due in May if he chooses to do so' and that 'the institution of the Commission of Enquiry ought not to be made a pretext for postponing the payment of his debts in so far as he is in a position to do so', the instruction went on; 'M. Waddington, having expressed a desire that you should act with your French colleague in urging this view, I sent you a telegram this morning authorising you to do so. At the same time I impressed on you the necessity that you should, in carrying out the above instructions, bear in mind that HMG consider that the payment of the tribute and the interest on the English shares of the Canal Company are obligations of a more binding character than any other and that they have a special interest in their practical fulfilment.'[90]

According to Lord Cromer who, as Major Baring, was the English Commissioner of the *Caisse*, 'the Commissioners . . . were of opinion that it would have been better not to pay the coupon . . . We were aware that the money could not be paid without taking the taxes in advance, a course to which we were opposed as being oppressive to the peasantry and also contrary to the true interests of the bondholders. Not only therefore did we abstain from putting any pressure on the Khedive to pay, but we even discussed the desirability of protesting against payment.' Commenting on HMG's insistence on payment, he wrote that they 'became in a certain degree responsible for the oppression which necessarily accompanied the collection of the taxes'. Discussing the reason for HMG's departure from their general policy that 'British subjects who invested their money in a foreign country must do so at their own risk', he recorded his opinion; 'There was evidently some special reason for so brusque a departure from the principles heretofore adopted. The reason is not far to seek. The Berlin Congress was then about to sit . . . Egyptian interests had to give way to broader diplomatic considerations. It was necessary to conciliate the French.'[91]

Vivian, disconcerted by his instructions, replied to Salisbury;

'In compliance with Your Lordship's instructions I have urged the Viceroy to meet the May coupon and have urged him to make every personal sacrifice to do so. His answer is that, if the British and French Governments insist, he will endeavour to meet the coupon at any cost, and responsibility for the consequences will rest with them. He says that the large deficit cannot be made good without ruinous sacrifices. Whatever the French may say, I know that the country is in extreme distress, that the coupons, if paid, will be wrung with ruinous sacrifice from the unfortunate taxpayer, and that proposals have already been made to collect the whole year's taxes in advance. I hardly think that HMG would like to countenance such methods. If the Viceroy really has put money by, he will not disgorge it without stronger measures than any government has hitherto put upon him, and the whole burden will fall upon the country.'[92]

In reply Salisbury told him: 'You have now done enough in favour of bondholders and it will not be necessary for you to press the matter further. You must keep in view two objects not easy to be reconciled. It is of considerable importance to us that the French Government should as far as possible be satisfied that we are co-operating with them heartily. On the other hand, you must not lose your influence with the Khedive by unduly pressing demands which he himself is convinced are unreasonable.'[93] He added that 'no representations on your part in favour of payment of debts can be pleaded in defence of any cruelty or pressure on the poor . . . It is desirable that the Khedive should pay his debts if he can without prejudice to his more binding obligations, such as justice to his subjects . . .'[93] A fortnight later, after the May coupon had been met, HMG were agitating about payment of the interest on their Suez Canal shares, which was due on 1 June.[94]

On 4 May, Vivian, reporting that the coupon had been met, with the assistance of various disguised bank loans (under the terms of the Goschen-Joubert settlement the Egyptian Government were debarred from contracting loans openly), wrote; 'The whole transaction is a very discreditable one; the country has been sucked dry to pay the coupon; the decree of 18 November has been evaded, if not violated, and the financial difficulties have been increased.'[95]

Meanwhile, the Commission of Enquiry, under the acting Presidency of Rivers Wilson, had opened its sittings on 14

April. Soon afterwards, Sherif Pasha, the Foreign Minister and Minister of Justice, was summoned by the Commission to give evidence before it in person, as it was entitled to do under the terms of the Decree. But Sherif resigned in order to avoid doing so. He was replaced in his offices by Riaz Pasha, a member of the Commission.

It had been arranged that the Commission should sit until August, and then adjourn until October, and that, before its adjournment, it should produce a preliminary report with a view to creating conditions which would enable a loan to be raised to deal with the judgment debts and with the unsecured floating debt generally. It was with this question of a loan in mind that the Commissioners, guided by Wilson, concentrated on two points: the surrender of the Khedive's personal autocracy to a Council of Ministers acceptable to European financiers; and the surrender of the Khedive's remaining property to the State. These were the two essential conditions for a loan. And it was clearly in mind that Nubar would be President of the new Council of Ministers.

This was a bitter pill for Ismail to swallow after the circumstances of Nubar's dismissal in 1876. But, possibly thinking that Nubar could be used to extricate him from his difficulties and then be got rid of, as he had been got rid of before, he did swallow it. In July, negotiations were opened with Nubar through Prince Husain, the Minister of Finance, for his return to Egypt.

Ismail was much more obstinate over his properties, about which he was asked for details in a questionnaire. He twisted and turned in all directions. He delayed answering the questionnaire. Then he offered to surrender the *Daira Khassa* and *Daira Sanieh* lands. But, since these lands were already fully mortgaged under the Goschen-Joubert settlement, the sacrifice offered was more apparent than real. He then offered to surrender 200,000 *feddans* out of the 450,000 *feddans* comprised in the other royal *Dairas*. Finally, he offered 288,762 *feddans* with an estimated income of £166,986 a year, retaining for himself 143,153 *feddans* with an estimated income of £223,645 a year. As these successive offers were refused by the Commission, who were determined that he should surrender the whole of his rural and urban property against a fixed Civil List, he complained to Vivian that the Commissioners were personally hostile to him

and denied their competence to sit in judgment on his acts.
But he got no sympathy from Vivian, who thought that he
'ought to make restitution on a large scale of the riches he has
extracted from the State to meet the debts the State has incurred'. He asked for authority to press the Khedive to accept
the Commission's demands.[96] But Salisbury was dubious.
Minuting Vivian's despatch, he wrote: 'I have a strong
impression that the proceedings of the Commission are wholly
wanting in commonsense. If they want to dethrone the Khedive,
their policy might lead to the desired result. But they do not
want to dethrone him. What then is the use of driving him to
desperation? It will not increase our hold on him. These ill-
gotten gains are an invaluable screw. But, once returned, the
screw is gone.' Salisbury's view was that enough pressure
should be put on Ismail to make him subservient to Anglo-
French policy, but not enough to break him. The Treasury
view, represented by Wilson, was more interested in the
immediate financial aspect. In this, he was supported by the
French Government. The Treasury view prevailed and led, in
the long run, to Ismail's deposition. At the time, Salisbury,
who was in Berlin at the Congress, told Vivian that he had
agreed with Waddington, the French Foreign Minister, that
'we shall together cordially support the Commission of Enquiry,
but avoid extreme measures and exigencies which might
bring about the dethronement of the Viceroy.'[97]

Towards the end of July Nubar, on his way back to Egypt
after having been assured by the Khedive that he would be
invited to form a Government, called at the Foreign Office. He
stressed the necessity of getting the Khedive to give up all his
estates. He told them that he was anxious to have Wilson as
Minister of Finance. The Foreign Office indicated that Wilson
could be made available if he were willing and told Nubar that
he would be supported by the British and French Governments.
They repeated Salisbury's warning about not pressing Ismail
too hard and said that, while they would not agree to any
Frenchman doubling the post of Minister of Finance with
Wilson, they would have no objection to a Frenchman taking
some other Ministry.

Rivers Wilson, who was corresponding, not with Salisbury
but with the Chancellor of the Exchequer and with Nubar,
went ahead without much reference to the views of the Foreign

Office. A settlement of the floating debt was becoming more and more urgent. With difficulty the Commission persuaded the Consuls-General not to press immediately for the settlement of the judgment debts, pending a general settlement, since this would mean that all floating debtholders would proceed to obtain judgement, and thus lead the country to bankruptcy. On 2 August Vivian reported that the Commission was still determined that Ismail should surrender all his lands. On 18 August, in reply to Salisbury's warnings that Ismail should not be pressed too hard, he expressed his agreement with the Commission, indicating that Ismail had no intention of abdicating and that it would not much matter if he did. This solidarity between the Commission and the Consuls-General (des Michels was even more anti-Ismail than Vivian) led to Ismail's yielding over his estates.

On 18 August Wilson presented the Commission's preliminary report to Ismail. In the first part the Commission made a scathing denunciation of the existing administration of Egypt. They found that the system of tax-collecting was arbitrary, that many of the taxes were unjustified and inequitable, that forced labour and military conscription were heavy burdens and retarded productivity, and that the Khedivial estates were cultivated almost entirely by forced labour. They recommended that the *corvée* should be restricted to works of 'unquestionable public necessity', that the taxation system should be regularised, and that the national Courts of Justice should be reformed.

Discussing the implementation of the Goschen-Joubert settlement, the Commissioners found that the Controllers had failed effectively to check abuses and recommended that no tax be collected except on the authority of a law officially promulgated, and that the exercise of the legislative power should be so guarded as to justify the eventual application of financial laws to all residents of Egypt irrespective of nationality. They recommended that a Reserve Fund be set up to provide for extraordinary expenses and for remissions of taxation in years of low Nile, that no taxes be collected in advance, that the *miri* be reviewed after the completion of a cadastral survey to provide for the adequate taxation of Ushuri lands, and that the customs tariff be revised.

In the second part of the report, the Commissioners estimated that the amount of unsecured outstanding debt for which provision had to be made amounted to £6,276,000, including £1,361,000 said to be owing to the Royal *Dairas* by the Treasury, which they considered should be written-off. They accepted Government expenditure estimates of £4,474,559 for 1878 and £4,529,559 for 1879 and estimated revenue for these years at £8,453,000 and £9,949,000 respectively. On this basis they drew up a balance sheet showing an accumulated deficit of £9,243,928 by the end of 1879. They stated that 'the confused accounts and irregular system of taxation render it as yet impossible to estimate the real revenue of Egypt or to do more than demonstrate the existence of a heavy debt which has to be made good', that 'the absolute power and control hitherto exercised by the Khedive throws upon him the responsibility for this condition of affairs', and that 'he cannot be released from this responsibility until time has been allowed for the introduction of a new system of administration, the central principle of which must be the limitation of the Khedive's absolute power, which has resulted in the present position'. They maintained that 'before any further burdens can be imposed upon the taxpayer, or any further sacrifices demanded of the creditors, the private property of the Khedive and his family are liable for the satisfaction of the debt'. The report went on to refer to the economic evils resulting from so large an accumulation of property in royal hands, took note of the Khedive's offer to relinquish part of it, and concluded by demanding the surrender of all his remaining properties in lands and houses in return for a Civil List.[98]

Having completed and presented their report, the Commissioners adjourned until October. Nubar, who had returned to Egypt on 15 August, 'energetically pressed the Khedive to accept the report spontaneously both as regards the limitation of his powers and the restitution to the State of his properties for the liquidation of the outstanding debt'.[99] Before the end of August Vivian was able to write that Ismail had unconditionally accepted the Commission's report 'without any pressure on my part'.[100] He added that Nubar would be invited to form a government, that Rivers Wilson would be invited to become Minister of Finance, and that a Frenchman would probably be appointed to some other Ministry.

On 28 August Ismail invited Nubar to form a government, by means of a Rescript in which he stated: '*Au lieu d'un pouvoir personnel je veux un pouvoir qui comprise une direction générale aux affaires, mais trouvant son equilibre dans un Conseil des Ministres. En un mot, je veux dorénavant gouverner avec et par mon Conseil des Ministres. Dans cet ordre d'idées . . . les membres du Conseil des Ministres doivent être tous solidaires les uns les autres.'* Nubar accepted the invitation, nominated the Egyptian Ministers, who included Riaz at the Ministry of the Interior, and asked the Khedive's authority *a 'laisser vacant pour un peu de temps encore le Ministre si important des Finances'*.

On 30 August Wilson and Vivian left Egypt for Europe on vacation. Frank Lascelles, from the British Legation at Athens, was left in charge of the British Agency.

There followed some complicated coming-and-going about Wilson's appointment and that of a French Minister. The French Government, which distrusted Nubar, were being difficult. Eventually, after a great deal of haggling which lasted until November, Wilson was officially gazetted as Minister of Finance and de Bligniéres, previously French Commissioner of the *Caisse*, as Minister of Public Works.

Meanwhile Wilson, as Minister of Finance designate, was busy in London and Paris arranging a loan on the security of the estates which Ismail had promised to surrender. It was not all plain sailing. Ismail procrastinated and it was not until 26 October that he promulgated a decree making over to the State, *'dans le but de permettre de régler la situation financière'*, all real property belonging to himself and his family, consisting of 425,729 *feddans* of agricultural property and houses bringing in an estimated income of £422,426 a year, in return for a Civil List. Then Rothschilds, with whom Wilson was negotiating the loan, insisted on a joint guarantee by the British and French Governments. Eventually, after much argument, and after the two governments had refused to give a guarantee, Rothschilds agreed to accept and the British and French Governments to provide, British and French Commissioners to administer the estates, which became known as the State Domains. A further difficulty arose when the French Government threatened to block the loan unless their requirements about the appointment of a French Minister were met. On 31 October, when all seemed to have been settled, a contract for a loan of a nominal £8,500,000 was signed between Wilson, acting for the Egyptian Government, and Rothschilds. The terms of the loan were not particularly favourable. The nominal rate of interest was 7 per cent; it was issued at 73 and the actual amount received was £5,992,000, which was sufficient to meet the whole outstanding amount of the unsecured floating debt. But, before Rothschilds had paid over all the money, another difficulty arose. In December, it was discovered that some of the lands pledged to the loan were encumbered by Mixed Court judgments and Rothschilds refused to advance any more money (they had already advanced £1 million) until these had been disencumbered. It was over a year before the matter was finally settled. During this delay the Egyptian Government were unable to settle with the floating creditors, although they had to pay for the service of the loan, which amounted to about £440,000 a year and which Rothschilds insisted on having remitted to them in accordance with the contract.

It had been agreed by the British and French Governments that the appointment of British and French Ministers should be followed by the suspension of the Control provided by the decree of 18 November 1876 incorporating the Goschen-Joubert settlement, on the understanding that the Control should be revived in the event of either Minister being dismissed from office without the consent of his government. A decree providing for the suspension of the Control on these terms was promulgated on 15 December.

Wilson and de Blignières returned to Egypt at the end of November and the new government started effectively to function as from that time. It laboured under several disadvantages. It enjoyed little or no popular support. Nubar, an Armenian and a Christian, was unpopular both with the Turkish aristocracy and with the Egyptian *fellah*. It had had no time in which to remedy the various abuses castigated by the Commission of Enquiry. It had inherited a desperate financial situation, made worse by an over-high Nile in the autumn of 1878, which proved almost as disastrous economically as the low Nile the year before. The proceeds of the Rothschild loan were not yet available for paying off the floating debt. They gained some popularity by paying off (by instalments) arrears in government salaries, but lost more as a result of various economies which they introduced. They reduced the strength of the army, thereby throwing some 2,500 officers out of employment.

It soon became clear that Ismail was still the real master of the situation. The government could only survive as long as he supported it with the prestige of his authority. Vivian saw this clearly enough, and realised that this support could only be obtained, if at all, by Ministers going out of their way to consult him and ask for his co-operation. Wilson, too, realised it in theory. While in Paris negotiating with the Rothschilds he had told Salisbury: 'If we only have fair play I have no doubt as to the result, but if the Viceroy is against us, or even luke-warm, our difficulties will be enormous.'[101] But, in practice, the government showed itself determined to exclude the Viceroy from any share in the business of administration.

In the result, as Salisbury had foreseen, 'the screw had gone' and there was no longer any lever with which to move Ismail. The inevitable crisis came in the middle of February 1879. Vivian had been warning HMG of impending trouble. Taxes and receipts on the 'affected' parts of the revenue were coming in slowly, and there was reason to believe that the Egyptian officials concerned were being encouraged by the Khedive to drag their feet. Ismail had convoked the Chamber of Notables, ostensibly to lay before them a proposal for an increase in the *miri* but actually, as Vivian believed, to use the prospect of increased taxation to stir up opposition to the government. Vivian also reported that 'serious discontent exists among officers of the army in consequence of a large number of them having been put on half-pay as a measure of economy while they are still owed heavy arrears of pay. I have brought this information privately to the knowledge of Ministers without result. Yesterday I received positive intelligence that the discontent was serious and that it was directed mainly against Nubar and Rivers Wilson.' He went on to state that he had mentioned it to the Khedive, who told him that Nubar's 'want of influence in the country and the natural ignorance of his European colleagues in all matters relating to internal admin-istration' were leading the government into difficulties. The Khedive complained that it had been Nubar's 'deliberate design to discredit his authority and he had no authority to put in its place'. Vivian, who clearly sympathised with the Khedive and disagreed with Wilson and Nubar, told Salisbury that 'in the interests of the success of the new order of things it is . . . absolutely necessary that the deliberations of the Council of

Ministers be strengthened by the counsels and authority of the Khedive and that he should be made directly and personally responsible for the issue'.[102]

On 18 February Nubar was waylaid and mobbed on his way to his office by a number of half-pay officers. Wilson, who was driving just behind him, came to his rescue. The two Ministers, with some difficulty and after a certain amount of manhandling, managed to gain their offices without serious injury. Here they were besieged by a group of angry officers until they were released by the Khedive who, appealed to by Vivian, took command of the situation and dispersed the officers.

After the incident, the Khedive summoned a meeting of the Consular Corps, told them that his present position of responsibility without power must be changed, and blamed Nubar for what had happened. Vivian, describing the incident by cable, told HMG: 'There is certainly an uneasy feeling of discontent and great jealousy at the large influence of the highly-paid European Ministers and officials which has become more apparent since the strong hand of authority was withdrawn. Yesterday's incident shows the weakness of the Ministry and the power of the Khedive, and I strongly recommend that his claim to a share in the counsels of his Ministers be allowed.'[103] At a subsequent meeting with the British and French Agents, Ismail told them that Nubar's resignation was necessary on grounds of public security and that he would in future preside himself over his Council of Ministers. When Nubar was told of this, he offered his resignation, which was accepted by the Khedive. Vivian reported: 'We thereupon warned the Khedive that we now hold him personally responsible for public order, as the events of yesterday prove that the Ministry has lost all authority and that the Khedive alone is able to maintain order. The troops would not have acted in the rioting unless the Khedive had ordered them to do so.' He added that the French Government had ordered de Blignières to remain at his post and that he had advised Wilson to do the same, 'but he seems inclined to tender his resignation at once. The Khedive meanwhile proposes to preside at the Council of Ministers and maintain the *status quo* until he knows the opinion of the British and French Governments.' Vivian went on to suggest that a British and a French warship be sent to Alexandria.

Next day Wilson showed Vivian a telegram he had sent to

Rothschilds blaming Nubar's fall on HMG's lack of support. Vivian told Salisbury that this accusation was 'entirely unjustifiable and I cannot admit that Nubar's fall has been caused by any want of proper support from me or my French colleague'.[104] He added that he had warned Nubar and Wilson of trouble and had been regarded by the latter as an alarmist. He also stated that he did not share Nubar's and Wilson's view that the incident of 18 February had been stage-managed by the Khedive.

HMG were clearly disturbed at the enmity which had developed between Wilson and Vivian, and which was a matter of common knowledge in Cairo. As soon as they heard from Vivian of the fracas of 18 February they instructed him to give the most 'cordial support to the policy of Rivers Wilson' and that 'all the influence of HMG must be at his disposal'.[105] The same day an identical note was sent to their respective agents in Egypt by the British and French Governments: 'You will state to the Khedive that the British and French Governments are determined to act in concert in all that concerns Egypt. They cannot lend themselves to any modification in principle of policies and financial arrangements recently sanctioned by the Khedive. The resignation of Nubar Pasha is, in their eyes, only a question of persons and cannot be implied as a change of system. Inform Rivers Wilson that the Cabinet are of opinion that his resignation at the present moment would be in the highest degree injurious to Egypt and to the general public interest, and HMG will give him all the support in their power if he retains his office.'[106]

In Wilson's view, 'all the support in their power' involved insistence on Nubar's reinstatement. But HMG were willing to accept his dismissal. This was probably due to the views expressed by Vivian and to the fact that the French were not enthusiastic about Nubar. But a few days later, probably moved by Rothschilds who had been moved by Wilson, and disturbed by the tone of Vivian's subsequent cables, in which he had withdrawn his suggestion for the sending of warships, had imputed no blame whatever to Ismail for what had occurred, and had uttered no word of sympathy for Wilson or Nubar, they adopted a harder line. Vivian was told that it was too late to countermand the order for warships 'even if it were desirable to do so'. They disapproved of Ismail's expressed intention of presiding over the Council of Ministers, and stated that Wilson's position would be 'difficult if not impossible if Nubar is not in some form readmitted to the Government'.[107]

But the French refused to support any British insistence on Nubar's reinstatement. Vivian also stated that 'any proposal for the re-entry of Nubar into the Cabinet . . . would be a mistake'. He recommended that the Khedive be advised to appoint Sherif in his stead. But HMG rejected this on the ground that Vivian himself had, a few months before, criticised Sherif as being too subservient to the Khedive. Eventually, the British and French Governments agreed to 'accept the Khedive's assurance of his willingness to defer to the opinions of England and France' provided (i) that the Khedive should not be present at meetings of the Council of Ministers; (ii) that Prince Taufiq, the Khedive's eldest son, and heir to the throne, should preside over the Council of Ministers; and (iii) that the British and French Ministers should have an absolute veto in the Council. In return for this it was agreed not to press for Nubar's reinstatement. The Khedive was to be warned that 'any future difficulty or disturbance will be looked upon as the result of his actions and the consequences will be very serious for himself'.[108] Thus matters were settled for the time being.

A new Council of Ministers was formed, with Taufiq as President and with Wilson, de Blignières and Riaz at their old posts at Finance, Public Works and the Interior respectively. After it had been formed, HMG, finding it 'difficult to understand the persistent differences of policy advocated by yourself and Mr Rivers Wilson', recalled Vivian to London for consultation, once more sending Lascelles from Athens to take over from him.[109]

Within two months, Ismail took another calculated risk in an endeavour to re-establish himself as master of Egypt. This time it led to his undoing.

When the Nubar Ministry was formed, the Commission of Enquiry remained in being and, after the autumn adjournment, went on with its task. By the beginning of April its final report, prepared principally by Baring, was ready in draft form. The financial settlement proposed need not be described here in detail as it had no immediate practical application. It started off from the assumption that Egypt was bankrupt and had been so since April 1876. It proposed a composition with Egypt's creditors consisting of a reduction to 5 per cent of the rate of interest on the funded debt, the payment of unsecured creditors at the rate of about 11s (55p) in the £, and the virtual cancellation of the *Muqabala*. It recommended the abolition of a number of the vexatious and inequitable taxes which had been levied over the past ten years, but proposed an increase in the *miri* paid on *ushuri* lands.

In a land where there are no official secrets, most of the report's recommendations were generally known before it was due to be published. Those for the abolition of the *Muqabala* and for the increased taxation of *Ushuri* lands were particularly obnoxious to the larger landowners, who were strongly represented in the Chamber of Notables, which the Khedive had convoked. Ismail took full advantage of this in the *coup* which he was preparing.

In the middle of March Vivian reported that the Khedive was trying to get rid of Riaz from the Ministry. HMG, in reply, instructed him to join with the European Ministers in insisting on Riaz' retention. Riaz stayed for the time being, but Ismail took no notice of the implied warning conveyed.

At the beginning of April, after Vivian had left, Lascelles reported that animosity against Riaz and the European Ministers was being stirred up by the *Ulema* and Notables, and that the Khedive was negotiating with the Notables to obtain their support for a financial plan which ignored the Commission of Enquiry's recommendations for abolishing the *Muqabala* and increasing the *miri* on *ushuri* lands.[110]

On 6 April Wilson and de Blignières had an audience with the Khedive at which they handed him an advance copy of the Commission's report. The Khedive 'received our remarks with outward courtesy',[111] but, immediately afterwards, sent each of them a curt letter dismissing them from office. On the same day he wrote to Sherif inviting him to form a Ministry.

On 9 April the Khedive summoned a meeting of the Consular Corps and, in the presence of a number of members of the Chamber of Notables, told them that 'the nation' demanded the formation of a purely Egyptian Ministry responsible to the Chamber of Notables. In consequence, Taufiq, 'yielding to the will of the nation', had resigned and been replaced by Sherif, who would form a Government according to the Rescript of 28 August 1878 in which the principle of Ministerial responsibility was set out. He added that 'the nation' protested against the declaration of bankruptcy contained in the Commission of Enquiry's report and that an alternative financial project, which 'had been submitted to him signed by all classes of the population', and which was in accordance with the terms of the Goschen-Joubert settlement, would be promulgated. Three documents were then distributed to the Consuls-General. The first was an address to the Khedive from the Chamber of Notables protesting against the acts, actual and contemplated, of the late Ministry. The second was a petition to the Khedive from a number of *Ulema* and Notables demanding constitutional government and protesting against the proposals embodied in the Commission's report, which had been submitted to the petitioners, who had prepared a counter-project for submission to the Chamber of Notables. The third document was the counter-project itself.

The counter-project estimated the 1879 revenue at a sum £800,000 higher than the Commission's estimate, provided for the payment in full of all Egypt's obligations (subject to a 'temporary' reduction of Unified loan interest to 5 per cent) and for the maintenance of the *Muqabala*, and made no provision for a Khedivial Civil List or for a reform of the administration. It was clearly impossible of execution and there was no intention in Ismail's mind that it should be executed. It was a temporary device adopted in the course of the rearguard action which he was engaged in fighting. It was promulgated in a decree dated 22 April which appointed Sherif as President of the Council of Ministers, requested him to form a government composed entirely of Egyptians, to prepare a Constitution, and to carry out in its entirety the financial plan which had been drawn up.

Sherif, in view of the decree that the European control over Egyptian finances be revived in the event of the dismissal of either of the European Ministers, invited Bellaigues de Bughas (who had replaced de Blignières as French Debt Commissioner) and Baring to assume the offices of Controller of Expenditure and Revenue respectively. They both declined on the ground that they could not associate themselves with a financial plan which they regarded as impracticable and with a change of system contrary to the engagements recently taken towards the British and French Governments. Sherif then asked the British and French Consuls-General to invite their Governments to nominate Controllers. At the same time several British and French officials at the Ministry of Finance resigned their posts. The following month Baring resigned as British Commissioner of the *Caisse* and was succeeded by Mr (later Sir) Auckland Colvin, an ex-Indian Civil Servant who had just resigned from the Ministry of Finance.

Neither the British nor the French Governments reacted strongly to Ismail's coup. HMG, in a despatch to Lascelles, after complaining about 'a grave and apparently international breach of international courtesy to friendly Powers' on the part of the Khedive, merely threatened that if Ismail continued to 'ignore the obligations imposed on him by his past acts . . . it will only remain for the two Cabinets to reserve to themselves an entire liberty of appreciation and action'.[112]

'For the moment, the success of the manoeuvre appeared complete . . . The Khedive had defied two powerful Governments; he had got rid of his European advisers, and he had appointed in their places a number of men who would implicitly obey his orders . . . European Governments might perhaps lecture him, but international rivalry was so intense that no common action of a serious nature was to be feared. He had indeed drawn a heavy draft on the credulity of Europe . . . Nevertheless, the scheme would probably have been successful if the financial plan which the Khedive had pledged himself to carry out had been based on any solid foundation. If he had been able to pay his debts no excuse would have existed for further interference from abroad. Unfortunately for the Khedive, his financial plan was impossible of execution.'[113]

The prime movers in Ismail's undoing appear to have been Rothschilds, who were intimately interested in Egypt's finances in that they had recently contracted for a loan of £8½ million on the security of the Khedive's estates. They were in close touch with Wilson who, not unnaturally, was very sore about the way in which he had been treated. Whether or not moved by Wilson, Rothschilds, having 'pulled strings both in Downing Street and on the Quai d'Orsay in vain',[114] approached Bismarck and secured the intervention of the German Government.

On 15 May the German Ambassador in London informed the Foreign Office that the German Consul-General in Cairo had been instructed to protest against the recent decree which 'in the judgement of the German Government was at variance with

I

the judicial reforms'.[115] This raised in a very acute form the question as to whether the Mixed Courts had jurisdiction over 'acts of administration which prejudice rights acquired by a foreigner' or whether such acts, not specifically directed against but only incidentally affecting foreigners, were sovereign acts unchallengeable in the Courts. A previous decision of the Mixed Court of Appeal had upheld this jurisdiction, which was generally supported by the European Governments. It was clear that the action of the German Government would encourage floating debtholders to press for execution of their claims, if judgment had already been given, or to seek judgments if they had not been given. And the German Government, in the light of its protest, might well be prepared to intervene in favour of German nationals who had obtained judgments. Other governments might follow suit and the whole concept of Anglo-French control over Egypt would be in danger.

So, on 30 May, the British and French Governments sent identical notes to their agents in Egypt stating that 'the decree of 22 April 1879, by which the Egyptian Government at its own discretion regulated the Egyptian debt, thereby abolishing existing recognised rights' was 'an open and direct violation of the international engagements entered into at the institution of the judicial reforms' and that the Viceroy would be 'held responsible for the consequences of his unlawful proceedings'. 'HMG understand that the German and Austro-Hungarian Consuls-General have made declarations on these lines . . . [and] are of the opinion that HH's assumption of modifying at his own unchecked discretion the contracts he has made with foreigners and to place these modifications above the authority of the Mixed Tribunals is inconsistent with the principles on which these Tribunals were established. You are instructed to associate yourself with the German and Austro-Hungarian protests against the decree of 22 April.'[116] HMG cannot have been very happy at having their hands thus forced and at having taken their stand on an interpretation of the powers of the Mixed Courts which was not supported by their own Law Offices nor by the Foreign Office Legal Adviser.

All the major Powers except Italy protested against the decree, following the lead of the German Government. Lascelles, after making his protest, cabled: 'The Egyptian Government now submit the financial dispositions of the decree to the

approval of the Powers which, if granted, will make them
internationally binding. They will then be promulgated in
another decree . . . The Egyptian Government will pay in full
the judgment creditors and all the European creditors of the
floating debt.'[117] In amplification of this cable Lascelles wrote:
'We protested against the pretensions of the Khedive to modify
arbitrarily and of his own authority the acquired rights of
Europeans in Egypt and to withdraw them from the jurisdiction
of the Mixed Tribunals. The Egyptian Government offers to
pay the European creditors of the floating debt in full and to
submit the rest of the financial proposals to the Powers . . . It
is manifestly unjust that an insolvent Government should treat
any class of its creditors more favourably than any other, while
the exclusion of the native creditors is inequitable. Nor do I
see how the Powers can approve of a financial plan and give it
the force of law if they have no opportunity of examining it. On
the other hand, they are bound to assist the Khedive in coming
to a fair arrangement with his creditors, and the proper course
for the Egyptian Government to pursue is to invite the Powers
to sanction the appointment of a Commission of Liquidation.'[118]

But the British and French Governments had had enough of
Ismail, and negotiations to get rid of him were already in train
at Constantinople. Sultan Abdul Hamid was not unwilling to
use the opportunity to re-establish Ottoman authority over
Egypt, which had been reduced almost to a nullity as a result
of the 1873 Firman issued by his predecessor Sultan Abdul
Aziz. He indicated that he would depose Ismail, revoke the
Firmans which had been granted to him by Sultan Abdul Aziz,
revert to the terms of the 1841 settlement, and confer the
Khedivate on Ismail's uncle, Halim who, under the terms of the
1841 settlement, was heir. (Mustafa Fazil was dead.) This did
not suit the British and French Governments, who thought that
a revocation of the 1873 Firman and a resumption of Ottoman
control over Egypt would hamper the Anglo-French financial
and administrative control which they were determined to
establish. They seem also to have thought that Taufiq would
be a more pliable instrument of Anglo-French control than
Halim, who was greatly under Ottoman influence, and whose
personal extravagance and incapacity for managing his personal
financial affairs were outstanding. And so they tried to prevail
on Ismail to anticipate deposition by abdicating in favour of

Taufiq. They promised him that if he abdicated he would get a handsome Civil List and that the succession would be guaranteed for Taufiq. If he did not abdicate and compelled the Sultan to depose him, neither of these advantages would be guaranteed. But Ismail, a gambler at the end of his tether, went on twisting and turning. He intrigued and bribed in Constantinople through his agent, Abraham Bey, who had been so lavish on his behalf in the past. He looked round in Egypt for that popular support which, only a few weeks before, had seemed so abundantly available. All was in vain. On 26 June he received a telegram from the Sultan addressed to the ex-Khedive and announcing his deposition. Simultaneously, a telegram arrived for Taufiq conferring on him the Khedivate. On 30 June Ismail left Egypt in the royal yacht *Mahroussa*. An eventful reign was at an end.

Notes

1. Derby-Cave, 6.12.75, FO 78/2538
2. Stanton-Derby, 24.12.75, FO 78/2404
3. Cave-Derby, 25.12.75, FO 78/2538
4. *ibid*, 20.12.75 and 1.1.76
5. *ibid*, 5.1.76
6. *ibid*
7. *ibid*, 15.1.76
8. *ibid*, 21.1.76
9. Minute in FO 78/2539A
10. Derby-Cave, 26.1.76, *ibid*
11. Derby-Cave, 26.1.76, FO 78/2539
12. Cave-Derby, 25.12.75, FO 78/2538
13. *ibid*, 5.1.76, FO 78/2539A
14. See Cave-Derby, 12.2.76, *ibid*
    No 121, Londres, 27.11.75
15. *Documents Diplomatiques Françaises, 1871–1914, 1me serie, T II, D*
16. See Stanton-Derby, 6.2.76, FO 78/2500
17. Derby-Stanton, 23.2.76, FO 78/2498
18. Cave-Derby, 18.1.76, FO 78/2539A
19. *ibid*, 1.2.76
20. *ibid*, 5.2.76
21. Derby-Stanton, 10.2.76, FO 78/2498
22. Derby-Stanton, 14.3.76, *ibid*
23. *ibid*, 13.3.76
24. *ibid*, 10.3.76
25. *ibid*, 6.3.76
26. This piece of Anglo-French financial jargon was used at the time, and will normally be used in this account, in referring to the revenues mortgaged as security for the Egyptian debt
27. Derby-Stanton, 27.3.76, FO 78/2498
28. *ibid*, 20.3.76
29. Stanton-Derby, 22.3.76, FO 78/2500. Rovers Wilson thought Ismail's objection reasonable. See his memoirs, *Chapters from My Official Life*, p 91
30. Hansard PDC, Vol 22, p 1418
31. Sabry, *L'Empire Egyptien sous Ismail et l'Ingérence Anglo-Française*, p 174
32. Derby-Stanton, 25.3.76, FO 78/2498
33. Some writers, e.g. Sabry, have taken the view that Disraeli's announcement was a deliberate attempt to drive Egypt into bankruptcy and one more move in a macchiavellian British attempt to assume control over Egypt. In fact, nobody seems to have told Ismail that it was intended to publish the report until the very last moment before publication. It would certainly have been better if the telegram of 25 March quoted above had preceded instead of following Disraeli's announcement in the Commons, and Disraeli might reasonably have foreseen the effect of such an announcement

34. Stanton-Derby, 6.4.76, FO 78/2500. The Decree was published on 8 April
35. For text of Cave report see Parliamentary Papers Commons, 1876, LXXXIII, 99, in FO 78/2539A
36. Allowing for the difference between the Egyptian pound and the pound sterling, this was the official budgetary estimate for 1875–76
37. A few weeks before, in conversation with Cave, he had estimated it at £12 million
38. Stanton-Derby, 17.4.76, FO 78/2502
39. Derby-Stanton, 21.4.76, FO 78/2498. The 'canal share annuities' were the 5 per cent interest on the shares bought by HMG which had been deprived of their coupons until 1894 as the result of an arrangement between Lesseps and Ismail in 1869 – see Marlowe, *The Making of the Suez Canal*, pp 253 and 303 - and which the Egyptian Government had agreed to pay HMG until that date
40. The floating debt to be consolidated consisted only of Treasury bonds which had for the most part been issued against loans of ready cash, and did not include current account indebtedness in respect of supplies to, or services for, the Government or *Dairas*
41. For details see Stanton-Derby, 8.5.76, FO 78/2502. Texts of Decrees in same volume
42. This is apparently a reference to a £5 million loan which had already been advanced by Crédit Foncier, for which a bonus of £2,740,800 had been provided
43. Derby-Stanton, 26.5.76, FO 78/2498
44. Wilson-Northcote, 8.5.76 and 13.5.76, FO 78/2502 and 2503
45. Northcote-Wilson, 18.5.76, FO 78/2499
46. Stanton had gone on leave prior to being transferred and Cookson was acting, pending the arrival of the Hon. H. C. Vivian, who had acted as CG three years before
47. Cookson-Derby, 7.6.76, FO 78/2503
48. *ibid*, 19.6.76. He was replaced at the Ministry of Commerce by another Englishman, Malan, whom the Khedive had recruited in England
49. Cookson-Derby, 20.5.76, FO 78/2750
50. *ibid*, 3.7.76
51. *ibid*
52. See text of opinion in FO 78/2750
53. See text of circular dated 30.8.76 in *ibid*
54. Vivian-Derby, 21.10.76, *ibid*
55. Vivian-Derby, 18.8.76, FO 78/2503, quoting contents of a letter received from Goschen
56. Derby-Cookson, 7.8.76, FO 78/2499
57. Vivian-Derby, 23.9.76, FO 78/2503
58. Later this arrangement was varied to provide for the issue of another £2 million of 5 per cent debentures, making £17 million in all, in return for which another £2 million of Consolidated Debt was surrendered to Ismail. The object of this manoeuvre was to enable Ismail to sell this stock on the market and so pay the debt owing to the British contractors for the Alexandria harbour works. But the price of this stock was so low that Ismail would only have been able to realise it at a price inadequate to settle this debt. In the event this £2 million worth of Consolidated

stock plus the Suez Canal Preference shares (the 'fifteen per cents') were placed as security for the £5 million advanced by Crédit Foncier. The Alexandria harbour contractors, Greenfield and Elliot, retained the lien on Alexandria port dues which had been provided in their contract as their security. As these port dues were part of the security for the additional debentures issued, Ismail had to hand back the £2 millions of Consolidated debt to the Caisse which had been surrendered to him, and pay 7 per cent interest on it, until such time as he was able to pay the contractors. The whole manoeuvre was an attempted device to expedite payment to Greenfield and Elliot. The Elliot was the Sir George Elliot of whom we have heard

59. Vivian-Derby, 11.11.76, FO 78/2503
60. See *inter alia* Vivian-Derby, 20.11.76, *ibid*. 'There is some agitation and strong feeling among the natives produced by the harassing over-taxation to which they are exposed, by the non-payment of wages and by the great misery and suffering which exists. This feeling is naturally and properly directed against the Khedive'
61. For what purports to be a detailed account of his murder see McCoan, *Egypt Under Ismail*, pp 191–204
62. Husain subsequently became Sultan of Egypt under the British Protectorate in 1914 after the deposition of Khedive Abbas II
63. See note 58 above
64. Derby-Vivian, 12.12.76, FO 78/2499
65. *ibid*, 13.12.76
66. See report by Baring attached to Vivian-Derby, 22.12.77, FO 78/2634
68. *ibid*, 13.8.77
69. *ibid*, 24.8.77
70. There had been a revolution in Turkey in 1876. Sultan Abdul Aziz had been deposed and replaced by Sultan Murad V. Under Murad, Midhat Pasha, the Grand Vizier, inaugurated a Constitution. This was followed by a counter-revolution. Murad was deposed and succeeded by Sultan Abdul Hamid II. The Constitution was suspended and Midhat sent into exile
71. Vivian-Derby, 6.1.77, FO 78/2631. Lord Tenterden, the Permanent Under-Secretary, minuted: 'I doubt if Vivian's advice is sound. It would be very unwise of the Khedive to refuse. He knows quite as well as anyone how to evade such an obligation, but repudiating it might be dangerous both to himself personally and to our interests in so far as they are concerned with the tranquillity of Egypt'
72. Derby-Vivian, 25.4.77, FO 78/2630. This reply was based on a Minute by Tenterden: 'The Khedive is in a dilemma. If he does not furnish the men, the Sultan may revoke the Firman of succession and possibly create a rebellion against the Khedive. On the other hand, the French and Russian Agents threatening a blockade is a strange proceeding. It is doubtful if the Russians would blockade the Canal and Alexandria in face of the Turkish fleet. But the sooner a hint is given to them not to attempt it the better. We would not suffer the route to India to be thus stopped; a collision with Russia would be inevitable. It seems to be a waste of words talking of pressure at Constantinople.' (Vivian had suggested putting pressure on the Sultan not to ask the Khedive for help.) 'The Sultan has a right to demand assistance

and it is little likely that anything would come of our representations.' In the event Ismail did send assistance to Turkey and no
hostile Russian action was taken against Egypt, in spite of the
presence of a Russian warship, *Petrovalovsk*, in the Mediterranean.
HMG told Russia: 'Any attempt to blockade or otherwise
interfere with the Canal or its approaches would be regarded as
a menace to India'

73. Vivian-Derby, 30.3.77, FO 78/2631
74. *ibid*, 9.8.77
75. Vivian-Derby, 27.10.76, FO 78/2503
76. *ibid*, 26.5.77, FO 78/2632, and 11.8.77, FO 78/2633. Rivers Wilson
    described Romaine as 'a good, well-mannered and a most
    honourable gentleman, but has not grit enough for his place.'
    Wilson, *op cit*, p 121. Baring thought Romaine was 'a dangerous
    lunatic who should be locked up'. Baring-Goschen, 28.12.77, FO
    633/2
77. Derby-Vivian, 23.10.77, FO 78/2630
78. Vivian-Derby, 7.7.77, FO 78/2633
79. *ibid*, 12.7.77
80. Lord Cromer, then Captain Baring, English Commissioner of the
    Debt, shared Vivian's views. See Cromer, *Modern Egypt*, Vol I,
    pp 26–7. Other Englishmen less closely in touch with the position,
    e.g. Edward Dicey, *England and Egypt*, p 247 – thought that the
    Goschen-Joubert settlement was viable and that the revenue
    estimate of £10 million on which it was based was a fair one.
    Dicey seems to have thought that independent estimates had
    been arrived at both by Cave and by Goschen and Joubert. In
    fact both missions took the same figure from the Egyptian budget
    for 1874–75 without any independent investigation
81. A report made by Baring the following summer, and sent to HMG
    with Vivian-Derby, 30.3.78, FO 78/2854, gives the following
    figures: Unified Debt £57.8 million, of which £27.9 million
    held in England, £23.9 in France and £6.3 million in Egypt.
    Preference Debt £16.9 million, of which £9.8 million held in
    England, £6.5 million in France and £0.6 million in Egypt.
    Privileged Debt £4.5 million all held in England. In an earlier
    report – see Vivian-Derby, 22.12.77 – Baring had stated that
    most of the secured £7.2 million of the unfunded debt was held
    either by Crédit Foncier or Comptoir d'Escompte
82. There was a further complication in that HMG were interested in
    the regular payment of the interest on their holding of Canal
    shares – see Note 39 – amounting to some £0.2 million p.a., and
    both the British and French Governments were interested in the
    payment of the Ottoman tribute which was 'affected' to the service
    of loans which British and French banks had made to Turkey
83. This agreement was not quite unanimous. A great many of the
    funded and secured debtholders, and to some extent the French
    Government, took the view that Egypt was able to pay her debts in
    full, and that Ismail's removal and the imposition of effective Euro-
    pean control were all that were necessary to ensure that she did so
84. Vivian-Derby, 23.2.78, FO 78/2853
85. Derby-Vivian, 8.3.78, FO 78/2851. A note on the draft states that
    the cable had been approved by the Chancellor of the Exchequer
    and by Mr Goschen

86. Nubar was not interested in 'constitutionalism' of the kind which had been tried, and which had failed, in Turkey. What he wanted was an efficient and partly Europeanised alternative to Ismail's despotism, with himself in charge
87. Vivian-Derby, 30.3.78, FO 78/2854
88. *ibid*, 13.4.78
89. HMG had instructed Vivian to make sure the tribute was paid. See Derby-Vivian, 12.3.78, FO 78/2851
90. Salisbury-Vivian, 30.3.78, FO 78/2851
91. Cromer, *Modern Egypt*, Vol I, p 35
92. Vivian-Salisbury, 18.4.78, FO 78/2854
93. Salisbury-Vivian, 20.4.78, FO 78/2851
94. *ibid*, 1.5.78
95. Vivian-Salisbury, 4.5.78, FO 78/2854
96. *ibid*, 8.6.78
97. Salisbury-Vivian, 17.7.78, FO 78/1851
98. For text of report see FO 78/2876
99. Vivian-Salisbury, 22.8.78, FO 78/2856
100. *ibid*, 23.8.76
101. Wilson-Salisbury, undated, FO 78/2852
102. Vivian-Salisbury, 15.2.79, FO 141/125
103. *ibid*, 19.2.79
104. *ibid*, 20.2.79
105. Salisbury-Vivian, 21.2.79, FO 141/123
106. *ibid*
107. *ibid*, 27.2.79
108. *ibid*, 8.3.79
109. *ibid*, 15.3.79
110. Lascelles-Salisbury, 4.4.79, FO 141/125
111. Wilson, *op cit*, p 191
112. Salisbury-Lascelles, 25.4.79, FO 141/123
113. Cromer, *op cit*, Vol I, pp 108–9
114. W. S. Blunt, *Secret History of the British Occupation of Egypt*, p 65. Blunt, who is not always a reliable source, relates that Wilson himself told him that on his return from Egypt he 'had gone straight to the Rothschilds in Paris and had represented to them the danger their money was running from the turn affairs had taken at Cairo and Alexandria. The Khedive intended to repudiate the whole debt and to shelter himself in so doing by proclaiming constitutional government in Egypt . . . He thus succeeded in alarming the Rothschilds and in getting them to use the immense political influence they possessed in favour of active intervention'
115. Salisbury-Lord Odo Russell (British Ambassador in Berlin), 15.5.79, copy in FO 141/123
116. Salisbury-Vivian, 30.5.79, FO 141/123
117. Lascelles-Salisbury, 15.6.79, FO 141/125. Vivian, returning to Egypt at the end of April after consultations in London, handed over to Lascelles as Consul-General in the middle of June
118. Lascelles-Salisbury, 15.6.79, *ibid*

12

The Coup de Grace

Ismail's deposition, at the instance of the British and French Governments, represented the firstfruits of that short period of Anglo-French political co-operation over Egypt which was inaugurated during the Congress of Berlin in 1878 and which replaced the previous more or less endemic rivalry between the two countries. Briefly, what had happened was this. The British Government in which Disraeli was Prime Minister and Salisbury Foreign Secretary, intent as usual on traditional British policy of preserving, as far as possible, the territorial integrity of the Ottoman Empire, intervened with the Powers in an attempt to secure in favour of Turkey a revision of the terms of the Treaty of San Stefano, which Russia had imposed on Turkey after defeating them in the war which had broken out in 1877. As a result of this intervention a Congress of the Powers was convened by Bismarck in Berlin. In preliminary conversations in Constantinople, Salisbury made a secret agreement with the Porte by which the island of Cyprus was to be leased to HMG, and British military Consuls installed in Asia Minor, in consideration of the assistance which England had promised Turkey at the Congress. The details of this secret agreement were 'leaked' in London during the course of the Congress as a result of the indiscretion of a Foreign Office clerk. The French Government, perennially suspicious of British designs on the Levant, were furious and nearly broke up the Congress. Bismarck, who wanted to appease the French in order to help them keep their minds off Alsace-Lorraine, succeeded in mediating an agreement between Salisbury and Waddington, the French Foreign Minister, by which, in effect, HMG conceded to France a free hand in Tunisia (which was annexed by France three years later) and equal 'rights' with Great Britain over Egypt. These equal 'rights' were soon interpreted by both Governments, and more or less accepted by the other European Powers, as conferring on Great Britain and France something like a monopoly of political interference in Egypt, always provided that this interference was exercised in consultation with, and in the general interests of, the European Powers as a whole. That is to say, the guardianship of the Ottoman Empire with which the Powers had vested themselves at the Treaty of Paris in 1856 was, in the case of Egypt, delegated to Great Britain and France.

HMG's reaction to Ismail's coup, before the German intervention had precipitated matters, was described by Salisbury in a letter to Northcote, the Chancellor of the Exchequer, on 11 May 1879. 'The Egyptian complaint is a complicated disease which will require patient treatment. We desire and must aim at several things not wholly consistent. We wish to keep clear of entanglements – that is to avoid relations with the Khedive which will put it in his power to insult us if we give him some temptation to do so. If this were all, the simple course would be to interfere as little with his internal affairs as we do with those of Italy. But we have a past which cannot wholly be sloughed off . . . We helped to set up the Commission of Enquiry and we received communication of his Reform Decree and of the Rothschild loan. Moreover we have a pecuniary interest in the payment of the tribute and the Suez Canal interest, and our capitalists have an interest in Alexandria harbour which we cannot afford to disregard. But above all these entanglements is the apprehension that if we stand aside France will become as dominant there as she is in Tunis . . . We cannot cut the tow-rope . . . But we must . . . keep abreast of France in any hold she has over the administration of the country . . . The Khedive is going straight to ruin and we cannot afford to be out of the way when the crash comes.'[1]

The crash was not long in coming. And when it came, HMG were closely associated with the French Government in the negotiations at Constantinople leading to Ismail's deposition. The two governments were determined that Sultan Abdul Hamid should not use the opportunity to instal his own candidate, Prince Halim, and revoke the various instalments of independence which Ismail had extracted from Sultan Abdul Aziz. They no longer had any interest in restoring effective Ottoman sovereignty. They wanted to control Egypt themselves, and to use the independence of Constantinople which

Ismail had secured to assist them in doing so. And so they secured Ismail's deposition, and Taufiq's succession, more or less on their own terms. And they compelled the new and seemingly compliant Khedive to appoint two Controllers – one British and one French – with powers which they hoped would be sufficient to bring some order into Egyptian finances, secure the interests of the bondholders, and see that the Egyptians did not get up to mischief. Salisbury had no illusions about the fragility of the control thus provided. As he told the British Ambassador in Paris: 'Actual authority we cannot exercise. With European Ministers the disbanded officers proved that two pairs of arms are no use against 2,000. The only control we have is moral influence, which in practice is a combination of nonsense, objurgation and worry. In this we are still supreme and have many modes of applying it – diplomatic Notes, Consular interviews, Blue Books. We must devote ourselves to the perfecting of this weapon. We must have complete knowledge of what is going on.'[2]

All depended on the continued compliance of Egypt's ruler and people with a form of control which had no armed force behind it and which, in Salisbury's words, was 'a combination of nonsense, objurgation and worry'. At first, this compliance seemed to be forthcoming. Sherif, the Prime Minister, made an unsuccessful attempt to induce the Khedive to promulgate a Constitution. Taufiq, with the backing of the British and French Consuls-General, refused. Sherif resigned and was replaced by Riaz, who had been a member of the Commission of Enquiry and the European Ministry, and who was regarded as a strong man. For the next two years, he and the two Controllers – Baring and de Blignières – ruled Egypt as a triumvirate in much the same despotic way as Ismail had done, although with rather more wisdom, and with a considerably greater regard for financial economy. For Egypt was technically bankrupt and the two Controllers regarded themselves – and had been appointed by the British and French Governments – primarily as representatives of the creditors in the administration of a bankrupt estate.

The first task was to arrive at an agreed liquidation of Egypt's indebtedness. The facts had been investigated and reported on by the Commission of Enquiry – of which all three of the triumvirate had been members. The implementation of the Commission's recommendations had been postponed by Ismail's coup. Now it was possible to proceed from where the Commission had left off. After a good deal of difficulty, an international Commission of Liquidation was appointed, by Khedivial Decree, to hammer out what was intended to be a final settlement. But the position had altered since the time of the Commission of Enquiry in that the British and French Governments had, in effect, assumed responsibility for the government of Egypt. They therefore had responsibilities towards the people of Egypt as well as towards the bond-holders, and their Consuls-General and Controllers were instructed to give 'earnest support' to the 'native government' during the deliberations of the Commission, which was presided over by Rivers Wilson, who had been solaced by a KCMG for his previous humiliations. In practice, this 'earnest support' resulted in agreement on a maintainable revenue figure more realistic than that relied on in the Goschen-Joubert settlement, and on a reduction in the rate of interest on the funded debt. But, except for the virtual abolition of the *Muqabala* (which was held almost entirely by Egyptians) there was no writing down of the capital sums standing to Egypt's debit.

The findings of the Commission were embodied in the Law of Liquidation promulgated on 17 July 1880. The figure of maintainable revenue was fixed at £E8,361,622 a year, of which £E4,987,988 a year was reserved for expenses of administration, leaving £E3,463,734 a year for the service of the debt, interest on which was reduced to 4 per cent. The *Muqabala* was abolished and arrangements made for the payment of some compensation to those who had contributed to it. Any surplus on the revenues 'affected' to the service of the debt was to be devoted to the extinction of debt and any surplus on the rest of the revenue was also to be so devoted to the extent of making up, together with any surplus on the 'affected' revenue, a sum equal to ½ per cent of the capital of the Unified Debt. Any additional surplus on the 'unaffected' revenue was to be at the disposal of the Egyptian Government. Any deficit on the 'affected' revenue was to be made good from the 'unaffected' revenue, whether or not there was a surplus on this.

It was a harsh settlement which imposed on the Egyptian Government – or rather on the Controllers – the necessity for a rigid economy and inhibited them from embarking on any major capital expenditure for the development of the country. In these circumstances, the form of government which became known as the Dual Control could not be expected to be popular. Its survival depended on the continuance of that habit of subservience which had been Ismail's legacy to Egypt's new governors. This proved to be a wasting asset. The events of the last few years, the winds of 'constitutionalism' blowing into Egypt from Western Europe, and even from Constantinople, the activities of a more or less free press, the growing influence of a native Egyptian landowning middle-class in face of the Turkish-Albanian-Circassian aristocracy, the use made by Ismail of the Chamber of Notables during his last few weeks of power, and the resentment felt against the European officials with high salaries introduced by the Dual Control, all combined to erode the habit of subservience and expose the nakedness of the power base from which the Dual Control operated.

A series of army mutinies drove Riaz from, and brought Sherif back into, office as Prime Minister. With the concurrence of the British and French Governments, acting through their Consuls-General and their two Controllers,[3] Sherif reconvoked the Chamber of Notables in an attempt to appease public opinion by erecting a façade of constitutionalism. But the Notables proved less subservient than of old. While admitting the validity of the financial settlement laid down in the Law of Liquidation, they tried to insist on the Chamber's control of the 'unaffected' part of the budget. This demand was held by the British and French to threaten the basis of the Law of Liquidation in that it posed the possibility of a series of budget deficits and the re-creation of a large floating debt. And so the demand was unequivocally rejected, thus throwing the Notables and a large section of public opinion into the arms of the already mutinous army. It soon became apparent that it was no longer possible to control Egypt by Salisbury's mixture of 'nonsense, objurgation and worry.' The great question arose as to whether the complex of private European interests which had grown up in Egypt over the past sixty years should be protected and sustained by the force of European arms. The representatives of these interests had no doubts on the matter, and the columns of newspapers were filled and the minds of statesmen infiltrated with demands for armed intervention. But the European Governments were hesitant, apprehensive and jealous of each other. And the parliaments of Europe were actuated by a desire for economy and, sometimes, by a sense of sympathy for the Egyptian people. For a few weeks during the winter of 1881–82 the French Government, with Gambetta as Prime Minister, seemed determined to compel a reluctant British Government into a joint armed occupation of Egypt as the only alternative to a unilateral French one. But Gambetta fell from office and a new French Government, with de Freycinet as Prime Minister, and under the influence of an economy-minded Chamber, began to think in terms of a possible accommodation with Egyptian insurgence. The other Powers, including Great Britain, were inclined to revert to the old formula – which had been so successful with Mohamed Ali forty years before – of a restoration of effective Ottoman suzerainty.

By this time Egyptian insurgence had reached a point at which the authority of the Dual Control had been reduced to a nullity. Although the Khedivial facade remained, the army, supported by something like a popular mass movement, had taken over the reality of power. It was apparent that armed force, applied from without, would be necessary to dislodge them. And it soon became apparent that the Porte, whose tradition was to compound with rather than attempt to subdue successful rebellion, would not oblige with armed force for the principal benefit of Egypt's European creditors. Although going through the public motions of supporting the more-or-less non-existent Khedivial authority, they were, in secret, negotiating with Ahmed Arabi, the leader of the Egyptian popular movement, who held the portfolio of Minister of War and was in fact the head of the Government.

Officially, and to a large extent in reality, HMG's apprehensions were strategic and not inspired by much concern for Egypt's English creditors. The opening of the Suez Canal twelve years before had greatly increased Egypt's importance as a vital link in the British system of Imperial communications. As Dilke, Under Secretary of State for Foreign Affairs, pointed out in the Commons England had a double interest in the Canal – commercial in that 82 per cent of traffic through the Canal was British, and political in that the Canal was 'the principal highway to India, Ceylon, the Straits, and British Burmah, where 250,000,000 live under our rule, and also to

China where we have vast interests . . . It is also one of the roads to our colonial Empire in Australia and New Zealand.'⁴ To the British Government, on the information which they received from Malet and Colvin, their Consul-General and Controller, the two alternative prospects facing Egypt were a chaos of fanaticism, looting and xenophobia on the one hand and, on the other, a military dictatorship hostile to England which might do a deal with Turkey and the Powers, or some of them, behind HMG's back. Either prospect threatened the Canal as an uninterrupted channel of communication.

The former prospect seemed to be underlined by a massacre of Europeans which took place in Alexandria in the middle of June. And so, faced with the equivocation of the Porte and the Powers at an international Conference convened in Constantinople, fearful at the prospect of a secret deal with Arabi by France or the Porte, or by both, and disturbed equally by the menace of the Egyptian mob and by the hostile motions of the Egyptian army, who were said to be erecting shore batteries trained on the British naval squadron which, for the past few weeks, had been in Alexandria harbour, the Gladstone Government moved reluctantly towards a decision to invade Egypt. Gladstone told the Commons: 'We must substitute the rule of law for that of military violence in Egypt, in partnership with other Powers if possible, but alone if necessary.' He sweetened the pill for his Liberal and Radical supporters, who were uneasy at the spectacle of a Liberal government pursuing an Imperialist policy at a time when 'imperialism' was still a term of abuse among true Liberals, by telling them that British intervention would be a means of bringing the Egyptian people 'hope . . . for free institutions . . . and . . . for the attainment of those blessings of civilised life which they have seen achieved in so many countries in Europe'.⁵

British armed invasion became almost inevitable on 11 July when, acting on authority rather reluctantly given by HMG, Admiral Seymour, commanding the British squadron in Alexandria harbour, bombarded Egyptian shore batteries after the Egyptian Government had ignored an ultimatum from him to dismantle them. (A French squadron, also in Alexandria harbour, withdrew on the orders of the French Government as soon as Seymour issued his ultimatum.) A month later, a British military force under Sir Garnet Wolseley invaded

Egypt and, on 13 September, defeated the main force of the Egyptian army at Tel-al-kebir, on the edge of the Delta, between the Suez Canal and Cairo. The British occupation of Egypt, which was to last for seventy years, had begun. The process of financial and economic colonisation had led, slowly unconsciously, but inexorably, to armed conquest.

By their occupation the British, willy-nilly, became the guardians and guarantors of all that complex of European privileges and property which had grown up over the previous sixty years. To the British Government, at the time, these privileges were comparatively unimportant. What really mattered to them was freedom of passage through the Suez Canal. Concern for this motivated the beginning, as it was to precipitate the end, of the British occupation of Egypt. But, for the Egyptian people, the construction of the Suez Canal was but one link in a long chain of events which perpetuated and intensified their seemingly endless servitude.

Notes

1. Iddesleigh Papers, Vol VII, BM Add. MS 50019
2. Salisbury-Lyons, 15.7.79, Lady Gwendolen Cecil, *Salisbury*, Vol II, p 355
3. Mr (later Sir Auckland) Colvin replaced Baring as British Controller in 1880
4. Hansard PDC, 3rd series, CCLXXII, 1720, 25.7.82
5. Hansard PDC, 3rd series, CCLXXII, 1586–90, 24.7.82

Sources

UNPUBLISHED

Public Record Office
FO 78 series
FO 141 series (from 1879)
FO 633 series (Cromer Papers), Vol II (1877–1880)

Quai d'Orsay, Service des Archives
Mémoires et Documents, Vols 1–18
Correspondence Politique Egypte, Vols 1–46 (1828–1869)
Documents Diplomatiques. Affaires d'Egypte, Vols 1–20 (1870–1882)

British Museum, Department of Manuscripts
Iddesleigh Papers, BM Add. MS 50019

PUBLISHED

State Papers
Parliamentary Papers (Blue Books), indexed in *A Century of Dip-
lomatic Blue Books*, edited by Harold Temperley and Lilian Penson,
Cass, 1966
British & Foreign State Papers, Vols 29–74, edited by Mr Lewis
Herslet (until 1870) and by Sir E. Herslet (1870–1896), published
by Messrs Ridgway & Co

Books
Abdul Rahman al Rifa'i, *Ahd Ismail*, 2 Vols, Cairo, 1948
Archaroui, Victor, *Nubar Pacha (1825–1899)*, Cairo, undated
Amin Said, *Tarikh misr min al-hamla al-fransiya ila naharan al-malikia*,
Cairo, 1959
Baer, Gabriel, *A History of Landownership in Modern Egypt (1800–
1850)*, Oxford, 1962
Bell, Moberly, *Khedives and Pashas*, London, 1884
Bevan, Samuel, *Sand and Canvas*, London, 1849
Blunt, W. S., *Secret History of the British Occupation of Egypt*,
London, 1906
Brinton, J. V., *The Mixed Courts of Egypt*, USA, 1930
Butler, A. J., *Court Life in Egypt*, London, 1887
Charles-Roux, F., *La Production du Coton en Egypte*, Paris, 1908
Charles-Roux, F., *Bonaparte, Gouverneur d'Egypte*, Paris, 1910
Claudy, Jean, *Histoire Financière de l'Egypte depuis Said Pacha
(1854–1876)*, Paris, 1878
Clot Bey, *Aperçu Général sur l'Egypte*, Brussels, 1840
Crabites, P., *Ismail the Maligned Khedive*, London, 1933

Cromer, Lord, *Modern Egypt*, 2 Vols, Vol I, London, 1908
Crouchley, A. E., *The Economic Development of Modern Egypt*, London, 1938
de Leon, Edwin, *The Khedive's Egypt*, London, 1877
de Lesseps, F. *Journal et Documents pour Servir à l'Histoire du Canal de Suez*, Paris, 1875–81
Denon, D. V., *Travels in Upper & Lower Egypt*, 1798–99 (tr.) London, 1803
Dicey, Edward, *England & Egypt*, London, 1881
Dicey, Edward, *The Story of the Khedivate*, London, 1900
Douin, G., *Règne du Khedive Ismail*, 4 Vols, Cairo, 1933–38
Duff Gordon, Lucie, *Letters from Egypt, 1863–65*, London, 1875
Duff Gordon, Lucie, *Last Letters from Egypt*, London, 1902
Egypt Exploration Society, *Who Was Who in Egyptology*, London, 1951
Farman, E. E., *Egypt and Its Betrayal*, USA, 1908
Gliddon, C. R., *A Memoir on the Cotton of Egypt*, London, 1841
Greener, Leslie, *The Discovery of Egypt*, London, 1966
Hamza, A. M., *The Public Debt of Egypt*, Cairo, 1944
Herold, J. C., *Bonaparte in Egypt*, London, 1963
Hoskins, H. L., *British Routes to India*, London, 1928
Jerrold, B., *Egypt Under Ismail Pasha*, London, 1879
Landes, D. S., *Bankers and Pashas*, London, 1958
Lane Poole, S., *The Life of R. H. Stratford Canning*, 2 Vols, London, 1888
Lesage, Charles, *L'Achat des Actions de Suez*, Paris, 1906
McCoan, J. C., *Egypt Under Ismail*, London, 1889
Malortie, Baron de, *Egypt, Native Rulers and Foreign Interference*, London, 1882
Marlowe, John, *The Making of the Suez Canal*, London, 1964
Mervan, Paul, *L'Egypte Contemporaine*, Paris, 1858
Muskau, Prince Puckler, *Egypt Under Mehemet Ali*, 2 Vols, London, 1845
Owen, E. R. J., *Cotton & the Egyptian Economy 1820–1924*, Oxford, 1969
Paton, A. A., *A History of the Egyptian Revolution*, 2 Vols, London, 1863
Rifaat, M., *The Awakening of Modern Egypt*, London, 1947
Rivlin, Helen A., *The Agricultural Policy of Mohamed Ali*, Oxford, 1953
Rothstein, Theodore, *Egypt's Ruin*, London, 1910
Sabry, M., *L'Empire Egyptien sous Ismail et l'Ingérence Anglo-Française (1863–1879)*, Paris, 1933
Scott, J. H., *The Law Affecting Foreigners in Egypt as a Result of the Capitulations*, Edinburgh, 1908
Temperley, H. W. V., *England & The Near East*, USA, 1964 (originally published London, 1936)
Wilson, Sir C. Rivers, *Chapters from My Official Life*, London, 1926

Published Articles, Pamphlets, etc.

Baker, Sir Samuel, 'The Reform of Egypt', *Fortnightly Review*, London, November 1882

Mulhall, M. G., 'Egyptian Finance', *Contemporary Review*, London, October 1882

Oppenheim, Henry, *Notes sur le Budget Egyptien pendant l'Année 1873–74*, Paris, 1874

Waghorn, T., *Egypt 1837*, London Library Pamphlet 106 (1837)

Waghorn, T., *Egypt 1838*, London Library Pamphlet 110 (1838)

Index

Galloway Bey, 15, 29, 33, 37
Galloway, J. A., 37–8, 39, 45, 72
Gambetta, M., 263
Geramb, Father, 12
Gessi, Romolo, 150
Gezira Palace, 106, 108, 224
Gibraltar, 34
Giglio (indemnity claimant), 72
Gisborne, Mr, 57, 73
Gladstone, Rt. Hon. W. E., 177, 264
Gondokoro, 143, 144, 145
Gordon, Major-General C. G., 140, 142, gov. of Equatoria, 145–7, g-g of Sudan, 147–50, feeling for Ismail, 150, 231
Gordon, Sir Robert, 30
Goschen, Charles, 97
Goschen, G. J. (later Lord), 221, 225, 226
Goschen-Joubert Mission (incl. G-J settlement), 221–5, 227, 229, 232, 236, 237, 239, 242, 261
Government of Bombay, 25, 27, 28, 32
Government of India, 133
Grant (explorer), 143
Granville, Earl, 201–2
Great Lakes, 129, 131, 132, 133, 143, 146
Green, Mr (acting British Consul-General in Egypt), 81, 92
Guardafui, Cape, 131, 132, 135, 137, 138, 140
Gulf of Suez, 25
Gura, Battle of, 142

Hami, Prince Al-, 72, 154
Hammont, M., 15
Harrar, 138, 139, 142
Hatti Sherif of Gulhané, 152
Helwan-les-Bains, 106
Hilali, Sh. Mohd. Al-, 147
Hill & Co., 35–6
Hill, Richard, 34, 35
Hirsch, Baron, 208
House of Commons, 31, 214
Hugh Lindsay, 27–8, 31–2
Husain Pasha, 224, 237

Ibrahamieh Canal, 126
Ibrahim Pasha, 21, 27, 43, 44, 46, 47

Imperial Ottoman Bank, 167, 169
India Board of Control, 24, 27, 30, 31, 40
Indian Mutiny, 55–6, 57
Indian Ocean, 31, 131, 132, 133
India Office, 183
Institut d'Egypte, 10
Ismail Ayub, 147
Ismail Pasha, 44, 57, accession of, 63, building boom in reign of, 105–6, character and extravagances of, 107–11, expenditure of, 111–17, speculations of, 119–26, imperial ambitions of, 131–3, relations of with HMG over Abyssinia, 135–6, efforts to suppress slave trade by, 139–40, 142–3, 144–5, appointment of Gordon by, 145, Gordon's feeling for, 150, obtains change in order of succession, 153–5, obtains title of Khedive, 155, difficulties of with Ali Pasha, 155–9, successful bribery by, 159–61, contracts 1st Oppenheim loan, 164–5, contracts railway loan, 165–6, contracts Daira loans, 166–7, buys land from Suez Canal Co., 168, appoints Ismail Sadiq as Finance Minister, 168, contracts 2nd Oppenheim loan, 168–9, increases Egyptian taxation, 169–70, signs Convention with Canal Co., 170–1, contracts Bishoffsheim loan, 171–2, contracts sundry short-term loans, 172–3, contracts 3rd Oppenheim loan, 173–4, sells Suez Canal shares to HMG, 175–6, applies to HMG for financial advice, 176–7, HMG's attitude towards finances of, 177–84, attitude to Mixed Courts of, 199–202, conversations with Cave, 207–9, negotiates with Outrey, 211–14, reactions to Cave Report, 214, sets up Caisse de la Dette, 217–19, harassed by Mixed Courts, 219–21, negotiates with G-J Mission, 221–3, liquidates Ismail Sadiq, 224, negotiates Daira debt with Goschen, 226, helps suzerain in war with Russia, 227, fights to stave off investigation into finan-